PSYCHOLOGICAL CONFLICT AND DEFENSE

PSYCHOLOGICAL CONFLICT AND DEFENSE

George F. Mahl

Yale University

Irving L. Janis, *Editor*

HARCOURT BRACE JOVANOVICH, INC.

New York   *Chicago*   *San Francisco*   *Atlanta*

ISBN: 0-15-572411-8

Library of Congress Catalog Card Number: 70-152582

Printed in the United States of America

ACKNOWLEDGMENTS AND COPYRIGHTS

The author wishes to thank the companies and persons listed below
for permission to use material in this book.

Textual Material

Opening quote: From Søren Kierkegaard, *Either/Or*, translated by
D. F. and L. M. Swenson, Princeton University Press, 1944, by
permission of the publisher.

Chapter 1   Opening quote: From Charles Augustin Sainte-Beuve, *Sonnet to
Ronsard*, translated by Jeffrey Mehlman.

Quotes from Breuer and Freud are reprinted from *Studies on Hysteria* (Standard Edition of *The Complete Psychological Works of
Sigmund Freud*, Vol. 2, 1955, edited by James Strachey) by permission of the Hogarth Press Ltd., Sigmund Freud Copyrights Ltd.,
and the Estate of Mr. James Strachey. *Studies on Hysteria* is published in the United States by Basic Books, Inc., Publishers, New
York, 1957, and the quotes are reprinted also by their permission.

2   Opening quote: Reprinted from *Narcissus and Goldmund* by Hermann Hesse, translated by Ursule Molinaro, copyright © by Farrar,
Straus & Giroux 1968. Reprinted by permission of Farrar, Straus &
Giroux.

Chapter 3   Opening quote: From K. F. Meyer, *Hutten's Last Days*, translated by James Strachey (Standard Edition of *The Complete Psychological Works of Sigmund Freud*, Vol. 10, 1955, edited by James Strachey), reprinted by permission of the Hogarth Press Ltd., Sigmund Freud Copyrights Ltd., and the Institute of Psycho-Analysis.

4   Quote from *Extracts from the Fliess Papers* (Standard Edition of *The Complete Psychological Works of Sigmund Freud*, Vol. 1, 1966, edited by James Strachey) reprinted by permission of the Hogarth Press Ltd., Sigmund Freud Copyrights Ltd., and the Estate of Mr. James Strachey. This material also appears in *The Origins of Psycho-Analysis: Letters to Wilhelm Fliess, Drafts and Notes, 1887–1902*, Basic Books, Inc., Publishers, New York, 1954, and is reprinted also by their permission.

Quote from Robert Waelder, "The Problem of the Genesis of Psychical Conflict in Earliest Infancy" in *International Journal of Psycho-Analysis*, 1937, 18, 406–73, by permission of *International Journal of Psycho-Analysis* and Robert Waelder.

5   Opening quote: From Denis Diderot, *Rameau's Nephew*, translated by Angela Richards (Standard Edition of *The Complete Psychological Works of Sigmund Freud*, Vol. 16, 1963, edited by James Strachey), reprinted by permission of the Hogarth Press Ltd., Sigmund Freud Copyrights Ltd., and the Institute of Psycho-Analysis.

Quotes from *Analysis of a Phobia in a Five-Year-Old Boy* (Standard Edition, Vol. 10, 1955, edited by James Strachey) reprinted by permission of the Hogarth Press Ltd., Sigmund Freud Copyrights Ltd., and the Estate of Mr. James Strachey. This material also appears in *The Collected Papers of Sigmund Freud* (5 vols., edited by Ernest Jones), Basic Books, Inc., Publishers, New York, 1959, and is reprinted also by their permission.

Quotes from Sigmund Freud, *The Interpretation of Dreams*, Basic Books, Inc., Publishers, New York, 1955, by permission of Basic Books, Inc. United Kingdom rights held by George Allen & Unwin Ltd.

6   Opening quote: Reprinted by permission of Charles Scribner's Sons and Constable & Co. Ltd. from *The Life of Reason* by George Santayana.

7   Opening quote: From D. H. Lawrence, "The Prussian Officer," in *The Complete Short Stories of D. H. Lawrence*, Vol. 1. All rights reserved. Reprinted by permission of The Viking Press, Inc., Laurence Pollinger Ltd., and the Estate of the late Mrs. Frieda Lawrence.

Quote from *Psycho-Analytic Notes on an Autobiographical Account of a Case of Paranoia* (Standard Edition of *The Complete Psychological Works of Sigmund Freud*, Vol. 12, 1958, edited by James Strachey) reprinted by permission of the Hogarth Press Ltd., Sigmund Freud Copyrights Ltd., and the Estate of Mr. James Strachey. This material also appears in *The Collected Papers of Sigmund Freud* (5 vols., edited by Ernest Jones), Basic Books, Inc., Publishers, New York, 1959, and is reprinted also by their permission.

Figure 5-2 Sears, P. S. Doll play aggression in normal young children. *Psychological Monographs*, 1951, 65, No. 323. Copyright 1951 by the American Psychological Association, and used by permission.

5-5 Photo courtesy of Dr. Georges Condominas.

5-6 Sigmund Freud Copyrights Ltd.

5-7 Sarnoff, I., & Corwin, S. M. Castration anxiety and the fear of death. *Journal of Personality*, 1959, 27, 374–85.

7-3 Sears, R. R. Experimental studies of projection, 1: Attribution of traits. *Journal of Social Psychology*, 1936, 7, 151–63.

9-1 Miller, N. E. Experimental studies of conflict. In J. McV. Hunt (Ed.), *Personality and the behavior disorders*. Copyright 1944 The Ronald Press Company, New York.

9-2 American Telephone and Telegraph Company.

11-2 Archives Photographiques, Paris.

11-3 Sigmund Freud Copyrights Ltd.

Table 10-1 Clark, K. B., & Clark, M. P. Racial identification and preference in Negro children. In E. E. Maccoby, T. M. Newcomb, & E. L. Hartley (Eds.), *Readings in social psychology*, 3rd ed. Copyright 1947, 1952, © 1958 by Holt, Rinehart and Winston, Inc. Used by permission of Holt, Rinehart and Winston, Inc.

*To Martha and to Barbara
and the rest of the next generation*

That which you have loved with youthful enthusiasm and admired with youthful ardor, that which you have secretly and mysteriously preserved in the innermost recesses of your soul, that which you have hidden in the heart: that you always approach with certain shyness, with mingled emotions, when you know that the purpose is to try to understand it.

SØREN KIERKEGAARD. Either/Or

PREFACE

The main goal of this book is to introduce the reader to the basic knowledge presently available about psychological conflict and defense. In my opinion, this basic knowledge is a distillate of much of the knowledge gained by Sigmund Freud and his followers over the past 80 years. This book emphasizes what seems to be the most pertinent and enduring portion of that work: those empirical observations and directly related clinical concepts of psychoanalysis which pertain to inner conflict and defense. The book is not a précis of psychoanalytic theory as a whole, nor is it concerned with the more abstract metapsychological concepts—such as psychic energy or ego and id—which are often invoked even in discussions about conflict and defense. Such a book would obscure the basic discoveries of psychoanalysis about conflict and defense. Besides, several such summaries exist that are excellent and readily available.

This book makes extensive use of clinical case material. Some of it has been excerpted from Freud's case reports; the rest comes from reports published by other analysts and from my own previously unpublished observations. This feature of the book is designed to acquaint the reader as fully as possible with the empirical referents, the real-life bases, of the psychoanalytic concepts presented. I hope that by doing this I am correcting a basic deficit in most textbooks, as well as aiding the reader to understand the concepts. Too few students have been presented with the concrete, empirical bases of some of the most fundamental psychoanalytic concepts.

This book is addressed to all serious students of personality dynamics who want to come to grips with some of the basic data and concepts about conflict and defense. Large numbers of such students are to be found in undergraduate courses in personality dynamics and in abnormal psychology. Many first-year graduate students in psychology and first-year medical students taking courses in personality may also find this book instructive, for the simple reason that very few undergraduate courses present the college student with the kind of material contained in it.

While this book emphasizes the contributions of psychoanalysts, it does not ignore the work of other theorists and researchers. At appropriate points the text discusses the work of individuals who approach the study of human behavior from other viewpoints—for example, some of the work of Neal E. Miller, the learning theorist and researcher, of George P. Murdock, the anthropologist, of Donald O. Hebb's co-workers, and of other experimental psychologists.

A common reason for bringing psychoanalytic thinking and learning theory together is to try to improve upon the psychoanalytic concepts either by translating them into learning theory terms or by reducing the former to the latter because these seem simpler or more universal or more objective or more testable in the laboratory. A common reason for citing various kinds of experiments bearing on psychoanalytic concepts is to test the validity of these concepts. I hope for the eventual unification of theories of behavior, and I value the rigorous, empirical evaluation of all concepts of any behavior theory. But these are not the reasons for the citation of nonpsychoanalytic references in this book. The primary reason for including such references here is to suggest that psychoanalytic observations and concepts dealing with the topic of the book and the work of scholars in other disciplines are mutually enriching. Thus I am equally interested in suggesting that stimulus-response psychology and conditioning theory cannot get along without Freud's "internal mental world" and in indicating that a particular psychoanalytic hypothesis can be, or has been, tested experimentally. In this way, future psychologists can see the mutual relevance of psychoanalysis and other approaches, and psychology will continue to progress toward the goal of a unified theory of human behavior with a sound empirical base.

This book was first published as Part II of *Personality: Dynamics, Development, and Assessment* (Harcourt Brace Jovanovich, 1969) by Irving L. Janis, George F. Mahl, Jerome Kagan, and Robert R. Holt, under the editorship of Irving L. Janis. Some topics are not treated as extensively in the present volume as they would otherwise have been, because they are discussed thoroughly in the other parts of the original textbook. This is especially the case with the discussions of external dangers, trauma, and bereavement and mourning. Since complete discussions of these phenomena were most relevant to Part I (*Stress and Frustration*) by Janis, the present volume limits its discussion of them and makes appropriate reference to the Janis volume.

Many people helped in the preparation of this book. The list of acknowledgments mentions a number of individuals, publishers, and organizations that kindly granted permission to use textual and illustrative material. Here I wish to express my thanks to those who gave more direct assistance. I thank Genoveva Palmieri for her devoted help in preparing the manuscript. I express my respect and gratitude to those persons who, by sharing their inner life with me in psychoanalysis, helped me gain for myself and attempt to convey a very real sense of the psychoanalytic concepts of conflict and defense. Each of my co-authors of the original textbook read one or more drafts of this book and gave me the benefit of his advice. I am especially indebted to Irving L. Janis for his meticulous and perceptive attention to several drafts.

George F. Mahl

CONTENTS

7

Projection, Over-Reactions, and Unconscious Homosexual Conflicts, 115

8

Over-Reactions and Unconscious Conflicts About Aggression, 127

9

Interference with Defenses and Reality Contact, 137

10

Defense Against Unpleasant External Situations, 151

11

Defense Against Drives and Affects, 171

12

Organization of Defenses and Individual Differences, 194

References, 205

Index, 213

PSYCHOLOGICAL CONFLICT AND DEFENSE

Let them say he dared too much;
the audacity was beautiful.

CHARLES AUGUSTIN SAINTE-BEUVE.
Sonnet to Ronsard

CHAPTER 1
ORIGINS
OF PSYCHOANALYTIC
IDEAS

Man is remarkable for the variety and scope of his capacities. He breathes, eats, drinks; he eliminates waste products. He reproduces. He perceives internal and external stimulation and can remember it. He can approach useful or enjoyable sources of external stimulation and he can avoid or destroy dangerous or unpleasant ones. He can satisfy his needs and wishes. He feels, in many different ways. He thinks and learns. He not only adjusts to a wide variety of environmental conditions, but he can also control and modify them to fit himself. Man does all these things in an interpersonal context. He reproduces, for example, with a mate, and they raise their children in the family group. He forms other groups for various purposes. These small groups function within still broader social contexts. As a social organism, man communicates, forms emotional interpersonal bonds, and shares values. And, of course, he does much more.

Man's capacities may also fail him, resulting in difficulties like those listed in Table 1-1. Broadly speaking, two conditions may produce such difficulties: the crises of real external stress and frustration discussed by Janis (1971) and inner, psychological conflict. In this book we shall focus on the latter, on internal, subjective factors, which are nearly always unconscious. As Table 1-1 indicates, no aspect of man's re-

Table 1-1 Examples of Behavioral Disturbances

Behavior class	Minor disturbances	Major disturbances
Eating	Temporary loss of appetite or over-eating upon entering college.	Chronic inability to eat, resulting in extreme weight loss and even death. Chronic overeating, resulting in obesity.
Elimination	Temporary constipation or diarrhea when starting a new job.	Chronic constipation or diarrhea, resulting in physical illness.
Autonomic responses	Sweating or fast heartbeat on a first date or during an examination.	Sustained sweating or fast heart rate.
Sexual activity	Impotency or frigidity when first at-tempting intercourse, or with a particular person.	Chronic impotency or frigidity.
Affective reactions	Unexplained passing anxiety when talking with an instructor. Episodes of irrational anger with a close friend.	Chronic, intense anxiety. Chronic sus-picious and angry behavior with everybody.
Perception	A student attending the funeral of a beloved teacher blots out the image of his dead body by "seeing" the open casket as closed. A student mishears his teacher's criticism as praise.	Hallucination that one's dead child still lives; a soda bottle wrapped in news-paper is experienced as the child. Hysterical blindness or deafness.
Memory	Forgetting the name of the speaker one is introducing to a seminar. Forgetting an appointment with a teacher one fears or dislikes.	Amnesia about long periods or critical events of one's life.
Thinking and learning	Inability to have thoughts and or-ganize them for a particular part of a term paper. Temporary inability to learn about a particular subject or to develop a particular motor skill.	Chronic inability to study or think during examinations, resulting in academic failure by an intelligent student.
Speech	Temporary flustering and occasional slips of the tongue in everyday speech.	Severe stuttering. Loss of capacity for speech. Mutism.
Social relations	Brief disruptions in friendships.	Extreme isolation of "the loner" on the campus or of the hermit. The "social butterfly" or "hail-fellow-well-met" type who is unable to form close friendships.

markable range of behavior is immune to impairment by unconscious processes. His social life, cognitive functions, emotional behavior, and even his life-sustaining biological functions are all susceptible to such impairment.

Since we shall be concerned largely with unconscious processes, which usually originate in childhood, rather than with here-and-now crises, we shall draw primarily on psychoanalytic case studies and secondarily on ex-perimental research. Most of what is known about the unconscious aspects of behavior has been learned through the use of the psychoanalytic method.

So far, the major contribution of systematic research to our knowledge in this area has been the occasional confirmation of hypotheses originating in clinical investigations, and this is likely to be true in the future. Experimental manipulation of "the unconscious" in the laboratory is extremely difficult, even if it were ethically justified.

Psychological conflict is the nexus of this book. A state of conflict exists when the individual is prompted to respond simultaneously in different and incompatible ways. In the kind of conflict we will be dealing with here, the *approach-avoidance conflict*, the individual is prompted both to approach a goal and to avoid doing so. Unpleasant emotional states, such as anxiety and guilt, motivate the avoidance reactions. Sometimes external stimuli, usually unrealistically perceived, arouse these unpleasant emotions; but more often very human propensities, such as love and hate, do so, because people often anticipate that some danger will occur if they engage in sexual or aggressive behavior. Avoidance responses are methods of preventing the unpleasant emotions and anticipated dangers from materializing. Since the avoidance responses have this protective function, they are called *defense mechanisms* or, simply, *defenses*.

Persons under extreme realistic stresses, as well as those involved in internal conflict, often use defenses to gain relief from their emotional distress. Laboratory and clinical studies have shown, for example, that parachutists about to jump often *repress* their fear, that people may *inhibit* and *displace* aggression when frustrated, and that those bereft by the death of a loved one often *identify with the lost person* to ease their grief and *turn aggression around upon themselves* to avoid a sense of guilt for the rage they feel at their deprivation. One purpose of this book is to examine a broad range of unpleasant external situations and to discuss in detail the process of defense against them. But we shall be concerned primarily with the unconscious inner conflicts involving defenses against anticipated dangers.

Most psychologists agree that Sigmund Freud is the towering figure in the area of conflict and defense, and we shall discuss in detail the discoveries of Freudian psychoanalysis about conflict and the unconscious determinants of behavior. Thus, in the process of discussing conflict and defense we shall also be presenting elements of an introduction to Freud—the best of Freud, which in the writer's judgment consists of the many empirical phenomena Freud "discovered" and the concepts most immediately related to them, not his most abstract theory. Of course, "the best of Freud" also includes the example he set as a person and as an investigator, especially his everlasting commitment to understanding real people and to the science of psychology. A background knowledge of Freud is one component of a thoroughgoing grasp of the psychology of personality. While concentrating on Freudian findings, we shall also discuss some major contributions by psychologists with other theoretical or methodological orientations, such as Neal Miller and Kurt Lewin. Some important experiments by other research psychologists will also be considered in our discussion.

Freud's contribution to the understanding of human behavior is indicated by Janis' volume on stress and frustration (1971), as for example in the discussion of his concept of the belated mastery of trauma and his views on the work of mourning. But these are only fragments of his total contribution, much of which we shall consider. Yet some psychologists take an extremely negative position about psychoanalysis (for example, Wolpe & Rachman, 1960), maintaining that the clinical evidence and hypotheses put forth by Freud and other analysts are merely fanciful speculations that have no place in a "scientific" psychology. However, those findings that become generally accepted among psychoanalysts are grounded in careful and prolonged studies of people's lives. Such is the case for the findings with which we will be concerned.

In this chapter we shall review the origins of Freud's ideas about conflict and defense. In the next two chapters we shall discuss and illustrate different kinds of conflicts and formulate a general paradigm for the approach-avoidance conflict. Then in subsequent chapters we shall discuss some typical conflicts of childhood and adolescence in our Western culture and their influence on personality development and adult behavior. If childhood conflicts are unresolved and continue to exist unconsciously, they give rise to inappropriate, disturbed behavior in adulthood. We shall discuss several kinds of such inappropriate adult behavior: for example, unrealistic perceptions and inappropriate emotional reactions to innocuous external stimuli, and conflictful sexual and aggressive behavior. In the course of these discussions the kinds of dangers people anticipate, the situations in which they do so, and the kinds of unpleasant emotions that result will all be examined. Some defense mechanisms must necessarily be discussed as we proceed, but a systematic consideration of all the known defense mechanisms is postponed to the final chapters.

If our discussions seem discursive, it is largely because of the nature of the subject matter and the limitations imposed by sequential, rather than simultaneous, presentation. It is impossible to present the subject matter of conflict and defense all at once or to present it in a neat series of steps. Instead, we shall take up some topics several times, drop them, and return to them again later. We do this largely because the intervening discussions would be disjointed if we postponed them or because they contribute to the background necessary for further examination of the topic. Our frequent use of case material may also add to the impression of discursiveness. This too is unavoidable. Freud's theories are based upon clinical case material; they are either incomprehensible or unbelievable without it. In addition, only case material conveys a sense of how psychological conflict *feels*. Without such a sense, *understanding* conflict is impossible.

The Historical Background

When we look into the origins of psychoanalytic ideas about conflict and defense, their empirical basis becomes clear. And by following Freud through his earliest discoveries, we come to appreciate the relationship between observation and inference in the clinical case study of a human personality. Although Freud's earliest concepts were subsequently modified because they were oversimplifications and grossly incomplete, they nevertheless included many key notions, such as unconscious motivation, conflict, repression, and other defenses.

When Sigmund Freud (1856–1939) started his neuropsychiatric medical practice in Vienna in 1886, he faced the problem of treating people who suffered from just the kinds of major disturbances presented in Table 1-1. Yet little was known about the causes of the disturbances or about effective ways to treat those patients. At first Freud used the conventional procedures, which were almost exclusively physical: baths, faradic electrical stimulation of various skin areas, massage, and rest cures. These failed, and toward the end of 1887 Freud turned to hypnosis, which was then moving to the center of psychiatric interest. In preparation for private psychiatric practice Freud had gone to Paris in 1885 and had seen the power of direct hypnotic suggestion demonstrated by Jean-Martin Charcot, the giant of French neuropsychiatry. In Charcot's form of treatment a patient suffering from a functional (nonorganic) impairment was hypnotized by the therapist and simply told that he would no longer have his symptom even after the hypnotic trance ended. At Charcot's command, people in wheelchairs got up and walked, mutes started to talk, blind people saw, amnesiacs remembered who they were. After witnessing these and other dramatic results, Freud tried direct hypnotic suggestion when he began to use hypnosis. But gradually he realized that this method did not always cure the symptoms and that the removal of one symptom was frequently followed by the appearance of others. Furthermore, he became bored with direct hypnotic suggestion; he was not learning anything about the puzzling conditions he was trying to cure. Fortunately, he remembered what an older colleague and friend, Josef Breuer, had told him a few years earlier about a clinical experience in which hypnosis was used in a different way.

THE PATIENT WHO HELPED DISCOVER PSYCHOANALYSIS

During the winter of 1880–81, Breuer undertook the treatment of a now-famous patient, known in psychoanalytic literature as Anna O. When he first examined her, Breuer saw lying in bed in her home a 21-year-old unmarried woman. Anna O. had taken to her bed some weeks earlier, exhausted and very upset from five months of helping to care for her very sick father. When he died in April 1881, Anna's condition grew worse. During the course of her illness, she had a severe nervous cough, bad headaches, a noticeable cross-eyed squint, and many other symptoms. She often had strange visual experiences; for example, objects often looked bigger than normal. There was a spontaneous rhythm to Anna's daily life. In the afternoon she would be irresistibly sleepy and would sleep until sunset; then she would spontaneously pass into a deep trance state, which she called "clouds." At night she would become excited and have frightening hallucinations and fantasies. She might sleep a few hours, but upon awakening in the morning she would continue in this excited and hallucinatory state until she again entered the somnolent condition in the afternoon. As nearly as Breuer could determine, this "illness" first manifested itself, and then in only slight ways, as the weeks of nursing her sick father passed by.

Breuer treated Anna from the winter of 1880–81 until June 1882, a little over a year. He saw her every two or three days, at times daily. Apparently he started to treat her by prescribing narcotics and by generally ordering her routine. But a warm personal relationship developed between Anna and Breuer. They talked, much more than doctors and patients usually do. And here Anna O. made her own contribution to the psychology of personality. If Breuer visited her during her evening trances, or spontaneous hypnotic states, she would tell him of all the terrifying hallucinations and fantasies she had had that day. Breuer listened! Afterward all the excitement, anxiety, and horror created by her daytime hallucinations and fantasies temporarily ceased, and she was "normal" that night. But if something prevented Breuer from visiting for a few days, she grew more disturbed. She herself perceived the therapeutic value of their talks and came to call it "chimney sweeping" or "the talking cure." The beneficial effect of Anna's "chimney sweeping" took Breuer by surprise, but once he recognized it he deliberately and systematically used the method. He intentionally visited her in the evening, when she would be in her spontaneous hypnotic state. She would talk; he would listen. She would usually feel and function more normally after telling him of her frightening mental experiences of that day.

But then something else began to occur. As Anna spoke about her current symptoms, she would recall earlier emotional experiences that were obviously related to her current symptoms. These recollections usually were of previous emotional reactions that included some version of the current symptom. *When she vividly relived these past experiences, including especially the first one, the current symptom would disappear.* Since her illness started while she was caring for her sick father, it is not surprising that most of these symptom-creating emotional experiences occurred at that time. About Anna's nervous cough, for example, Breuer discovered:

> She began coughing for the first time when once, as she was sitting at her father's bedside, she heard the sound of dance music coming from a neighbouring house, felt a sudden wish to be there, and was overcome with self-reproaches. Thereafter, throughout the whole length of her illness she reacted to any markedly rhythmical music with a *tussis nervosa* [nervous cough]. [Breuer & Freud, 1893–95, p. 40]

Her cross-eyed squinting was a remnant of an incident when her father asked the time from his bed and she brought her watch very close to her nose to look at it as she fought back the tears and sadness she felt for him; the fact that things looked larger than usual was a repetition of the apparent increase in size of the watch dial. The spontaneous rhythm to her life—drowsiness in the afternoon and wakefulness at night—seemed to repeat her daily pattern when she was nursing her father: She would nap in the afternoon and sit up with him at night.

Once Breuer realized that her spontaneous hypnotic states facilitated the therapeutic recall of such significant experiences, he supplemented them with induced hypnosis. Through this combined use of spontaneous and induced hypnosis, Anna obtained relief from many of her symptoms. Thus, in the period from 1880 to 1882, patient and doctor collaborated in developing a new use of hypnosis for the investigation and treatment of psychological disturbances: cathartic, or abreactive, hypnotherapy.

Breuer did not apply his technique to other patients, but he told Freud about it in the fall of 1882. In 1888 or 1889, frustrated with the results of direct hypnotic suggestion, Freud tried Breuer's method and found it more satisfactory. It was just as effective and, more important, it seemed to shed light on the *causes* of the patient's symptoms. They *seemed* to be indirect expressions of forgotten memories of intensely unpleasant, overwhelming emotional experiences, for they disappeared when the memories were recalled with abreaction (reliving) of their emotional content. The memories were forgotten only in the sense that the individual was not aware of them; they still persisted "in the unconscious," fresh and dynamically pressing for expression and doing so in symptoms. This was a new hypothesis about mental aberrations—a brilliant searchlight penetrating the darkness for the curious, inquiring, and ambitious Freud. Little wonder that he now relied mainly upon abreactive hypnotherapy.

FREUD'S FIRST "PSYCHOANALYTIC" CASE STUDY

Soon, however, something happened that decisively influenced Freud's views about conflict and his therapeutic-investigative method. Freud found that he could not hypnotize every patient who came into his office. In view of his and Breuer's hypothesis, this posed only a practical problem. If he could enable the patient to recall the forgotten memories by some other means, the symptoms should still disappear. But how was he to do this? Here Freud recalled something he had recently observed in France in the clinic of Hippolyte Bernheim (1840–1919), another outstanding psychiatrist of the time:

> I was saved . . . by remembering that I had myself seen Bernheim producing evidence that the memories of events during [hypnosis] are only *apparently* forgotten in the waking state . . . . He had, for instance, given a woman in a state of [hypnosis] a negative hallucination to the effect that he was no longer present, and had then endeavored to draw her attention to himself in a great variety of ways, including some of a decidedly aggressive kind. He did not succeed. After she had been woken up he asked her to tell him what he had done to her while she thought he was not there. She replied in surprise that she knew nothing of it. But he did

not accept this. He insisted that she could remember everything and laid his hand on her forehead to help her to recall it. And lo and behold! she ended by describing everything that she had ostensibly not perceived during her [hypnosis] and ostensibly not remembered in her waking state [Breuer & Freud, 1893–95, pp. 109–10].

Freud coped with the unhypnotizable patients in a similar way and described the results for the first time in the case history of Lucy R. (Breuer & Freud, 1893–95).

Lucy R. was 30 years old, unmarried, and serving as a governess to the children of a widowed Viennese industrialist. She was referred to Freud primarily because she had lost her sense of smell and was bothered constantly by olfactory hallucinations. She smelled things that were not there. During her treatment with Freud, she hallucinated the odor of cigar smoke.

Freud unsuccessfully tried to hypnotize Lucy. When he decided to proceed without hypnosis and asked her to try to recall times when she had really smelled the odors of her hallucinations, she insisted that there were no such times. He insisted that there must have been, urged her to remember, insisted that she would remember (but not *what* she would recall), pressed on her head with his hands, and in general *pitted his will and efforts against her contrary insistence and desire.* As a result of a series of such clashes between herself and Freud, Lucy did recall several very painful emotional experiences that she had forgotten but that were obviously related to her olfactory symptoms. About cigar smoke, for example, she remembered an occasion when her employer had entertained two men from his factory at luncheon in the house. After lunch the men smoked cigars. As they were leaving for their offices, one of them, who was especially fond of the children, started to kiss them goodby. At this their father became angry and shouted, "Don't kiss the children!" This reaction upset Lucy very much. She was secretly in love with her employer and fantasied that she would marry him some day, but now she doubted that he was the right kind of man for her.

But this episode had also reminded her of a still earlier one, which she recalled next. A woman, an acquaintance of the father, had visited one day and had kissed the children on the lips. This too had infuriated their father. Afterward he released his anger on Lucy, saying that it was her responsibility to see that no one ever kissed the children's mouths and that he would discharge her if it ever happened again. It is easy to imagine the disappointment and heartbreak Lucy felt as she concluded from this outburst that he did not love her and as she was reminded of this episode by the other related one. Two days after Lucy recalled the earliest of these memories, her symptoms disappeared. She no longer had olfactory hallucinations, and her sense of smell returned. She was no longer depressed over her disappointment in love; she was reconciled to it, at least for the time being. Her treatment ended on this note.

We have called Lucy R. the first "psychoanalytic" patient because hers was the first treatment described by Freud that proceeded without hypnosis—that is, in which the essential tool for bringing unconscious thoughts and feelings into awareness was largely *verbal communication* between Freud and a patient *in the usual waking state* of consciousness. Although Freud later modified his method in many ways, as have other succeeding analysts as well, psychoanalysis still retains the goal of making conscious the unconscious, and it still relies exclusively upon interaction channeled through words. We put the term "psychoanalytic" in quotes because Freud guided and exhorted the patient in a specific direction: toward the recall of memories. *Free association* by the patient, which may lead in any direction, was not yet the basic feature in the treatment technique. It had become so, however, by 1900, when Freud's classic work *The Interpretation of Dreams* was published.

Key Concepts
from the Early Case Studies

When Freud found that he could force the recall of memories without hypnosis, he gradually stopped using hypnosis altogether. He tried out his new technique on a wide variety of symptoms in addition to hysterical ones affecting sensory experience. These included fears, compulsions, obsessional thinking and behavior, paranoid thoughts, and psychotic hallucinations.

REPRESSION

In all these cases the use of insistence, urging, and pressure on the head appeared to overcome the amnesia for memories. Freud felt that his effort overcame a resisting force in the patient. This subjective experience became a crucial datum stimulating his creative thinking. Freud hypothesized that *his use of force produced memory recall because it overcame a force that was preventing the spontaneous emergence into awareness of memories.* And, he hypothesized further, *this force that maintained the patient's amnesia had produced the amnesia in the beginning.* The "forgetting" of his patients, then, was not to be regarded as true forgetting at all. It was not like the usual fading of memory. Nor was it attributable to organic brain deficiencies or to any other type of physiological weakness. It seemed that the perceptions and thoughts of unpleasant emotional experiences were actively forced out of consciousness and actively kept out of consciousness; that is, they were *repressed*.

UNBEARABLE AFFECT
AS THE CAUSE OF REPRESSION AND CONFLICT

Why was the memory repressed in the first place? Because of the *unbearable affect*, or unpleasant feelings, stemming from it, Freud answered. The unbearable affect might be in direct response to real or imagined perceptions; Lucy's hurt and disappointment, for example, were direct responses to her employer's angry outbursts and to the shattering of her fantasy that he loved her enough to marry her. Or the unbearable affect might arise from the individual's moral standards, as it did in the case of Anna's guilt over her desire to be off dancing to the music she heard nearby instead of nursing her father. One of the basic laws of human experience, Freud maintained, was the *pleasure principle.* By this he meant that there is a basic tendency in human behavior to avoid unpleasant experiences and to seek out pleasant ones. Repression of the memory was in accord with the forces of the pleasure principle, for the expulsion of the memory from consciousness prevented the related unpleasant feelings from developing. For example, by repressing her memories Lucy spared herself the reliving of the painful feelings that were part of the original experiences. The basic function of repression, Freud hypothesized, was exactly this attempt at defense against experiencing the unbearable affect.

The preceding remarks cover only half the forces Freud thought were involved in neurosis. The other half consisted of forces inherent in the intense emotions themselves, in those urges toward expression or "discharge" that characterize emotions. Thus, at the time of the original repression the repressive forces were pitted against these expressive forces. And with the repression of the memory, Freud hypothesized, an emotional "charge" remained associated with the unconscious memory trace. This "charge," too, constituted a force tending toward "discharge." Thus, in sustained repression the repressive forces were continually pitted against the expressive or "discharge" forces of the pent-up emotions.

With such working hypotheses, which were based on concepts then popular in physics, Freud could account for many of his observations. Symptoms could be attributed to indirect "discharge" or expression of the pent-up emotional charge associated with the repressed memory trace. Freud's ability to produce recall of the repressed memory by his efforts of will and urging of the patient could be explained as the overpowering of the repressive forces inherent in the pleasure principle. And the abreactive recall was therapeutic, Freud argued, because with the emergence into consciousness of the repressed memory the pent-up emotional "charge" was now "discharged." With this, he thought, the necessary condition for symptoms was abolished.

From this historical sketch it is apparent that the concepts of conflict and defense were among the first developed by Freud. The sketch also shows the original empirical bases and behavioral referents for these concepts. Conflict and defense have remained principal concepts in psychoanalytic theory, although more precise formulations were given later, as we shall see. In fact, their specific content changed several times as Freud observed new instances of unconsciously motivated behavior, saw old and seemingly understood symptoms in a new light, and modified his conceptual scheme accordingly. Thus, the nature of the conflicting forces, the personality components involved, and the role of conflict and defense in adjustment are all viewed quite differently today than they were in this

Figure 1-1 Freud's "laboratory" in Vienna, where he made nearly all his discoveries.

While his patient lay on the couch, Freud sat in the armchair behind the head of the couch. The reclining position of the patient derived from the period when Freud had used hypnosis. He continued to use this position to facilitate relaxation and free association by the patient. Freud sat behind the patient to minimize the influence of his facial expressions and other visible reactions on the patient's flow of associations and to enable himself to relax, free from being watched by patients for many hours each day. Not having to be continually "on guard," Freud could thus listen more carefully, and respond more perceptively, to the patient's free associations. This general physical arrangement is now part of the standard psychoanalytic situation throughout the world.

initial phase of psychoanalysis. It is with the present meanings of these concepts, of course, that we will be most concerned. But these present meanings are better understood if we know their beginning.

FREE ASSOCIATION AS THE CENTRAL PROCEDURE

The historical sketch also shows Freud in action—observing keenly and attempting to understand and explain his empirical observations. To do the latter he drew readily on the ideas of others that appeared useful,

Figure 1-2   Freud's study and desk in Vienna.

Here Freud worked on his many papers and books. Here, too, he conducted consultations with patients, who sat in the armchair in the left foreground.

but he was not handcuffed by tradition or fashion. When old methods failed, he devised new ones. Freud soon realized, for example, that abreaction of unpleasant experiences was of limited therapeutic value and that the use of both psychological and physical force and pressure was fraught with both therapeutic and investigative dangers.

Accordingly, he modified his technique along lines mentioned earlier, making *free association* its cornerstone. In this procedure the individual abandons his customary conscious control over his behavior and gives free verbal expression to every thought, feeling, or impulse of which he becomes aware. Under these conditions the extent to which overt behavior is determined by unconscious conflicts increases, and the nature of those unconscious determinants is more accessible to observation. Thus, the *freedom* of *free* association means freedom from the conscious inhibition and other forms of control over *verbal* expression.

Largely through the use of free association, Freud saw things that others could not see or overlooked. Where explanatory concepts were lacking or inadequate, he invented new ones. Always, however, his speculation was geared to observation; his formulations derived from facts as he saw them and were maintained only as long as they seemed to account for the facts. He was never interested in idle speculation or in creating fairy tales.

Repression Investigated Experimentally

Freud often resorted to metaphors and failed to define precisely some of his principal terms, but that is often the case with pioneers who open up new fields of research. In the course of opening up research on human conflict Freud made basic clinical discoveries that stimulated a great deal of research by psychologists using the more rigorous techniques of experimental psychology. Even his earliest discoveries about the repression of unpleasant memories had this stimulative effect. For example, many systematic studies have now been performed by psychologists that clearly demonstrate that the memories of unpleasant experiences are "forgotten" more readily than others. This has been shown for spontaneous real-life experiences (for a review of such studies see Sears, 1943, and Cofer & Appley, 1964) and for unpleasant experiences induced experimentally by temporarily threatening subjects' self-esteem—for example, by telling them that they have failed in experimental tasks (Rosenzweig, 1943; Alper, 1948; Glixman, 1949, for example) or by arousing pain and fear reactions.

A study by Diven (1937) illustrates one way of investigating repression experimentally. Diven placed college students in an apparatus that made it appear that they were part of an electrical circuit originating in a wall socket. He presented a series of stimulus words to each subject and asked him to associate with as many words as he could for 12 seconds. Periodically *red* and next *barn* recurred in the list of stimulus words. Each time *barn* was presented, the subject was given a mild electric shock at the end of his 12-second association period. Although the shock was delivered only at these times, nearly half the subjects never became aware of the connection between *barn* and the occurrence of the shock. After periods of delay varying from 5 minutes to 48 hours this entire procedure was repeated, except that the shocks were now omitted. At the outset of this second test the subjects were asked to remember as many of the stimulus words in the first test as possible. Throughout the experiment, Diven recorded the electrical activity of the subjects' skin (the psychogalvanic skin response), which indicated how emotionally upset his subjects were.

The results? As a result of the experimental procedure, *barn*, *red*, and other words with a *rural* meaning produced changes in the electrical activity of the skin. Of particular interest was the finding that this occurred just as often in those subjects who were not aware of the fact that *barn* always preceded the shock as in those subjects who were. When the subjects tried to recall the stimulus words at the outset of the second test, they recalled many more "neutral" words than "traumatic" words—*red, barn, rural words*, or *whatever word had followed barn*. Furthermore, this temporary memory loss was greater for those subjects who were not aware of the timing of the shock than it was for those who were. Finally, some of Diven's results suggested that the longer the delay (he called it, aptly, "the incubation period") between the two tests, the greater were the effects of the shock in the "unconscious" subjects.

Diven's experiment was stimulated by Freud's early ideas about the repression of unpleasant emotional experiences. It shows the fruitfulness of these early ideas and the possibility of subjecting them to experimental scrutiny even though they represented only a fragment of the truth, as we shall see.

Our sketch of Freud does not reveal the whole complex man who developed a momentous new psychology, that Freud about whom Thomas Mann wrote as follows in celebration of his eightieth birthday:

> as physician and psychologist, as philosopher and artist, this courageous seer and healer has for two generations been a guide to hitherto undreamed-of regions of the human soul. An independent spirit . . . a thinker and investigator who knew how to stand alone . . . he went his way and penetrated to truths which seemed dangerous because they revealed what had been anxiously hidden, and illumined dark places . . . and made even his opponents indebted to him through the creative stimulus they derived from him. Even should the future remould and modify one result or another of his researches, never again will the questions be stilled which Sigmund Freud put to mankind [Quoted in Jones, 1957, pp. 205–06].

The reader interested in these aspects of Freud should see Jones's biography (Jones, 1953, 1955, 1957), which also covers much of the long, intricate history of Freud's ideas subsequent to the phase we have discussed.

Thomas Mann referred to the possibility that the future may require that various parts of Freud's thought be modified. Colby, in *The Skeptical Psychoanalyst* (1958), presents an extreme view of this possibility. He concludes that many of Freud's ideas, as was true of some of Darwin's and Newton's, will turn out to be wrong or so drastically changed that their future form will bear little resemblance to the original ideas. What about this possibility of change? What are its implications for the reader's attitude toward the rest of this book?

Certainly psychoanalytic thought will change in the future. Any viable science changes. New facts will be discovered. They will give rise to new concepts. New ways of thinking about old facts will also emerge. Such evolutionary changes occurred repeatedly within Freud's own work. We have already seen signs of them in the historical sketch presented in this chapter. Although we cannot continue the historical approach throughout these pages, we shall pick up briefly the historical thread of Freud's thinking in Chapter 4. And throughout this volume we shall refer to landmarks in the development of his observations and ideas. Other psychoanalysts have already carried Freud's thinking beyond the point it had reached when he died in London in 1939. (He was 83 when he died, a refugee from Nazi-occupied Vienna.) We shall refer to some of these.

All science is a process, not a dogmatic, static body of knowledge, and psychoanalysis is no exception. What the following chapters present is our current basic knowledge about conflict and defense—in particular, the part of our knowledge that is least likely to undergo radical change, for our focus is on empirical-clinical observations that have been repeatedly confirmed and on those concepts of Freud that are tied directly to these observations.

Oh! To love a woman! To be a priest! . . . Oh, happy is the man who is sawn in two or pulled apart by horses!

VICTOR HUGO. The Hunchback of Notre Dame

The younger girl with the braids was leaning out of the window.

"Goldmund!" she whispered. He stood and waited.

"Are you coming back?" she asked. Her timid voice was no more than a breath.

Goldmund shook his head. She reached out with both hands, seized his head; her small hands felt warm on his temples. She bent far down, until her dark eyes were close before his.

"Do come back!" she whispered, and her mouth touched his in a child's kiss.

Quickly he ran through the small garden, toppled across the flower beds, smelled wet earth and dung. A rosebush tore his hand. . . . "Never again!" commanded his will. "Again! To-morrow!" begged his heart.

HERMANN HESSE. Narcissus and Goldmund

CHAPTER 2
TYPES
AND EXAMPLES
OF CONFLICT

B efore we examine conflict and defense in detail, it will be useful for us to take a broad, general view of the subject. As noted earlier, we speak of *conflict* when a person is prompted simultaneously by incompatible response tendencies.

The Four Basic Types of Conflict

Lewin (1931) and Miller (1944) have shown that there are four basic types of conflict situations. Since the types were first named with reference to tendencies to approach or avoid goals, they are most readily described in those terms. The term *goals* refers to external objects or to definite activities, such as specific thoughts or specific overt responses, around which behavior is organized. In this sense we may speak of both *positive* and *negative* goals. Positive goals are those objects or activities an individual is impelled to approach; negative goals are those he is impelled to avoid. For the sake of clarity, we shall assume that no more than two goals are involved in a conflict; actually, any number of goals may figure in a given conflict. We shall also assume that the incompatible response tendencies are of equal strength, although this is not always true.

THE FOUR TYPES DEFINED

Approach-Approach
Conflict
Here the individual is prompted simultaneously and to an equal degree to approach two desirable but mutually exclusive goals. The child who must choose between two equally attractive toys, the student who must select one of two equally valued courses, the adult who must pick one of two equally desirable jobs, are all in approach-approach conflict situations.

Approach-Avoidance
Conflict
Here the individual is prompted to approach a single goal at the same time that he is prompted just as strongly to avoid it. The child who wants to pet a dog he is afraid of, the adult who desires but fears intimacy, the student who is impelled yet ashamed to speak before his classmates, are in approach-avoidance conflicts.

Avoidance-Avoidance
Conflict
Here the individual is prompted to avoid two goals or two courses of action. The high school graduate who abhors going on to college and equally dislikes going to work, the individual who is equally ill at ease talking with both men and women at a party, the voter who dislikes the presidential candidates of both the Democratic and Republican parties, are in avoidance-avoidance conflict situations.

Double Approach-
Avoidance Conflict
In this case each of two goals or lines of action invokes an approach-avoidance conflict. Upon close examination, what appear to be simply avoidance-avoidance or approach-approach conflicts are frequently seen to be double approach-avoidance conflicts. Thus, it is very possible that the high school graduate just mentioned is in the more difficult position of wanting to go on to college and also to work at the same time that he dislikes each. Each of the two alternatives prompts approach and avoidance behavior. Anna O. was probably in this type of conflict situation as she sat by her father's bedside that night, both wanting and not wanting to stay there caring for him and at the same time wishing she were at the dance next door but feeling guilty about this desire and then repressing it.

**General Principles:
Approach and
Avoidance Gradients**
Many properties of behavior in these various conflict situations have been discovered through clinical and experimental observation. One of these properties is that *the approach and the avoidance tendencies become stronger and stronger the closer in time or space one is to the goal.* If a student wants to go to college, he becomes more interested and involved in preparing to go as the time for going approaches. If he wants to avoid it for any reason, all of his attempts to do so will increase in vigor as the time comes.

These variations in the strength of the approach and avoidance tendencies are conveniently known as the *approach gradient* and the *avoidance gradient.* Miller (1944) and Brown (1948) have proposed that *the avoidance gradient is steeper than the approach gradient.* Figure 2-1 illustrates these relationships. Clinical and experimental observations (for example, Miller & Murray, 1952; Murray & Berkun, 1955) strongly suggest that the facts of behavior fit this model very frequently. We are not concerned at the moment with the nature of this evidence or with the exceptions to the model. We shall examine the figure in more detail shortly. For the moment it should be noticed that both the approach and avoidance tendencies get stronger as a person nears a goal and that the avoidance gradient is the steeper of the two—that is, the avoidance tendency increases more sharply than the approach tendency as one gets nearer the goal. Of course, the directional "pull" of the two tendencies is opposite: the stronger the approach tendency, the stronger the pull *toward* the goal; the stronger the avoidance tendency, the stronger the push *away* from the goal. (This is what the arrows on the approach and avoidance gradients indicate.)

Lewin and Miller made clear how different the behavior is in the various types of conflict situations. These differences are due to the kinds of tendencies involved and to the gradient property of the tendencies.

**Approach-Approach
Conflict**
The approach-approach conflict is quickly and easily resolved. Assume that an individual is in a state of equilibrium: His two approach tendencies are equally strong. For a moment he will be unable to choose between two goals. Very soon, however, one or the other goal will become more desired than the other, even though ever so slightly. A shift in attention or some additional extraneous stimulation might produce this change. However it is produced, that change will be enough to tip the balance. At this point the individual will start to approach that goal. As he moves nearer, his tendency to move nearer still will become stronger, and this strengthened tendency will then

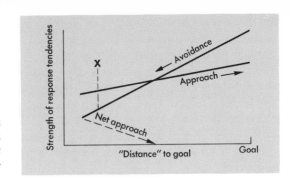

Figure 2-1 The approach and avoidance gradients in a simple approach-avoidance conflict. (Adapted from Miller, 1944)

move him still closer to that goal. Since there is no opposing avoidance tendency, a snowballing of approach behavior to the particular goal in question will occur, and the original state of conflict will cease.

Approach-Avoidance
Conflict   The introduction of avoidance tendencies alters the situation drastically, as an examination of the approach-avoidance conflict reveals. Remember that in this case the individual is prompted to approach and avoid the same goal, to make and to refrain from the same response. Remember, too, that in our model the avoidance gradient is steeper than the approach gradient. In this instance we are assuming that the avoidance gradient is of sufficient overall strength to cross the approach gradient.

Suppose an individual is at point X in Figure 2-1. At that point his approach tendency is stronger than his avoidance tendency. Thus, the individual will start to approach the goal. As he approaches the goal, however, his more sharply rising avoidance tendency eventually will be stronger than the approach tendency. At this point the individual will retreat from the goal. Soon he will reach a point where his approach tendency is again stronger than his avoidance tendency, and he will again start to approach the goal. And so he might continue oscillating. In general, we can say the individual would be trapped in the approach-avoidance conflict situation. His avoidance tendency would prevent him from reaching the goal he strives for; his approach tendency would prevent him from ever giving up that goal.

The "edge" the approach tendency has over the avoidance tendency is shown by the "net approach" line in the diagram. That edge decreases steadily as the individual approaches the goal, and it disappears at the point where two gradients meet—that is, where the two tendencies are of equal strength and there is neither a net approach nor a net avoidance. Net approach is simply a convenient quantitative way of representing the comparative strengths of the two opposing tendencies.

There is quite a difference between the approach-approach and the approach-avoidance conflict. The former is easily resolved and results in some form of satisfaction: One or the other goal is attained. The latter introduces negative factors (such as fear and guilt), which give rise to the avoidance tendency. It results in the frustration of both the approach and the avoidance tendencies, and it creates the distress of sustained conflict per se. We assume that approach-avoidance conflicts produce the kinds of chronic symptoms experienced by Anna O. and Lucy R., which we discussed in the preceding chapter. We saw there how Lucy, for example, loved her employer and at the same time was driven to suppress that love by her fear of being rejected and humiliated by him. Her constant preoccupation with cigar smoke appeared to be an indirect expression of these conflicting feelings, for the smell of it reminded her of him—both how attractive he was and how cruel he could be. Lucy was also chronically fatigued, which can be attributed to her prolonged state of conflict.

Double Approach-Avoidance Conflict

The double approach-avoidance situation also produces misery but of a somewhat different type. Remember that in the double approach-avoidance conflict the person is prompted to both approach and avoid two different goals simultaneously. To bring out the contrasting features of this situation, we shall again assume that the avoidance gradient is steeper than the approach gradient and also that it is of such overall strength that it crosses the approach gradient. The state of the individual in these circumstances is diagramed in Figure 2-2. As a result of the conflict over approaching goal A, the individual's net approach tendency for goal A progressively decreases as he comes nearer to it and becomes zero before he reaches the goal. The same state of affairs is true with regard to his net tendency to approach goal B.

What will the individual do if he is at point X? He will approach B, since the tendency to do so is stronger at that point than the tendency to approach A. Soon, however, the tendency to approach A will be the greater. When it is, he will start to approach A, retreating from B. And so on. This simultaneous action of the two incompatible net approach tendencies will prevent him from reaching either goal. Yet he will be trapped in the situation. The donkey who starved to death because he couldn't choose between

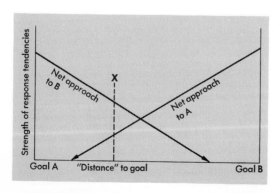

Figure 2-2 The net approach gradients in a double approach-avoidance conflict. (Adapted from Miller, 1944)

two equally attractive piles of hay was trapped in such a double approach-avoidance conflict. In his case it was greed that gave rise to the two avoidance tendencies. The thought of giving up one pile while he ate the other produced his eternal dilemma and his eventual starvation. The young man who cannot choose between a beautiful but stupid girl and a less beautiful but intelligent one is caught in the same kind of situation. The double approach-avoidance conflict situation is clearly a distressing one: In it are the aversive factors underlying the avoidance tendencies, the frustration of the four general response tendencies (two approach tendencies and two avoidance ones), and the tension created by the conflict itself.

Avoidance-Avoidance Conflict   What about the avoidance-avoidance conflict? Since there are no approach tendencies to maintain the conflict, the individual will leave the field entirely, avoiding both goals. While momentarily distressful, this conflict permits of a ready solution and relief in a free-field situation. However, escape from the field may be, and very frequently is, blocked by physical or psychological barriers. (The latter are often additional avoidance tendencies.) If so, the individual is trapped in the conflict situation.

Our study of conflict psychology must return now primarily to the empirical discoveries and theory of psychoanalysis concerning the approach-avoidance conflicts. For convenience we shall generally use the simple term *conflict*, by which we shall always mean approach-avoidance conflicts. Nearly every human approach-avoidance conflict is part of a double approach-avoidance conflict, in fact part of a whole series of interrelated double approach-avoidance conflicts. But in our examples we shall focus on only the most salient *single* approach-avoidance conflict. This is sufficient for an exposition of the basic principles of conflict and defense.

We shall begin by considering real conflicts experienced by three different people. For now we shall discuss only those aspects of their lives that are directly relevant to the specific conflicts with which we are concerned. In later chapters we shall add further information about these three people and about the case studies of Freud that we shall cite.

Examples of Conflict

A PERCEPTUAL CONFLICT: DUANE

Duane, a man who is considered psychiatrically normal, had the following unusual perceptual experience at the time of his father's death. Dutifully present during the prescribed hours for the "viewing" of the body by friends and relatives, Duane spent much of the time virtually alone in the room. Several times he walked up to the open casket and looked for long moments at his father's body.

Duane knew and could see that his father was dead. He could see this from the grotesquely distorted mouth position produced by the clumsy mortician. He could see it from the pancake make-up on his father's face. He could see it from the utter stillness of his father's body. And yet, episodically, he saw his father alive, as if he were restfully sleeping. Especially vividly he saw the rise and fall of his father's chest as he breathed deeply, easily, and regularly. Why did Duane experience this perceptual conflict?

The death of his father was a very painful loss for Duane, as the loss of a loved parent is for anyone. But it also frightened him because it aroused fearful memories of three earlier deaths—the death of his mother in his early childhood, the death a few years later of his grandfather, who was in effect the boy's father (his own father having remarried and abandoned the boy to his grandparents until adolescence), and the death of his grandmother during his adolescence. A new and special instance now occurred with the death of his father. Thus, the sight of his dead father aroused an intensely painful and fearful sense of loss.

There were other reasons why the sight of his dead father was unpleasant. When Duane was told that his father was seriously ill and might die, he consciously hoped that he would. That would free Duane of responsibility for an ailing old man who would intrude on his life. And, at first, he was relieved to hear that his father had died. In both instances these thoughts and feelings made him feel guilty. This complex reaction had lasted very briefly when it first occurred, but Duane remembered it for a moment soon after he first saw his dead father. Then he banished such thoughts from his conscious thinking.

The sight of his dead father, then, was acutely unpleasant for this man: It aroused a painful *grief reaction* based on his love for him and a *fear reaction* based on a latent childlike need for him; but it also rearoused the *guilt* stemming from his wish that his father would die and from his sense of being relieved and freed by his father's death, and he saw before him the fulfillment of these guilt-laden wishes. It was as if he coped with the disturbing vision of his dead father by distorting the final perception— by seeing his father alive, not dead. To the extent that he saw his father alive, one could say that he *denied* the realistic perception that he was dead.

The behavioral processes are diagramed in Figure 2-3. With one exception (to be mentioned in a moment), the components diagramed are known, they are facts. The solid arrows represent inferred causal relations. The gray arrow is an arbitrary notation indicating that the inaccurate perception interferes with the occurrence of the accurate perception. The label "denial" is the technical psychoanalytic term for this type of substitution of an inaccurate perception for an accurate one.

But there were also reasons for Duane to perceive his father accurately, and these we have not yet discussed. One reason was the simple fact that Duane's perceptual processes, like those of other normal adults, would automatically tend to be accurate. There are, of course, *motives* for realistic perception. Thus, a desire to look at his father's body is listed in Figure 2-3 as one of Duane's approach motives. That he did want to look at his father can be inferred from his behavior. He was not physically forced to go to

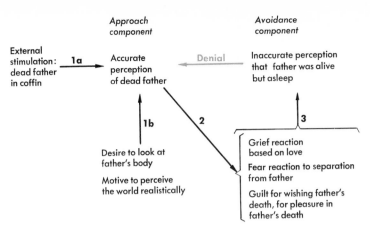

Figure 2-3   The approach-avoidance conflict instigated in Duane by his father's death.

The presence of Duane's dead father's body and the approach motives (the desire to look at his father and to perceive the world realistically) prompt the accurate perception of his dead father (1a and 1b). But this accurate perception produces a complex, unpleasant emotional state in Duane (2), which in turn prompts his inaccurate perception that his father is alive (3). This inaccurate perception replaces, or denies, the accurate perception. As a result, the intensity of the unpleasant emotional state is decreased. Thus, the perceptual denial defends Duane against painful emotional experiences. (In all of the schematic diagrams gray arrows and labels indicate defenses.)

the coffin, stand by it, and gaze on his father, yet he did just that. We infer that both his love and his thinly veiled pleasure at his father's death motivated him to approach the coffin and look at his father's body. And we can also infer that he wanted to perceive accurately, for nearly every adult learns that it is to his advantage to do so.

Diagrams like that in Figure 2-3 will be used throughout this volume. Therefore, it might be worthwhile to focus attention on this first one to be sure it is clear how the diagram schematizes what we know about Duane's experience. Recall that we have singled out for explanation one aspect of his experience: his perceptual conflict. This was manifested in the oscillation between the accurate perception of his father as being dead and the inaccurate perception that his father was alive but asleep.

In terms of the approach-avoidance conflict model, we can regard the accurate perception of his dead father as both the goal and the approach behavior. The two black arrows numbered 1a and 1b represent diagrammatically the fact that this approach behavior was instigated by both the external stimulus of his father's body and by the two approach motives, his wish to look at his father and his desire to perceive it realistically. The black arrow numbered 2 represents the fact that the accurate perception of his dead father aroused in Duane a sense of grief, of separation fear, and of guilt over his wish that his father die. These unpleasant emotions in turn motivated Duane's inaccurate perception, as represented by the black arrow numbered 3. This misperception is defensive avoidance behavior in terms of the approach-avoidance conflict model, and the unpleasant emotions are avoidance motives. We can see that the substitution of the inaccurate perception for the accurate one would provide Duane with some temporary reduction of his sense of grief, fear, and guilt by obliterating momentarily the vivid reminder of his father's death.

In the remainder of this chapter we shall examine two additional examples of conflict. Then in the next chapter we shall present a general paradigm concerned with the elements of conflict and their interrelations common to all our examples.

A SEXUAL CONFLICT: ED

A young man, whom we shall call Ed, periodically attempted to find sexual satisfaction in masturbation and in premarital intercourse with his fiancée. However, in both circumstances he felt uneasy, tense, and sweaty, and a vague sense of impending doom engulfed him afterward. Hence, Ed avoided both activities most of the time.

Conscious guilt and shame were very important causes of Ed's discomfort. He did not want anyone to know about his masturbation, and, despite a boastful attitude toward his premarital intercourse, he preferred that no one know about it. Mere discretion or a sense of privacy was not his only motivation; he felt that both acts were sinful and relieved evil urges on his part. He discovered a still more powerful and previously unknown source of his discomfort as he explored his behavior day after day in psychoanalysis: He feared that his genitals would be cut off if he engaged in these activities. This fear was unconscious; it manifested itself most clearly in frightening dreams that only occurred following an increase in either masturbation or intercourse. After one such upsurge in sexual activity, for example, Ed dreamed that he had a fatal illness and was in a hospital. The doctors had removed an organ from his body and wrapped it up. It made a small, elongated package. As Ed told the dream to his analyst, the shape of the package reminded him of the shape of a penis.

Following another upsurge in sexual activity, Ed dreamed that one of his testicles was quite large owing to a tumor growing within it. A man, presumably a doctor, was going to cut it off. Ed's view of his sexuality as a fatal and evil cancerous process as well as his fear that he would be castrated were very thinly disguised in these dreams. While thinking about this dream, he remembered suddenly that he had dreamed something similar when he was about 7 years old: "A woman had cut off my penis and was starting to slice the end of it the way my mother sliced bananas for my cereal. This woman had cut the penises off all the little boys in the world. She looked like a witch."

The content of these nightmares, their close temporal correlation with active phases in his sexual life, and his associations to them strongly sug-

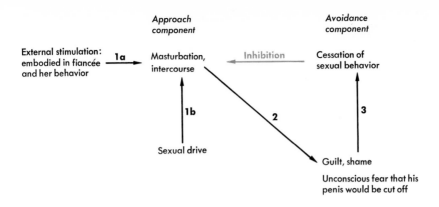

Figure 2-4   Ed's approach-avoidance sexual conflict.

The combined effects of his fiancée and his sexual drive prompt Ed to engage in sexual behavior (1a and 1b). But such activity arouses conscious guilt and shame and unconscious castration anxiety (2), which in turn motivate Ed to stop engaging in sexual behavior (3). He does so by actively inhibiting the actions he wants to perform. As a result, he no longer experiences the guilt, shame, and fear. Thus, the inhibition has defended him from very unpleasant emotional experiences, but at the expense of his losing full sexual gratification.

gest that Ed's uneasiness, tension, sweating, and sense of doom associated with masturbation and intercourse were surface manifestations of an unconscious fear of castration, a fear present in his childhood and still operative in his adult life. It appears that sexual behavior activated this fear and that he avoided the danger of castration by inhibiting his sexual behavior.

Recent experimental studies of dreams and sleep suggest that similar inhibition occurs even during dreams. Fisher, Gross, and Zuch (1965; see also Fisher 1965a, b) found that penile erections accompany more than 90 percent of the rapid eye movement periods of sleep, which indicate reliably that a person is dreaming. However, preliminary data suggested that nightmares involving disguised castration anxiety and conflicts over unconscious incestuous wishes caused the erections to disappear.

A diagram of Ed's sexual conflict, including the known behavioral components and the inferred causal relations, is presented in Figure 2-4. *Inhibition* is the psychoanalytic term for the type of cessation of sexual activity manifested by Ed. The term implies that this cessation functions *actively* to prevent such sexual behavior as masturbation and intercourse. It is distinct from passive cessation, such as that which follows sexual gratification.

AN EATING CONFLICT: EDIE

Edie was a young woman who periodically could not eat. When she tried to eat at such times, she would feel nauseated and would be afraid she might choke on a piece of food because it would be so big it would get stuck in her throat. Physicians could not find any medical basis for her difficulty, and there was nothing wrong with the size bites she took. Nor was anything wrong with her appetite. In fact, eating was one of her favorite activities. Furthermore, eating the foods she liked best bothered her the most. The whole picture is one of a psychological conflict of the approach-avoidance type. The ordinary human need for food, but particularly her special relish for it, strongly motivated her to eat. Yet her nausea and fear of choking motivated her to avoid it.

If Edie had ever actually eaten foul food, so spoiled that it made her sick to her stomach, or if she had ever actually choked on food, she could have had a conflict resulting from simple conditioning. But as far as she could remember, she had had no such experiences.

A retrospective view of her analysis shows that her eating conflict was based on another conflict. The nature of this other conflict and of its relation to the eating conflict will become apparent from some of the relevant information. We are going to reach a strange conclusion. To make that conclusion as credible as possible, we have selected the least inferential information available. Only close attention and fitting together of details of scattered descriptions and seemingly isolated episodes of Edie's life were required to formulate the following material, not "deep interpretations." To avoid giving the wrong impression, however, we must point out that the mutual relevance of these various items of information and the way we have fit them together are all part of a *retrospective account* of portions of Edie's psychoanalysis. During an actual psychoanalysis, separate items of information are embedded among many other items. They do not emerge in a logical sequence, and the meaning of each is not crystal clear at the time it occurs. But gradually the bits form a consistent pattern, converging on a unique formulation that appears to account for them.

The Origin and Early Form of the Eating Conflict

As a child Edie had always been an "eating problem" for her parents, but her present severe problem started in her adolescence. Following a high school dance, she and her date went to a local teen-age hangout, where they ordered cheeseburgers, one of her favorite foods. As she ate she felt nauseated. On a few subsequent dates, which also included a stop for cheeseburgers, she again felt nauseated and was afraid she might vomit and strangle on the vomitus or on a fresh bite of the cheeseburger. During this period, she was not affected this way if she ate with girls or at home; it only occurred with boys. Edie's discomfort and fear were so intense that she stopped eating with her boyfriends.

For the next 7 years, she avoided eating when in the presence of a man. This restriction prevented her from developing any sustained, intimate relationship with a man. She would date a man up to the point when he would ask her to dine with him, whereupon she would refuse without explaining why. That would be the last she would hear from some men. Those who took her out again would sooner or later again suggest a dinner date and would be curious about her rejections, which she still refused to explain. Eventually even these persistent men would stop calling her, or she would simply refuse all dates with them. Her reasoning then was that she was too ashamed to explain her fears about eating with them and that she could not cope with their curiosity about her unpredictability in accepting dates with them.

Two things are striking at this point: the specific relation between Edie's eating conflict and her heterosexual life, and the far-reaching effect it had on that life. This effect is especially curious if one stops to consider it. It seemed perfectly logical to Edie that her inability to eat with men and her reluctance to tell them why should preclude every potential intimate male relationship. But it is not logical. If Edie unconflictfully wanted intimacy, she could have obtained it in spite of her eating conflict. Many men would not have been driven away by it, and some would have been interested by it. People pursue love despite even more severe handicaps. The fact that she did not do so makes one wonder if she also had a sexual conflict, and if it might be intimately connected with her eating conflict.

Edie was, in fact, very conflicted in her sexual life, both during adolescence and for a long time after the onset of her eating conflict. Her sexual desires were strong, but so were her anxiety and guilt about them. Even during late adolescence her sexual life was minimal, and any kissing or necking and petting were sources of great anxiety and guilt. She had been raised to believe that any kind of sexual activity not immediately connected with having children was sinful and would eventually be punished harshly by her parents and God. The severity of Edie's upbringing is indicated by the fact that her parents never shared the same bedroom after her younger sibling was born when Edie was 3. Her parents always gave as the reason for this drastic step their decision not to have any more children. Previously, sexuality had been a necessary evil for them; now it was an unnecessary one, to be avoided at all costs.

Thus, the speculation that her sexual life was quite conflictful is correct. But we have not yet seen the further evidence that there is a relation between this and her eating conflict.

Concomitant Variation in the Eating and Sexual Conflicts

Lonely and frustrated in her early adulthood, desperate that she might never enjoy a normal life, Edie met a young man to whom she revealed her eating conflict. He mothered her with his own cooking and with a great deal of tolerance and sympathy. At the same time, she was waging a painful conscious struggle to overcome her sexual conflict. Finally she achieved a temporary and partial victory over both of her conflicts: She was able to eat with this man and to be sexually intimate with him. She was not completely free of discomfort in either circumstance, but at least she was able to achieve enough gratification to give her a new life. In fact, she soon married him.

The fact that both conflicts changed at the same time suggests that they might have been related. We could confidently conclude they were if we saw repeated instances of such covariation.

By the time Edie undertook psychoanalysis, her eating conflict had become sporadic and was no longer limited to the situation of eating in the presence of a man. The very frequent psychoanalytic interviews over a period of several years provided a unique opportunity to observe the psychological context of the fluctuations in severity of her eating conflict.

At the time she started psychoanalysis, Edie's sexual conflict had been intensified for a few months. For many reasons, which we will not go into, she was not enjoying a pleasurable spontaneous sexual life with her husband. At the same time, her eating conflict had flared up again. She complained especially of her inability to eat hamburgers, which were still among her favorite foods. Things continued in this way for nearly a year, but then she reached a point where there was a marked reduction in her conflict over sexuality. She was able for a while to tolerate her rich erotic feminine capacities. While this change affected many aspects of her life, it was most directly shown in frequent and enjoyable intercourse with her husband. What happened to her eating conflict now? It too disappeared. For the first time since she entered analysis she was eating hamburgers, and her general pleasure in eating was very great. This kind of thing happened again several times. When her sexual anxiety, guilt, and inhibitions decreased, so did her conflict over eating. Thus, there was clearly a relation between these two conflicts.

Can we go further and say what the nature of that relationship was? For example, was one conflict a necessary condition for the other? The most plausible answer seems to be that her sexual conflict was the cause of her eating conflict. Three types of observation suggest that this was the case.

1. Other information in her analysis very strongly suggested that her becoming an "eating problem" was the residue of a severe childhood neurosis around the ages of 5 and 6. This neurosis involved a severe childhood sexual conflict. Before the neurosis came about, she was a beautiful, rounded, feminine little girl with wavy hair; after it appeared, she became unattractively "stark" (to use her own word), dour, and thin, and she wore her hair in a straight, tightly drawn style.

2. We know that her sexual conflicts in adolescence preceded the eating conflict that emerged at that time.

3. In her analysis her sexual conflict always *appeared* to change before her eating conflict did. We can only speak of *appearance* here, for patients do not always let analysts know such things precisely when they happen.

We have seen that Edie's eating and sexual conflicts varied together. And we have reason to believe that they did so because her sexual conflict was the necessary condition for her eating conflict. Did her analysis bring to light any explanation for these two aspects of her eating conflict? It did.

Hunger and Eating as Substitutes for Genital Desires and Sexual Behavior

One day Edie and her husband were visiting a local museum; suddenly she was struck with an overwhelming wish to have intercourse with him. They rushed home, but something in the situation momentarily stimulated her sexual anxiety and guilt to a slight degree. Thereupon she was seized with an equally urgent hunger. For a moment she could not decide whether to eat and then have intercourse or vice versa, so equally balanced and peremptory were these two desires. The outcome was a quick bite of something from a refrigerator shelf on the way to the bedroom.

Notice that the arousal of a strong sexual wish and then inhibition of that wish *preceded* the appearance of her strong hunger. Notice also that eating was nearly as desirable as intercourse. It is as if hunger and eating were substitutes for sexual desire and sexual gratification.

If they were, that would explain the covariation of the two conflicts and the dependence of the eating conflict on the sexual conflict. When her sexual conflict was intense, leaving her sexual desires inhibited and frustrated, eating became a substitute activity and acquired a new meaning: it was *sexual activity* providing actual erotic gratification. This being true, it now became the source of anxiety and guilt. Thus, *this woman's eating conflict was a substitute for her sexual conflict.* This is "the strange conclusion" we mentioned in the beginning. It is strange, yet it seems inescapable in view of the evidence. Exactly the type of evidence we have cited led Freud and other psychoanalysts to construct their hypotheses about the unconscious motivational conflicts that underlie surface inhibitions, hysterical symptoms, and other forms of neurotic behavior.

Sexual conflicts have different effects in different people. Edie developed an *eating* conflict because her previously established attitudes or fantasies, of which she remained unaware, made eating and sexuality *equivalent* for her. Her eating conflict did not arise by chance that night she was eating cheeseburgers with her boyfriend after the high school dance. Nor was chance responsible for the fact that it retained its peculiar form for 7 years and kept her from becoming intimate with a man. Many other means could have been used to solve that problem. The eating conflict had to be the solution for Edie because of its sexual equivalence. It is in this sense that symptoms and their behavioral effects are psychologically determined and have a specific "unconscious meaning," in Freud's terms. (Why that equivalence came to be, we have not considered. We have only been concerned with showing that there was such an equivalence.)

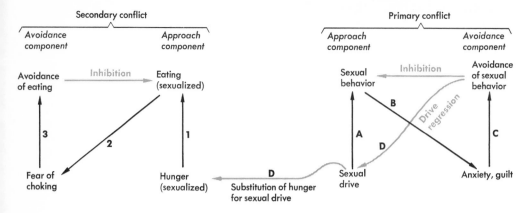

Figure 2-5   Edie's manifest eating conflict and her more basic, underlying sexual conflict.

Edie's sexual drive prompts her to engage in sexual behavior (A). But even the slightest tendency to do so, such as wishing to or thinking about it, arouses anxiety and guilt (B). These painful emotions motivate her to avoid sexual behavior by actively inhibiting it (C) and to regress to an earlier form of sexual desire— oral cravings. Thus, Edie not only inhibits her sexual behavior but also substitutes hunger for sexual desires (D). Hunger, now sexualized, prompts her to engage in highly sensual, sexualized eating (1). But to eat, especially in the presence of a man, produces in her a fear of choking (2). This fear motivates her to avoid eating, to actively inhibit it (3). In this way she defends herself against the fear of choking and, indirectly, against the primary conflict over sexuality.

The diagram in Figure 2-5 schematizes the basic processes that we have discussed in this example of conflict. *Drive regression* is the psychoanalytic term for the process of substituting a developmentally earlier drive and its resultant behavior for a developmentally later drive and its resultant behavior. In Edie's case hunger and eating were substituted for the sexual drive and sexual behavior. As we shall see in Chapters 4 and 12, there are good reasons to believe that oral stimulation constitutes an earlier form of sexuality than does genital behavior and that Edie had defensively returned to this earlier stage.

In this chapter we have presented three examples of approach-avoidance conflicts. In the example of Duane we focused on his perceptual conflict; he oscillated between "approaching" the realistic perception of his dead father and avoiding that painful experience by hallucinating that his father was breathing and thus still alive. Ed's conflict consisted of the oscillation between "approaching" sexual gratification and actively avoiding it. Edie suffered from two interrelated approach-avoidance conflicts: her sexual conflict and her eating conflict. Within each conflict she would oscillate between the relevant gratification and the avoidance of it. In addition, she oscillated between the two conflicts, now approaching sexual gratification, now avoiding it by regressing to eating, but then having to avoid that pleasure because of its sexual significance.

In each case, of course, we have focused only on certain aspects of what were highly complex situations. We saw, for example, that conflicting approach and avoidance motives operated behind the drama of the conflicting overt responses we have just mentioned. Thus, a wish that his father be dead and the conflicting guilt over this wish were among the underlying motives causing Duane's perceptual conflict. This motivational conflict produced many other effects on Duane's behavior that we did not discuss. The same was true in the other two examples.

In fact, I am no clever work of fiction;
I am a man, with all his contradiction.

K. F. MEYER. Hutten's Last Days

CHAPTER 3
BASIC CONCEPTS
OF CONFLICT
AND DEFENSE

I n the preceding chapter we became familiar with a few concrete examples of conflict. Now we can go on to discuss some important features common to all of them. The starting point of each example was an instance of impaired behavior—a faulty perception of reality, a sexual disturbance in a young man, an eating disturbance in a young woman.

Psychological Determinism

In each instance the behavioral impairment was caused by conflict, by psychological rather than biological processes. In this sense each instance was a special case of the most fundamental principle of psychoanalysis: the principle of exceptionless psychological determinism. This principle states that in a biologically intact human being every aspect of behavior is determined by psychological factors. It insists that there are no accidents or coincidences in human behavior and that there is no such thing as a meaningless pattern of behavior.

Although Freud did not create the idea of psychological determinism, he did make a revolutionary contribution to it: He extended the concept to include forms of behavior, such as hysteria, dreams, and many aspects of psychotic behavior, that previously had not been regarded as psychologically caused, and he relentlessly applied the principle to *details* of behavior that had been largely ignored. Slips of the tongue, memory lapses, and other forms of what Freud called "the psychopathology of everyday life," as well as "random" thoughts, including free associations, all appeared to him to be psychologically determined. Revolutionary at the time, this extension is still heatedly contested by biologically oriented psychologists and psychiatrists. However, the general principle of exceptionless psychological determinism is accepted at least implicitly by many behavioral scientists.

Not that psychoanalysis ignores the role of biological factors in behavior; on the contrary, they are assumed to be the ultimate basis of all behavior. The emphasis on *psychological* determinism merely means that many aspects of human behavior, including conflict and its results, cannot be attributed to biological aberrations. They seem to be caused by such psychological processes as motives, emotions, stable personality traits, fantasies, anticipations, and so forth.

Nor are sociological or cultural factors ignored. Indeed, psychoanalysis has always insisted that these factors play an important part in the development and functioning of the personality. Psychoanalysis does maintain, however, that society and culture influence behavior only through their impact on the psychology of the individual. These influences alter or mold psychological processes within the individual and thus become part of the "internal" psychological determinants of behavior.

The adjective "exceptionless" is redundant, of course, but it serves to emphasize that no behavioral detail is exempt from psychological causation. Thus, Edie's sexual conflict caused not only her eating conflict but also the specific conditions in which it arose and the specific form it took during the 7-year period. If we had examined the other two examples as minutely, we would have found that their specific details too had to be exactly as they were: that there were reasons why Duane hallucinated breathing movements on the part of his dead father rather than something else and why Ed's sexual fears were expressed specifically in medical terms. The relentless application of the principle of exceptionless psychological determinism as a working assumption greatly enhances the understanding of human behavior.

The Conflict Paradigm

We have examined several specific instances of conflict, but what are the patterns and principles common to all approach-avoidance conflicts? What is the essence of the psychological determinism of the results of conflict?

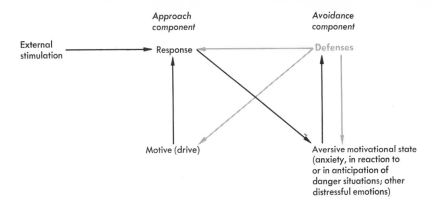

Figure 3-1   *The general approach-avoidance conflict paradigm.*

An external stimulus or an approach motive or, more often, a combination of the two instigates an approach response. In turn, the approach response evokes distressing emotions, which are usually some kind of anxiety—anticipatory fear, shame, or guilt. The distressing emotion motivates defenses, which have the effect of ending or preventing the painful emotion. Some defenses interfere with the approach motive or drive; some interfere with the approach response; and some are oriented directly against the unpleasant emotions.

We began our search for such generalizations in the last chapter, where we discussed the four basic types of conflict as categorized by Lewin and Miller: approach-approach, approach-avoidance, avoidance-avoidance, and double approach-avoidance. We saw that these categories are based on the kinds of competing response tendencies operating in the conflicts. We then discussed some general principles of conflict behavior: the approach and avoidance gradients and their behavioral consequences in the four classes of conflict.

We can now arrive at a general model, or paradigm, of conflict by extracting the common features from the schematic diagrams used earlier to describe specific conflicts. What we obtain is the following formulation, which is also illustrated in Figure 3-1. Approach-avoidance conflicts involve opposing response tendencies. One of these tendencies, conveniently called the "approach" tendency, is instigated by external stimulation (for example, Duane's perception of his dead father), by internal motives or drives, or by the combined action of external stimulation and internal motivation. This response (the approach tendency) in turn gives rise to an aversive motivational state in the individual. An aversive motivational state is an internal condition, such as pain or fear, that impels a person to bring it to an end. At times this aversive state is a direct response to the perceptions of the external situation. The grief and sense of painful loss experienced upon seeing the dead body of one's parent is such a direct response. In most human conflicts, however, there is no such current basis in reality for the aversive motivational state. Yet the individual is acting *as if* some *dangerous situation* actually did exist or as if he will suffer some dangerous consequences because he has responded as he has. He appears to be *anticipating a danger situation.* Ed was clearly doing this, for example, when he feared that someone would cut off his penis because he was intimate with his fiancée. So was Edie when she feared her parents' and God's punishment for her sexual behavior.

The aversive motivational state also includes from time to time other distressing feelings that we cannot so readily describe as anticipations of danger situations, such as the fear of being separated from a loved one, the guilt and shame that appeared in the examples, and other distressing affects, such as disgust and depression, that did not appear in our examples. But closer inspection in later chapters will show that it is possible to conceptualize these aversive states as reactions to or anticipations of danger situations.

Once produced, the aversive, unpleasant state motivates the individual to respond in ways that enable him to avoid it and the anticipated danger situation. Since these responses have this protective effect, they are called *defense mechanisms,* or simply *defenses.* There are many different kinds of defenses. Even our limited number of examples illustrated several different kinds. In the first example Duane distorted his perception of his father by *denial.* The other examples involved *inhibition* of actions that would have been instrumental in obtaining satisfaction: Ed was inhibited in his sexual behavior, and Edie was inhibited in both eating and sexual behavior. Another defense mechanism, *regression,* in this case from genital to oral-alimentary desires, was also involved in Edie's conflict. In Ed's case we saw still another defense, *repression,* in his obliteration from awareness of the ideational content of his fears—that he would be castrated. Repression very commonly involves obliteration from consciousness of the approach motives as well as the avoidance motives. Later we shall examine the whole array of known defenses; the important point right now is to realize that there are different kinds and that the process of defense can affect different aspects of behavior—such as the perceptual, the ideational, the motoric—and different components of the conflict paradigm.

All the defenses, however, have the same result of avoiding or decreasing the aversive motivational state, of avoiding or mitigating a perceived or anticipated danger situation. Some defenses do so by altering perceptions that cause distress; others do so by altering the drives or responses that indirectly bring about the aversive state; still others do so by interfering with the aversive states themselves. The three gray arrows of Figure 3-1 depict such various orientations of defenses.

Do Conflict and Defense
Ever Concern Trifling Matters?

At first glance, the products of conflict and defense often seem trivial and foolish. It is a temptation to view in this light such events as the transitory perception of respiratory movements in a dead body and an outbreak of anxiety over eating a cheeseburger—a temptation often yielded to by experts in human behavior as well as by the layman. But this appearance is deceptive. Death, ambivalence composed of love and hate for a father, sexual desires, fear of parents and of God, shame and guilt—all these and more of the most significant aspects of human life lie behind such seemingly insignificant phenomena as the surface events. Our examples are not exceptional; the investigation of any product of conflict and defense leads to the same order of vital factors in life and to the same degree of complexity.

Conscious and Unconscious Conflict

The examples make clear the extent to which unconscious processes are involved in conflict; we saw that the very fact of there being a conflict may not be known to an individual. While Ed was aware of having a sexual conflict and of some of the conflicting motives, he was not aware of the very important fear that his penis would be cut off. That fear manifested itself only in disguised form in his nightmares. Edie knew, of course, by the time she started analysis that she had a sexual and an eating conflict, but she was not aware of the relationship between them or of the key factors involved in each. Obviously, some of the most significant aspects of the lives of these people were unconscious. Consciousness and significance are not equivalent in human psychology.

One can place conflicts on a continuum representing the extent to which conscious and unconscious processes are operative. No conflicts are completely free from unconscious influences, but some are relatively free; in such instances the person is aware that he is in conflict and knows what his conflict is essentially about. And such conflicts, too, may involve very significant aspects of life. The conflict of the frightened but honorable soldier and that of the parent who must punish the child he loves are familiar examples.

It makes a great deal of difference, however, just how free a conflict is from unconscious influences. This difference is shown in three ways: (1) the degree to which the conflict is realistic or appropriate, (2) the process by which the conflict is resolved, and (3) consequences of the conflict.

APPROPRIATENESS

Conscious conflicts are usually appropriate to the external or internal situation, while unconscious conflicts are seldom appropriate. The conflict of the normal soldier about to enter battle is highly realistic and appropriate; Edie's conflict over eating was highly unrealistic and inappropriate. Conflict is highly appropriate if one is knowingly about to commit an opprobrious act but not if one is merely daydreaming; yet daydreams greatly disturb people whose unconscious wishes are gratified by this means.

RESOLUTION

To resolve most conscious conflicts, people think, reason, and make decisions. Furthermore, they do these things to a degree appropriate to the seriousness and complexity of the issues. Thought and decision making play little or no part, however, in the resolution of unconscious conflicts. Instead, the individual resorts automatically and unknowingly to the defense mechanisms. This is what occurred in each of our examples.

Sometimes people do engage in a great deal of thought when unconscious conflict is involved, but in a manner that is quite inappropriate. The thinking has a ruminative quality, and decisions are very late in coming or never come at all. And the amount of thinking bears no relation to the issue at hand. When her eating conflict was activated, Edie would often spend a great deal of time considering whether, and what, to eat. She did this briefly that day she and her husband rushed home from the museum. That rumination and indecision was due to a momentary, unconscious increase in her sexual conflict. In extreme cases of this kind of inappropriate thinking people cannot decide such simple things as whether to say Yes or No to the simplest question, whether to turn right or left, or which shoe to put on first. Freud speculated that Hamlet's indecision about avenging his father's death was due to a conflict over his unconscious hostility toward his father.

CONSEQUENCES

Of course, conscious conflicts do not always have a happy ending, even though they are more easily resolved than unconscious ones. Sometimes we choose not to do something we desire to do. We feel regret, but we are able to tolerate our frustration or disappointment. Often we sympathize with ourselves, comforting or rewarding ourselves with a substitute satisfaction, or we let our friends and family do so for us.

The outcome of unconscious conflict resolution by defense mechanisms is quite different. Defenses impair behavior, as we have already seen. But still more disadvantages follow. They prevent a person from becoming aware of the true nature of his anxieties and thus from modifying them through reappraisal and relearning. Moreover, they provide for no real gratification of needs and thus leave the individual in a frustrated, pent-up state. There is a price, then—often a very great price—for the relief of anxiety and the security from imagined dangers achieved through the process of defense. The relief is particularly expensive because this is not the end of the matter, especially where internal needs are the primary instigators of the conflict. They still motivate the individual, usually driving him with even greater intensity. The opposing motives are unchanged. The result is perpetuation of the conflict, in the same or disguised form, and further defense. An endless process of conflict and defense is the typical outcome of unconscious conflict.

When Edie resolved her sexual conflict in adolescence with repressions and inhibitions, her sexual needs continued at a high level of intensity, partly because they were completely unsatisfied by even indirect means and partly because of the physiology of adolescence. They were then transposed from her sexual apparatus and functions to her alimentary system and functions. Eating became a substitute for sexual behavior. But eating now became the source of conflict and the target of defense. At first this "new" conflict was a restricted one, only a step removed from her sexual conflict: She became panicky and unable to eat cheeseburgers whenever she was with a boy. Her specific phobic avoidance of this situation was a temporary resolution of conflict by means of a defense that did not alter the unconscious conflict. She then developed a conflict over eating anything in the presence of a man and resolved this by phobic avoidance. Finally, eating under any circumstance became embroiled in conflict. And she still had her sexual conflict! The defensive attempt to resolve her adolescent sexual conflict thus initiated a repetitive process that continued for many years and that involved progressively larger segments of her behavior. Whenever she decreased her defensive resolution of her sexual conflict, gradually in her developing relationship with her future husband or episodically in her analysis, her eating conflict vanished.

The differences between conscious and unconscious conflicts that we have been discussing and illustrating are generally observable phenomena. They rank among the most significant discoveries made by Freud.

The Role of the Past

As the facts about the conflicts unfolded in our examples, they led in each case to significant events in the remote past of the individual's life. The causes of the present manifestations of conflict included behavioral components stemming from the past. The series of painful losses of "parents" that started in Duane's early childhood gave a special quality and intensity to the "pain" caused by his father's death. The young man who dreamed that his penis was cut off had had very similar dreams in his child-hood. Edie's eating and sexual conflicts in adulthood were related to con-flicts in early adolescence and to her situation at the age of 5 or 6, when she started to change from a vivacious, plump little girl into a thin, stark person, fleshless and sexless. These are but some of the connections between the later conflicts and the earlier experiences of these people.

Past experiences significantly influence all present behavior, including conflict behavior. Generally speaking, present behavior has *evolved* from past behavior and experience into its current form. The speech of the adult, for example, has developed from the early vocalizations of the infant. Here past is to present behavior as the seed is to the plant. In the case of conflict, however, the usual progressive transition is arrested. Memories of old ex-periences remain fresher, more susceptible to arousal by current events, and thus more important as determinants of present behavior. Needs and wishes of childhood, fears related to their fulfillment, and the resulting conflicts all persist into the present, only slightly disguised and modified as a result of the inevitable maturation and socialization of the individual. Earlier de-fenses, too, tend to persist with relatively little change. The phrase *repetition of the past* is more descriptive of conflict behavior, and the phrase *develop-ment from the past* is more descriptive of unconflicted behavior.

Freud discovered that the past has these consequences when it has been excluded from consciousness. *Unconscious* memories, fantasies, fears, conflicts, and defensive patterns of response all remain relatively *unchanged with the passing of time.* (This is one of the things Freud meant when he said "the unconscious is timeless.") Being unconscious, they are cut off from the psychological growth of the individual, which is largely tied up with con-scious experience. When these unconscious remnants of the past become conscious, their present influence is greatly diminished. Memories frequently recalled lose their impact on behavior; fears consciously experienced can be reassessed in view of the current external reality; old modes of behavior cease to be automatic when the person becomes aware that he is following them.

The Adaptive Value
of Conflict and Defense

When they find themselves unable to control and tolerate their emotional distress, many people attempt to avoid it as quickly and directly as possible. This is the essence of the process of defense. While it tem-porarily relieves the person from his unpleasant affect, defense is usually ultimately ineffective, because it does not change the real sources of the emotional distress. Duane's perceptual denial, for example, did not change the fact of his father's death or his pleasure over it. In one sense, Duane did not even perceive his father realistically. But these maladaptive features are of no consequence from the standpoint of the process of defense so long as its essential goal is achieved—the quickest attainment of the maximal degree of emotional equanimity possible under the circumstances. Our major emphasis has been and will be on the maladaptive results of conflict and defense, because these are the most thoroughly investigated ones. But conflict and defense can be of adaptive value.

ADAPTIVE CONFLICTS

We have indicated that some conflicts may be realistic and appropriate; they may also be useful. For example, the soldier who goes into battle after coming to grips with the realistic conflict between his loyalty to his comrades and devotion to the cause of his country on the one hand and his fear of death on the other is quite likely to be more resolute and courageous than the soldier who had no such trial conflict in thought. Because he is also consciously frightened, the soldier who has the conflict is motivated to protect himself. He will be attentive to his own performance, alert for signs of danger, and effective in battle—all for his own safety as well as for the success of the mission. (The operation of similar principles in realistic conflicts associated with the threat of impending surgery is discussed in Janis, 1971, pp. 95–105.) It seems fairly clear, then, that realistic conflict can be adaptive.

ADAPTIVE DEFENSES

Defenses, too, can be adaptive. For example, an accurate perception of an external situation completely beyond the individual's control would overwhelm him and render him incapable of action. Perceptual distortion by denial could enable this individual to function temporarily, perhaps long enough for the external danger situation to pass.

Another example is that in which external reality is accurately perceived but the anxiety it evokes is repressed and inhibited just long enough for the individual to perform adequately. Epstein and Fenz (1965) found that skilled parachutists experienced considerable anxiety prior to the time of jumping but repressed this anxiety just before and at the critical moment of jumping. If they did not do this, the act of jumping might be seriously interfered with and even be impossible for some individuals.

Still another instance where defenses serve an adaptive function is that in which basic drives are suddenly intensified in a situation where their gratification would be highly maladaptive. Puberty in a member of modern society is a case in point. For example, the early adolescent in our culture must resort to some degree of defense against his rekindled, intense sexual and aggressive urges. Otherwise he becomes a "delinquent" and is treated as a "misfit." Society does not tolerate him, and he is cut off from the established avenues for further growth and development, such as school and relatively unsupervised participation in peer groups.

In all these instances the defenses operate unconsciously and add to the unconscious forces operating in the individual. Thus, they pose a risk for the individual in addition to providing him with adaptive mechanisms. To be adaptive, the defenses must be elicited selectively, used to the minimum degree and for the minimum time necessary for the purpose of adaptation. And eventually the unconscious forces created or maintained by the defenses must be temporarily diminished by catharsis or gratification. Epstein and Fenz observed just this process. After completing their jumps, the experienced parachutists' repressions ceased, and they *then* experienced anxiety.

It is a temptation to say that unrealistic conflict could never be useful or adaptive, but here we must be cautious. Impaired functioning can indeed always be traced back to unrealistic conflicts, but it is not a foregone conclusion that all unrealistic conflicts result in maladaptive behavior and in only impaired functioning. We shall soon discuss, for example, how sons often feel jealous of the relationship their fathers have with their mothers. In these circumstances the sons usually repress their rivalrous anger because of unrealistic fears of their fathers' retaliation and because they also love their fathers. Thus, this is an unrealistic conflict. Yet it promotes the sons' identification with the moral standards of their fathers; this identification is essential for the sons' psychological growth. As another example, many outstanding creative achievements in art and science seem to be related to unrealistic conflicts.

Heinz Hartmann (1939, 1950, 1952, 1955), one of the leading contemporary psychoanalytic theorists, has proposed still another adaptive result of defenses with his concept of the "change of function" of defenses. This concept holds that defenses, which originate in conflict, may later be used for reasons that have relatively little to do with conflict. Thus, Hartmann suggests, defenses may become *autonomous* from conflict, "conflict-free." He refers to some of the same types of changes that Gordon Allport (1937, 1961) has described in his discussion of the "functional autonomy of motives." A girl who represses her sibling rivalry, for example, and resorts to excessive loving of her sister in order to maintain that repression is simultaneously learning how to get along affectionately with another female. As she grows up, she may come to enjoy warm, close relationships with other women, including her sister, for their own sake, not because she is still struggling with hatred for her sister. In Chapter 8 we shall present some clinical observations about a woman whose life approximated this pattern.

In the meantime, we shall examine more closely some of the other characteristics of conflict and defense that we have been discussing. Since one of the most important is the childhood origin of many conflicts appearing in later life, we shall now turn to certain aspects of the emotional life of children. In this way we shall more completely understand such conflicts as the one Duane experienced when his father died, the one that disturbed Ed's sexual life, and those involved in Edie's unusual attitudes about eating.

Welcome is every organ and attribute of me, and of any
man hearty and clean,
Not an inch nor a particle of an inch is vile, and none
shall be less familiar than the rest.

WALT WHITMAN. Song of Myself

CHAPTER 4
CHILDHOOD SEXUALITY AS A SOURCE OF CONFLICT

We have all heard that Freud discovered that our sexual life starts in childhood, not with puberty and adolescence. But we may not all have a clear idea of exactly what it was he discovered or of the kinds of observations that led to his discovery. The next two chapters present Freud's major discoveries about childhood sexuality and the ways it influences adult life. They also illustrate the kinds of observations that led to these insights about human behavior. Before we begin, we must make clear the limited aims of these chapters: We shall be discussing only one dimension of childhood, albeit one of the most significant ones, and even the treatment of this dimension will be incomplete. Our focus on childhood sexuality will enable us to see more clearly the nature of the persisting conflicts and defenses that underlie behavioral disturbances in many adult men and women.

A Return to History

Childhood sexuality and the associated aggression due to sexual frustration and jealousy were not products of Freud's imagination, nor were they his a priori assumptions. Rather, the existence of sexual and aggressive impulses, wishes, fantasies, anxiety, and conflicts in childhood and their significance for the behavior of the adult were *forced upon* Freud's attention by his clinical observations and the attempt to understand symptoms to which they give rise.

We saw in Chapter 1 that Freud's earliest view was that neurotic symptoms were caused by *unconscious memories of real experiences,* which consisted of intolerable emotional responses to external stimulation. This was his explanation for the symptoms of Anna O. and Lucy R., for example. Freud had no sooner stated this theory than he started to modify it. First he extended it along its original line to what seemed a necessary conclusion. He had been impressed from the beginning with how frequently the repressed memories were of traumatic *sexual* experiences and with the fact that a *series* of overwhelming experiences extending back into the person's early life seemed to be involved. Many of his patients abreacted memories of sexual experiences dating from their childhood. So it seemed then. Consequently, only a few years after *Studies in Hysteria* started to appear in 1893, Freud published several papers (1896a, 1896b, 1896c) in which he stated that the basic overwhelming experience involved in neuroses was always a sexual one incurred before puberty at the hands of an older person. Memories of having been sexually aroused or abused in childhood by nursemaids, older siblings, or other adults, for example, seemed to be at the source of hysterical symptoms. Thus Freud arrived at his *seduction theory of neuroses.*

FREUD'S DISCOVERY OF CHILDHOOD SEXUALITY

Four years later, in *The Interpretation of Dreams* (1900), Freud maintained instead that conflicts involving childhood sexual and hostile *wishes,* not memories, were the basic causes of neuroses. He had reevaluated the likelihood that adults seduced or sexually stimulated children as frequently as his patients' accounts of their childhood indicated. More important, he had discovered that what had seemed to be repressed memories of real, externally imposed childhood sexual experiences were actually *unconscious fantasies* elaborated in the service of the child's *internal* sexual impulses and conflicts. Often these impulses and conflicts involved the child's own parents, as we shall see. Fantasies of sexual stimulation by adults could serve as wish fulfillments of the child's own desires, analogous to the function of conscious daydreams. These fantasies might also serve as "defensive fictions," the function of which was to conceal from the person himself conscious knowledge of his own still earlier, childhood masturbatory and other erotic actions. The individual could feel relieved of responsibility for his sexual excitement and "misbehavior," for example, by fantasying that adults had caused it. These discoveries were related to something else Freud had come to realize: Reality and fantasy, truth and fiction, are not distinguished in unconscious thinking. Unconscious fantasies, memories of such fantasies, and unconscious memories of real events all seem equally real when one becomes conscious of them. By all these interrelated observations and realizations, then, Freud had discovered by 1900 that conflicts over sexual and hostile impulses dating back to childhood were crucial in the causation of adult conflicts. At the root of many conflicts in the adult man was an unconscious childhood desire to have sexual satisfaction with his mother and to eliminate his father as a rival. In adult women, like Anna O. and Lucy R., unconscious sexual wishes for the father and jealousy of the mother were involved. Freud named this constellation of forbidden desires and fantasies the *Oedipal complex*.

It was not easy for Freud to make these discoveries. The major difficulty, of course, arose from the pioneering nature of his work. He was one of the few people studying these problems, and all of his colleagues considered neurosis to be a disease of the nervous system. There were also personal difficulties. To make these discoveries, he had to admit to himself that his seduction theory had been wrong. To publish his discoveries, he had to publicly acknowledge his earlier error. It is easy to imagine how distressing this admission was for a physician still trying to establish himself professionally and scientifically; a physician, furthermore, who, with Breuer, had proposed a radical new theory and published his new discoveries.

From a study of Freud's letters to his friend Wilhelm Fliess, one senses another obstacle to his discovery of childhood sexuality, an obstacle repeatedly encountered even today in the training of analysts—a disbelief, or a reluctance to believe, in its validity. As early as the spring of 1897 Freud doubted his seduction theory, and he nearly abandoned it in the fall of that year. But then he appeared to hesitate for over a year before he was finally convinced in the belief that "to the question: 'what happened in earliest childhood?' the answer is 'nothing.' But the germ of a sexual impulse was there . . . [Freud, 1892–99, Letter 101, p. 276]." An important aspect of his reluctance to recognize the importance of the person's *own* childhood sexuality must be attributed to the fact that this discovery stemmed in a large part from the first psychoanalysis in history—his own self-analysis. Thus, in addition to the usual obstacles on the path to momentous insights, Freud had to overcome his own conflicts, without the help of another analyst, in order to discover childhood sexuality.

Now we must see what Freud meant when he said of childhood, "the germ of a sexual impulse was there." However, we shall not limit ourselves to what he meant at that time, although the germinal ideas for much that follows were then in his mind.

The Psychosexual Life of the Child

In a very broad sense Freud discovered that the human being's erotic, sensual life starts in childhood, and he delineated a sequence of developmental stages of childhood eroticism (1905b). He also recognized that the child's erotic life has extensive psychological ramifications, which go far beyond simple bodily pleasure and include his inner mental life and his early relations with other members of his family. The term *psychosexual* refers to these two aspects of the child's emotional life.

THE THREE STAGES OF CHILDHOOD EROTICISM

During the first year or so of life, childhood eroticism is dominated by the pleasures caused by stimulation of the mucous membranes of the mouth. This is the *oral stage*, and the passionate thumb-sucking of many very young children is one typical manifestation of it.

In the second year, according to Freud, the child's erotic life comes more and more under the dominance of his anal membranes. Now his chief sensual delight is derived from rectal stimulation provided primarily by his own excretory activities but also by such forms of stimulation as his own touching of his anal region, cleaning and bathing by his parents, and enemas. The preoccupied pleasure of the defecating child and his contentment after he has just evacuated a large stool, often after a period of deliberate retention designed to increase its size, is typical of this *anal stage*.

Sometime during the third year or the first part of the fourth, genital stimulation and excitations start to provide the child with his most intense sensual pleasures. This is the *childhood genital or phallic stage*. Phallic or clitoral masturbation is now a typical occurrence. No observant adult can help seeing this either in open and unmistakable behavior or in more covert forms, such as rubbing against people and objects in play or rhythmical thigh-pressing.

Aggressive Aspects   There is an aggressive aspect to each of the stages, too. In the oral stage, after he has teeth, the child delights in biting. As he is developing bowel control, and often afterward, the child enjoys defying his parents by defecating according to his desires, not theirs. He can now be especially willful and stubborn and cruel in many ways. The phallic stage is usually accompanied by delight in penetrating and destroying things, but the most prominent feature of the child's aggression in this phase involves his parents, in ways to be discussed shortly.

The oral, anal, and phallic eroticism of childhood, Freud reasoned, are different, age-appropriate manifestations of the same eroticism characteristic of postpubertal life. Many people have claimed that Freud thereby widened the meaning of "sexuality" to include all pleasure-seeking behavior and that "sexuality" in psychoanalysis lost its usual meaning. On the contrary, Freud was insisting that we recognize the *sexual* quality of all three stages of childhood eroticism. The oral and the anal are just as sexual as the genital, and the childhood genital pleasures are just as sexual as those of adulthood.

Freud based this conclusion on several converging empirical observations and lines of reasoning that render it less mysterious or bizarre than it seems to be at first glance.

The Biological Similarity of the Three Zones

To begin with, the biological structure and functioning of the various zones are similar. The mouth, anus, and genitals are all lined or covered with mucous membranes and are richly supplied with blood vessels and sensory receptors. When stimulated from within or without, they become engorged with blood and give rise to intense sensations. Sensations in the various zones do differ, but they have a common quality Freud often described as an "itching," which is usually experienced as a craving for further stimulation in the form of rhythmical, abrasive contact with some object. This stimulation may be provided by rhythmical thumb-sucking, rubbing of the anus with the fingers or the passing of a stool, or various kinds of masturbation of the genitals. All these activities may be regarded as masturbatory. A commonly observed phenomenon also indicates that excitations in the various zones are closely related: In baby boys, erections frequently accompany oral and anal stimulation.

The Relationship Between Childhood Eroticism and Adult Sexuality

Freud supported the sexuality of the three stages with a second group of observations and inferences. These concerned an apparent relationship between the eroticism of childhood and the sexual life of adults—normal adults, perverts, and psychoneurotics. In the complexities of the adult sexual life of these three groups Freud perceived the operation of oral, anal, and, of course, genital eroticism, and he concluded that the sexual significance of such eroticism in adulthood was either a residue, a continuation, an unconscious persistence, or a return of the sexual significance of this same eroticism in childhood.

Thus, he noted that pregenital eroticism plays an important role in the sexual foreplay or byplay of the normal adult. Sensual kissing is a familiar instance. Childhood oral eroticism appears here as a residual, subordinate process. The fact that intercourse is the major goal of adult sexual activity Freud called *genital primacy*. The usual fate of pregenital sexuality is to become a preliminary to the main goal.

In many perversions, however, oral or anal eroticism is paramount. Orgasm is possible for many perverts, for example, only by sexual union via the mouth or anus or only if there is a great deal of oral and anal stimulation. Such a condition, where childhood pregenital eroticism continues to play the dominant role it played in the pregenital phases of development, is an example of *fixation*.

The situation of psychoneurotics was perceived by Freud as somewhat more complex. A typical configuration here is: inhibition of overt genital eroticism, substitution of unconscious fantasies centered in fixated oral and anal eroticism, and overt symptoms caused by the wishes expressed in these unconscious fantasies and by defenses against such wishes. The unconscious fantasies involve the same wishes experienced consciously and gratified openly in the sexual perversions. If he had no conflict about these wishes and fulfilled them in overt behavior, the psychoneurotic would engage in the same kinds of sexual activity enjoyed by perverts. But of course he does have conflicts about them and thus is markedly different from perverts. As Freud explained, the psychoneuroses are the negative of the perversions.

The configuration just outlined operated in the example of the eating conflict presented in Chapter 2. Eating was a substitute for genital behavior for Edie. But the conflict over eating, as became clear in her psychoanalysis, was a conflict over unconscious fantasies of sucking, biting, and feeding on a penis. While these fantasies never became fully conscious, derivatives of them did. Thus, she one day said that one of the happiest moments in her life was a particular time when she was eating a hot dog a boy had given her. As she ate it and the small group of peers about her were silent, she felt an intense state of peaceful bliss. On another occasion late in her analysis the nausea she experienced upon eating reminded her of a strong bout of nausea and feelings of disgust she had experienced in adolescence when a boy told her he had "creamed his jeans." Eating was such a sensual experience for this patient because it was a disguised gratification of her unconscious desires to suck, bite, and feed on a penis, but by the same token it was the object of severe inhibitions.

In addition to discovering that pregenital eroticism was of sexual significance in the adult lives of psychoneurotics, Freud also discovered that these forms of eroticism had been especially prominent in their childhoods. It appeared that they had returned to earlier forms of sexual eroticism when frustrated in their genital behavior by external circumstances or by their own internal conflicts. When we discuss the Oedipal complex, it will be apparent how that aspect of childhood sexuality, which subsumes a great deal of the child's genital eroticism, is also often continued into adulthood and becomes the source of neurotic conflict.

**The Interchangeability
of the Excitations** A third reason for regarding oral and anal
eroticism as sexual is that excitations in the
oral, anal, and genital zones, and their related gratifications, are interchangeable. This property of interchangeability is at the basis of the psychoneurotic phenomena that we have just discussed, but it manifests itself in other ways as well, which would not be regarded as neurotic. For example, adults who have been accustomed to normal genital gratification frequently manifest an upsurge in oral and anal interests if they are deprived of intimate contact with members of the opposite sex. Perhaps without realizing it, most of us become more interested in food and eating or our bowel functioning—depending upon our individual make-up—when there are occasional interruptions in our genital sex life. We do in miniature and without conflict what many psychoneurotics wish to do on a grand scale but cannot do. The normal limits of such behavior are often exceeded in situations of prolonged deprivation. Men in all-male schools and army camps and in prison often become intensely involved with their food, even to the point of strongly protesting about it on unrealistic grounds. And they often become excessively preoccupied with bowel movements and flatus. The prominence of "latrine humor" is a typical derivative expression of this preoccupation.

In *Ulysses*, James Joyce portrays the flow of Leopold Bloom's subjective experience after finishing his breakfast. As the episode begins, Bloom is in a reverie about his youth stimulated by a letter from his daughter, Milly, in which she mentions the attentions of some young men.

Seaside girls. Torn envelope. Hands stuck in his trousers' pockets . . . singing. . . .

Those girls, those girls,
Those lovely seaside girls

Milly too. Young kisses: the first. . . . Mrs Marion [Bloom]. Reading lying back now, counting the strands of her hair, smiling, braiding.
A soft qualm regret, flowed down his backbone, increasing. Will happen, yes. Prevent. Useless: can't move. Girl's sweet light lips. Will happen too. He felt the flowing qualm spread over him. Useless to move now. Lips kissed, kissing kissed. Full gluey woman's lips.

· · ·

The cat, having cleaned all her fur . . . stalked to the door. . . . Wants to go out. . . .
He felt heavy, full: then a gentle loosening of his bowels. He stood up. . . .

· · ·

A paper. He liked to read at stool. Hope no ape comes knocking just as I'm.

. . .

He kicked open the crazy door of the jakes. . . . The king was in his counting house. . . .

Asquat on the cuckstool he folded out his paper turning its pages over on his bared knees. . . . No great hurry. Keep it a bit. . . .

Quietly he read, restraining himself, the first column and, yielding but resisting, began the second. Midway, his last resistance yielding, he allowed his bowels to ease themselves quietly as he read, reading still patiently. . . . Hope it's not too big bring on piles again. No, just right. So. Ah! . . . He read on, seated calm above his own rising smell [1961, pp. 67–69].

In the latter part of this excerpt Joyce portrays succinctly and honestly the anal pleasures many adults secretly experience. The excerpt also shows the close association that may exist between sexuality and anal eroticism. Notice how quickly Bloom's desire to defecate follows upon his sexual reverie and how the reverie is toned with the nostalgic regret that he will never again experience the excitement of those first young kisses. Could Bloom be turning from his disappointing sexual reverie to a substitute, anal form of pleasure? Did Joyce knowingly and deliberately juxtapose the sexual reverie and the sensual defecation because he, the perceptive artist, knew of the frequent close connection between sexuality and anality? Or did his own unconscious thought associate these two images? Or is the anal episode to be simply attributed to the fact that Bloom had finished breakfast a short while before? And are we to regard it as mere coincidence that the pleasurable anal episode so closely follows the sexual reverie? Only a rigorous study of the associative context of all excretory episodes in *Ulysses* and probably in Joyce's other works as well, and of Joyce himself, would enable us to answer these questions. The mere fact that we can ask such questions, however, illustrates the stimulative effect of Freud's ideas about pregenital sexuality and of the relentless application of the principle of exceptionless psychic determinism. Incidentally, Joyce's use of the image "The king was in his counting house" in this anal context is an artist's recognition of a symbolic unconscious equation of feces with money that Freud frequently observed operating in his patients and in dreams of normal people.

The Development of Object Relations

The three psychosexual stages are defined by the regions of the body dominating the child's erotic life, and the progression from one stage to the other is defined by changes in the dominant erotogenic zone. There is another aspect to the child's sexual life, which Freud also discovered. The important people in the child's life—including the child himself and his parents—necessarily become involved in his erotic life. The emergence of this interpersonal dimension, which is called in psychoanalytic writings the *development of object relations,* makes the child more than a biological assemblage of erogenous body parts. It contributes greatly to his becoming a social creature, and specifically a *human being.*

NARCISSISM

The Greek myth about Narcissus epitomizes a very important aspect of human object relations: self-love. Upon seeing his reflection in the water, Narcissus sat transfixed in self-adoration and self-absorption. Unable to give up looking at his image, he eventually died of starvation.

Self-Love and Feelings of Omnipotence

Young children love themselves nearly as much as Narcissus did, frequently manifesting their narcissism in the same way when they look in the mirror with unabashed, shameless admiration. But the most important expression of the child's self-love is the cherishing of his body and its parts, his good bodily sensations, and his body products. All those things he conceives of as his—toys, clothes, bed, parents—are also loved in an extended narcissism. When he forms a concept of himself, probably in the second half of his first year, he loves *himself* too. One indication of this is his love of his own name and his angry hurt in any teasing play with his name.

Another aspect of the child's narcissism, in addition to his self-love, is his sense of omnipotence. Much of the time he acts as if he feels in control of the world about him, as if he believes that his wishes, gestures, and cries *in themselves* determine events in the external world. He does not seem to realize that his behavior is effective only because his parents are disposed to react to it.

Narcissism as the First Stage of Object Relations

When Freud developed the concept of childhood narcissism and incorporated it into psychoanalysis (1914a), he also speculated that it was the first developmental stage of human object relations. The most important reason for this speculation was his observation that severely disturbed psychotics who have abandoned normal adult love relationships react in ways that resemble the narcissistic behavior of very young children. Daniel Paul Schreber, who was a German judge before he became mentally ill, described his own paranoid schizophrenia in his memoirs, which Freud studied (Freud, 1911). Schreber lost interest in the people about him (they seemed to constitute a shadow world) and at the same time acted as if he loved himself and as if he felt omnipotent. He would pass the time standing half-naked in front of his mirror, all the while experiencing erotic, voluptuous bodily sensations. His sense of omnipotence revealed itself in his delusion that God had selected him alone as a love object and was gradually transforming him into a woman. He was going to bear a new race of men, fathered by God. Such phenomena of schizophrenia are associated with the abandonment of normal human relationships, with the loss of close human contact in old-fashioned "insane asylums," and with a great deal of oral and anal activity resembling that of very young children. Hence Freud thought it plausible that the narcissism of cases like Schreber was a result of regression to a stage of object relations that preceded relationships with other people, to the stage of loving only oneself.

Later Manifestations of Narcissism

While we cannot say exactly how and when narcissism develops in childhood, it seems certain that it does. It also appears that as we grow up we lose most of our narcissism. But we never give it up entirely. Adults, too, like to look at themselves in mirrors, literally and figuratively. The pride we feel in recognizing in ourselves something worthwhile, or in having our accomplishments recognized and reflected in the attitudes of other people, can be considered a normal, healthy bit of narcissism. Freud also noted several other manifestations of narcissism: the usual concern we feel for ourselves when we are sick, the satisfaction of knowing we are loved, and some of the pleasure parents derive from loving their children, who are extensions of themselves. It is just as certain, of course, that the child comes to love others too, a development that is correlated with decreasing narcissism. It is time now to consider this aspect of the child's life.

In nearly all that we shall say about the child's love of others, we shall be speaking about the child in our Western civilization—a monogamous, patriarchal culture in which the basic social unit, the *family*, consists of the biological (as well as psychological) mother and father and their children. It is in such a child that we are naturally most interested, and the emotional relationships and conflicts of just such a child have been more thoroughly studied than those in other cultures.

SEXUALITY IN FAMILY RELATIONSHIPS

The parent-child relationships in our culture involve erotic feelings in both parent and child. We shall discuss only some of these feelings operative in the child.

Preoedipal Attachments to the Mother

The Oedipal complex is one of the most important results of the child's passionate feelings for his parents, but it is a relatively late phenomenon of childhood. Freud regarded it as one aspect of a developmental process starting in earlier, preoedipal erotic attachments of both the girl and the boy to the mother. Freud reasoned that the early erotic attachments developed because the child obtained erotic stimulation from the mother in the course of the biologically necessary activities in which they engage—nursing, bathing, comforting, toileting, and so forth. In nursing, for example, the child not only is fed but also experiences the erotic pleasures of sucking and of being warmed against his mother's body, rocked, and murmured to. It seems quite plausible that children should come to long for erotic oral stimulation from their mother as well as to long for food from her. This type of erotic longing is reinforced and expanded in content. Each step in the child's psychosexual development, outlined earlier, introduces new kinds of erotic gratifications into the changing mother-child relationship.

Toileting   After weaning, the most intense interaction between mother and child is focused around toileting and toilet training. This involves a great deal of physical contact between the mother and the child's excretory organs. From this interaction children may develop a longing for anal stimulation by their mothers and often by their fathers, too, for the father is likely to share in this aspect of child rearing. The parents' interest in bowel training contributes further to an anal-erotic current in the parent-child relationship. Parents are pleased with and proud of signs that the child is developing bowel control, and they transmit these feelings to the child, who comes to share in them and to learn that a bowel movement brings him his parents' love. His excretory process becomes an important medium for expressing his love for his parents as well as for obtaining their love. Thus, what is very pleasurable for autoerotic reasons takes on an interpersonal meaning and becomes even more pleasurable and object related.

Erotic-Genital
Stimulation   As the boy and girl enter their third or fourth year, they long for erotic-genital stimulation by their parents, especially by the mother, and they express interest in her genitals. This change in the primary form of erotic attachment to the mother reflects the fact that the child's genitals are becoming his primary source of erotic pleasure and the child's related growing awareness, however primitively conceived, that his parents have a genital love life.

Soon boys and girls start to follow separate lines of development. A boy continues his primary erotic attachment to his mother. Indeed, he develops a passionate, though childlike, genital love for her that is a forerunner of his heterosexual loves of adolescence and adulthood. At the same time, his filial love for his father becomes complicated by jealousy and hostility toward him because he is a rival, and more successful, lover of his mother. In this way the boy typically develops his positive Oedipal complex. Although the little girl never gives up all her sexual attachments to her mother, she does turn away from her mother as a primary erotic love object and comes to focus her sexual longings upon her father. She too develops an Oedipal complex—passionate love for her father and jealous hostility toward her mother.

In the next chapter we shall discuss the Oedipal complex in detail, but first we shall discuss the little girl's turning to the father to keep our developmental portrayal intact. Freud often said that the emotional life of women was an enigma. It was not until the middle 1920's that he thought he might have discovered the most significant cause for the girl's turning to the father—a constellation of thoughts and feelings that he called *the female castration complex* (Freud, 1924, 1925b).

THE FEMALE CASTRATION COMPLEX

While still erotically attached to her mother, the little girl discovers that boys have penises and that she does not. This discovery is a severely traumatic experience that threatens her narcissism and is experienced as a painful loss of her self-esteem, as a sense of inferiority. Common results of this mortifying blow are the development of penis envy (to be discussed in Chapter 6), a repression of clitoral eroticism and an associated aversion to masturbation, and the change in object relations with which we are concerned now. The girl usually blames her mother for the fact that she does not have a penis, and she turns to her father in the hope of getting a penis substitute from him, a baby.

The female castration complex thus consists of the girl's loss of self-esteem and a sense of inferiority because she does not have a penis, usually the angry blaming of her mother for this "defect" in herself, and the longing for a penis substitute to restore her lost self-esteem. The female castration complex provides the motivations for the development of the girl's positive Oedipal complex.

A Clinical
Example

The following excerpts from observations made by a female analyst illustrate the appearance of the castration complex in one of her little daughters. The parenthetical remarks are quoted from the original source; bracketed comments have been added by the present writer.

A little girl of three years old whose upbringing had presented no difficulty in her first year and little serious difficulty in her second and third years, suddenly began to shew signs of trouble. She was heard one day saying to herself, "Mummy has smashed me up." At about the same time it happened that when her mother was drying her after her bath the little girl displayed great anxiety every time the mother approached her genitals with the towel.

.   .   .

Some months before this episode, this child and her [somewhat older] sister . . . had seen a little boy naked when they were playing on the beach. Probably this was the first time that they had noticed the difference between the sexes.

. . .

It happened that, at about the same time that she made the remark I have recorded and displayed anxiety lest her mother should touch her genitals, the children's father went into the nursery and tried to shake hands with them. The younger of the two refused to give him her hand, saying, "I won't give you my hand, I will only give you my finger." When her father asked in amazement why she did so, she replied, using her own childish terms, that it was because he had a penis and "a little bag." [Is the little girl substituting her finger for the penis she fantasies she has lost? She may be defensively *denying in action* that she does not have a penis.] (Her knowledge of the scrotum could only have been derived from the incident on the beach several months previously; it had never been mentioned in the conversations between her elder sister and the grown-ups.) It is true that she only said this once. Only a few hours later, when her father, hoping to elicit the same reply, again asked her to give him her hand, she refused, as she had done before, but gave as her reason, "because you've got an apron." [Has she now made her father into a woman, who wears an apron instead of a penis? This might be a *denial in fantasy* of her father's masculinity.] . . .

From that time on, certain difficulties arose which might perhaps be called symptoms. At meals the child did not want to have her meat cut up and wished to take all her food only in large pieces, not divided up in any way, so that in fact it was impossible for her to eat them. For instance, she would not allow anyone to break off a piece of cake for her, and so forth. A dog which she knew was once brought to see her when it had just been shaved and the effect was to give her a shock. [All these details are symbolic substitutes for her concern with the integrity of her own body. We can surmise, for example, that she does not want to see food cut up because it stimulates her thoughts that her genitals had been cut up.] She became more and more preoccupied with the idea of "big and little" until she could think of nothing else. . . . She also evolved a theory that she had once been big and had only just become little.

. . .

The little girl also developed a transitory symptom in the shape of a tic. On one occasion she took hold of her nose and asked if it was a big one. This gesture very soon became a tic: every moment she put her fingers to her nose. [Now her nose seems to be a symbolic substitute for a penis. By touching her nose constantly she may be again *denying in action* the perception that she does not have a penis.] At this point her mother intervened with an interpretation and gave a suitable explanation that nothing had been taken away from the child, that all boys and men were from their birth like the little friend whom she had observed, that all girls and women, including her mother, were like herself and that the one form was just as nice as the other and that some day she would have children. At first this interpretation had no effect, but its effect was instantaneous when it was repeated by the other child, the [older] sister. . . . The tic vanished the same day.

Finally the child developed a habit of blaming her mother for everything disagreeable which happened. If she dropped anything, it was her mother's fault, although the latter was often nowhere near: she should have looked after her better. The same explanation applies here—the child was reproaching her mother, who was really "to blame for everything," seeing that she had not borne the little girl as a boy [as reported to Waelder, 1937, pp. 453–56].

A Baby as a Fantasy Substitute for a Penis

The idea that having a baby is a fantasied substitute for having a penis is at first very strange. But psychoanalytic evidence leaves little doubt about this equivalence in unconscious thinking, especially that of many women who have been psychoanalyzed.

Most women will admit to, or give evidence of, a wish that at least their first child be a boy. Many have the same wish but keep it a secret. The present writer observed five women before, during, and after pregnancy in either psychoanalysis or long-term, intensive psychotherapy. In one case the writer observed a second pregnancy as well. In each instance the woman secretly preferred to have a boy. The emotional depth and importance of this preference was strikingly shown in the woman with two pregnancies.

She maintained until just before delivery of her first baby that she was impartial, in spite of the fact that she used to assert that the world regarded females as "second-class citizens." But the moment she gave birth to a girl she was aware of a sense of disappointment. For an instant she consciously wished her baby were a boy. When she heard the next day that a friend of hers had just given birth to a boy, she felt extremely jealous and angry. That little boy immediately became severely ill. She was then horrified by a fleeting awareness that she was glad of it, for he might die and her jealousy would be satisfied. Because these thoughts were so alien to her conscious values and attitudes and guilt-producing, she repressed them. Within two months she was in the throes of a severe depression that had a paranoid quality. The guilt produced by her reactions to having had a girl instead of a boy was a very important determinant of that profound disturbance. Subsequently she gave birth to a boy. During the pregnancy she was nearly incapacitated with anxiety, but with the birth of a boy there was no postpartum reaction. Instead there followed a long period of an equanimity she had never previously shown in a 7-year period of analytic and psychotherapeutic observation.

This preference for boy babies cannot be attributed solely to the women's internalization of our cultural evaluation of the male, for another type of evidence emerges in psychoanalyses of women. Their dreams and associations concerning their babies often show the unconscious phallic meaning of the baby, as in the following example. Another young woman had the following associations and dream during a 10-day period in her fifth month of pregnancy. (Significantly, the dominant theme of her conscious everyday life at this time was her competitiveness with men, typified by a minor automobile "accident" in which she angrily cut in front of a man who was about to pass her in an adjoining lane of a one-way street.)

One day the patient's free associations included an image of an *erect penis* seen in profile. As she described it, she thought of the profile of her nose and her embarrassment that it turned up at the end. [Compare the nose–penis equation in the example of the little girl.] Her next thought was of how her *"belly is really beginning to stick out now."*

In her next analytic hour, as she was wondering whether her analyst's *penis* was *erect*, she felt her abdominal muscles contract. Then she said that she was actually actively doing this. She then realized that lately she had been contracting her stomach muscles to *make* her *"belly into a hard, protruding ball . . . to make the baby stick out hard."* Her *competitive driving* and the auto "accident" occurred 2 days later. This was the only auto mishap in 6 years of analytic observation.

Two analytic hours later she reported the following dream: She was lying down and was looking down her body at her abdomen. She saw her pregnant abdomen sticking up. The baby inside was moving rapidly and extensively, causing the wall of her abdomen to be pushed way out in places as though the baby was pushing out with a leg here, a leg there, an arm here and then there.

Then a place on her abdomen was pushed out, making a protuberance a few inches long, about the size of a thumb. This protuberance was either from her navel or near it.

Her associations to the dream were that the baby might have had an erection, which was causing this protrusion near her navel. Then she recalled that as a little girl she had thought her navel was her penis. She further recalled that in the previous two hours of her psychoanalysis her competitiveness with men had been discussed. She realized that she did compete with men and needed to "cut them down to size."

The unconscious equating of parts of the female body and especially of a baby with a penis has been observed in many women during psychoanalysis. Evidently this equation in fantasy, together with her castration complex, leads the girl in her transition from her preoedipal attachment to her mother to her choice of her father as her primary love object. Freud assumed that the boy and the girl reach the Oedipal stage of their psychosexual development around the fourth year. The girl reaches it in the manner we have discussed. The boy reaches it as a result of the involvement of his developing phallic eroticism in his already positive attachment to his mother, which dates back to his first awareness of her as a distinct person. In the next chapter we shall take a close look at the Oedipal complex and its impact on adult life.

> *If the little savage were left to himself [and had] the violent passions of a man of thirty, he would strangle his father and lie with his mother.*

DENIS DIDEROT. Rameau's Nephew

CHAPTER 5
THE OEDIPAL CONFLICTS AND THEIR EFFECTS

D iderot's striking statement, which was also quoted by Freud (1915–17), epitomizes the positive Oedipal complex. This complex is an emotional constellation of two components: (1) an intense conflict over erotic love for the parent of the opposite sex and (2) an intense conflict over jealous, rivalrous hatred for the parent of the same sex. The Oedipal conflicts significantly influence children's emotional and fantasy relationships with their parents at around the ages of 3 to 6. What kind of evidence led Freud to the discovery of the Oedipal conflicts? How is the Oedipal complex manifested in the behavior of the child and the adult?

Manifestations of the Complex

We shall devote most of this discussion to the Oedipal complex in the male, taking account of the fact that nearly all of Freud's published observations concerned the male. Three basic lines of evidence can be extracted from Freud's writings on the Oedipal complex: (1) direct observations of childhood behavior and fantasies, (2) childhood memories recalled by patients in psychoanalysis, and (3) observations of themes or events in adult behavior that can best be understood as indirect results of a persisting repressed, and thus unconscious, Oedipal complex. In the following paragraphs we shall sample these three classes of evidence.

MANIFESTATIONS OBSERVED IN CHILDREN

In 1909 Freud reported the observations made by the father of a 5-year-old boy, whom Freud called Little Hans (1909a). The father, who was a layman sympathetic to Freud's ideas, made these observations as he tried to help Little Hans overcome an intense fear of horses. His method was psychoanalysis, modified in keeping with Little Hans's age and the father's inexperience, and aided by occasional consultations with Freud. This was the first "child analysis" in history. (Nowadays, a father would not be encouraged to try to treat his own child but would be helped in finding a suitable specialist in child therapy.)

Many of the father's observations concerned things Little Hans did and thought as a result of his Oedipal complex. For example, the boy enjoyed getting into bed with his mother, where they would hug and caress each other. He also asked her to touch his penis because "it's great fun." He would masturbate and have sexual fantasies about his mother and playmates as he did so. He described one such episode as follows. (His opening remark refers to masturbation, and the events he describes as he masturbated were taking place in fantasy. Grete is a female playmate.)

> I put my finger to my widdler just a very little. I saw Mummy quite naked in her chemise, and she let me see her widdler. I showed Grete, my Grete, what Mummy was doing, and showed her my widdler. Then I took my hand away from my widdler quick. . . . the chemise was so short that I saw her widdler [p. 32].

Little Hans also enjoyed being in the bathroom with his mother when she went to the toilet. "He goes on pestering me till I let him," she said. He had fantasies that he would some day marry his mother and that they would have children.

Little Hans's Oedipal jealousy and hostility took such forms as being inappropriately aggressive in roughhousing with his father, defying his father's occasional attempts to keep him from getting into bed with his mother, fantasying that he, and not his father, was married to his mother, and wishing that his father would be dead so that he could have his mother all to himself.

These are some of the least inferential observations about Little Hans's Oedipal complex. Many child analysts have replicated these findings.

Using doll-play materials similar to those illustrated in Figure 5-1, Pauline Sears (1951) and a group of colleagues observed how normal boys and girls—3, 4, and 5 years old—expressed aggressive fantasies concerning their mothers and fathers. More than 100 lower-middle-class and upper-lower-class children from the Midwest were given the opportunity to play freely with the doll family, which consisted of a father, mother, boy, girl, and baby. Observers recorded everything the children did in this projective play. Later the researchers carefully defined criteria for judging whether play behavior was aggressive and then counted the number of times aggressive behavior had occurred in the doll play. They also determined how frequently the aggressive behavior was directed toward the various members of the doll family.

The results that interest us concern the mother and father dolls. As Figure 5-2 shows, the girls directed much more aggression toward the mother doll than toward the father doll; the boys expressed more aggression toward the father than toward the mother doll. Such results cannot be explained simply as reactions to how the children were disciplined and frustrated (in the usual sense of that word) by their parents. These results are highly consistent with the pattern of aggression one would predict if he assumed that these young children were in the throes of their Oedipal complex.

Sears included a sample record of the play of a 4-year-old boy named Mike. The following excerpt from the record shows the vividness with which Mike fantasied that all sorts of misfortunes should descend upon his father:

Figure 5-1 The doll house and part of the doll family used in Sears's study of children's aggressive fantasies concerning their parents.

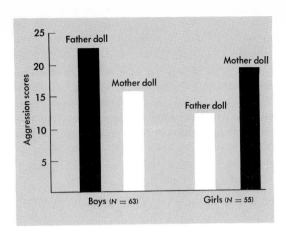

Figure 5-2 Results of the doll-play aggression study. (Based on data from Sears, 1951)

chair goes on top of the old man . . . Mother kicks him [father] backward out of house . . . the girl kicked him back again . . . toilet sits on F [father] . . . someone goes phooey on the old man . . . he [father] falls . . . F has to go to jail . . . table smashed on top of him . . . the house is burning . . . Daddy is going to stay in and burn . . . F falls in fire . . . chair smashes his head in . . . [Father] lying in bed and burning . . . someone piles furniture on top of him [father]. He's all smashed up . . . [Father has] to sleep in tub—pokes his head down—jams him in [Sears, 1951, pp. 40–41].

Neither Diderot nor Freud exaggerated the intensity of the hostile designs the little boy has on his father.

MANIFESTATIONS REVEALED BY CHILDHOOD MEMORIES: THE RAT MAN AND THE WOLF MAN

Freud's adult patients recalled doing and thinking in their childhood the same kinds of things that were directly observed in Little Hans.

The Rat Man (Freud, 1909b), for example (so named because of his obsessional thoughts about rats), recalled that in his fourth, fifth, and sixth years he begged his governesses to let him engage in sexual play with them and enjoyed crawling under their nightgowns, undressing them, and touching their genitals. He could recall that he had erections in these early years, too. The governesses, of course, were maternal substitutes, for they took care of him. He could also recall a thinly disguised Oedipal death wish directed toward his father: In his childhood he feared that if he thought about his strong wishes to see some of his little girl friends naked, *his father might die.*

Another patient, called the Wolf Man because of a childhood phobia of certain pictures of wolves and a nightmare about wolves, recalled similar childhood events, after painstaking work in his analysis. (The study of the Wolf Man is the best published example of Freud's analytic work [Freud, 1918].)

Like the Rat Man, the Wolf Man was cared for largely by governesses and maids rather than by his mother, so his Oedipal behavior, too, was directed toward them. Once, in the middle of his third year, he saw a nursery maid named Grusha, whom he loved very much, on her hands and knees scrubbing the floor. When he saw her he urinated in front of her, an act Freud interpreted as the effect sexual excitement had on him at that time. The psychoanalysis of the Wolf Man produced a mass of indirect evidence that he had seen either animals having intercourse or his parents in the same position, which Freud believed was why the sight of Grusha in that position, with her buttocks prominently raised, had such a stimulating effect. He reasoned that it must have triggered an overt, displaced expression of the boy's early Oedipal longing for his mother. (We shall consider this inference further in a moment.) When the Wolf Man was nearly 4, his sister, who was two years older, seduced him into sex by-play and handled his penis. As she did this, she said that his nurse, Nanya, used to do this with other men. The boy loved Nanya as much as any woman in his life at that time, so within a few weeks he tried to repeat the erotic experience with Nanya by masturbating in front of her.

The recapturing of memory fragments from the Oedipal period similar to those of these two patients of Freud is a very common occurrence in psychoanalyses. Individuals differ, of course, with respect to the clarity of recall, the explicitness of the erotic and hostile dimensions of their childhood behavior, and the extent to which adults had encouraged their overt sexual behavior. Sometimes the memories are of real events; sometimes they are memories of fantasies.

INDIRECT MANIFESTATIONS OBSERVED IN ADULTS

The fate of the Oedipal complex is repression, which usually starts in the fifth or sixth year. But many themes and events in the later life of almost any person can best be understood if one assumes that there really was an Oedipal complex in childhood and that it continues to influence behavior after its repression. These later forms of behavior become evidence, or manifestations, of the Oedipal complex to the extent that one accepts the validity of such explanations. And, as we shall see, the full significance of the early experiences or fantasies recalled in fragmentary fashion in adulthood, as in the case of the Rat Man and the Wolf Man, is fully realized only retrospectively, following a careful study of their aftermath in later life.

Actually, observations of indirect manifestations in adult behavior were primarily what led Freud to his discovery of the Oedipal complex. One form of behavior, dreaming, was especially important in this regard.

By the time he wrote *The Interpretation of Dreams* (1900), Freud had studied a large number of dreams—his own, his patients', and other people's as well. He observed that many adults reported dreaming of the death of their parents. When he examined these dreams, he detected a pattern: "that men . . . dream mostly of their father's death and women of their mother's [p. 256]." He also observed at this time that "many men dream of having sexual relations with their mothers, and speak of the fact with indignation and astonishment [p. 264]." These dreams, he thought, must be produced by repressed Oedipal wishes, both the hostile and the erotic, that originated in childhood but persisted into the dreamer's adult unconscious mental life. Since they are defended against in everyday behavior, they find expression in the wish fulfillments (which are usually disguised) of dreams.

At the time he was making these observations and inferences about dreams, Freud was observing in the symptoms and behavior of his patients what he thought must also be indirect results of repressed Oedipal wishes or memories.

**The Rat Man
and the Wolf Man
as Adults**
The Rat Man's and the Wolf Man's later lives clearly illustrate this phenomenon. We mentioned that when he was a boy, the Rat Man had sexual fantasies and feared that his father would die if he had such fantasies. The Rat Man's later sexual life remained closely tied to the theme of his father's death.

1. When he fell in love in adolescence, he had the obsessive wish that his father would die. Then, he fantasied, his girlfriend would love him because she would feel sorry for him.
2. A few years later, when he was again in love, he used to imagine that if his father died he would have enough money to marry.
3. When he first engaged in intercourse, the obsessive thought flashed through his mind, "This is glorious! One might murder one's father for this! [Freud, 1909b, p. 201]."
4. His father died when the Rat Man was 21, whereupon he experienced an uncontrollable upsurge of desires to masturbate.

This pattern seems best explained as a manifestation of persisting, repressed Oedipal wishes. The recalled childhood fear that his father would die if the boy had sexual fantasies would then be viewed as but a fragmentary manifestation of the Oedipal complex.

The diagram in Figure 5-3 illustrates how we can conceptualize adult manifestations of the hostile component of the Oedipal complex as the results of an unconscious approach-avoidance conflict.

Turning to the Wolf Man, we should remember the childhood scene with Grusha: The little boy saw this nursery maid on her hands and knees,

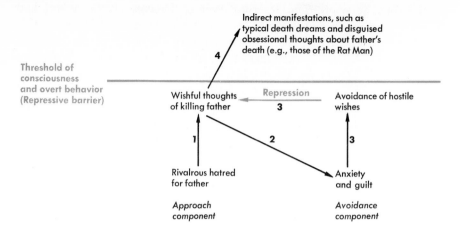

Indirect manifestations, such as
typical death dreams and disguised
obsessional thoughts about father's
death (e.g., those of the Rat Man)

4

Wishful thoughts   Repression   Avoidance of hostile
of killing father   3   wishes

1   2   3

Rivalrous hatred   Anxiety
for father   and guilt

Approach   Avoidance
component   component

*Figure 5-3   How adult manifestations of the hostile component
of the unconscious Oedipal complex might result from an approach-avoidance conflict.*

*Most adult men have repressed the unresolved residues of their
childhood conflicts involving their Oedipal jealousy of their
fathers. The heavy gray line represents this fact. In the case of
unconscious conflicts, the "threshold of consciousness and overt
behavior" is a barrier resulting from the active process of repression; it is not a simple threshold analogous to sensory thresholds,
which may be crossed merely by increasing the intensity of the
stimulus. When intensified for any reason, the individual's rivalrous hatred for his father can make him unconsciously wish to
kill his father (1). Even though unconscious, such a wish evokes
unconscious anxiety and guilt (2), which motivate the intensification of the repression of such death wishes (3). At this point
the individual is left with very strong wishes to kill his father, but
they are blocked from becoming conscious by a very strong repression. Such "dammed-up" death wishes frequently produce
strange conscious experiences, such as dreams about the death of
the father, or simply of an older man, and isolated, bizarre
thoughts about one's father's death when one has intercourse or
engages in some other sexual behavior (4).*

with buttocks made prominent, scrubbing the floor; he then urinated in
front of her, which Freud interpreted as a sign of Oedipal sexual excitement. In judging the significance of this episode and its relation to his adult
sexual life, one is bound to be influenced by these further facts in the Wolf
Man's life:

1. "From his puberty he had felt large and conspicuous buttocks as the most
powerful attraction in a woman; to copulate except from behind gave him scarcely
any enjoyment. [Freud, 1918, p. 41]."

2. Early in adolescence he was attracted to a servant girl working in his home, but he kept his distance from her. One day, however, he was overwhelmed with love for her when he saw her kneeling on the floor scrubbing it.

3. Late in his teens he came upon a peasant girl kneeling by a pond as she washed clothes. He fell violently in love with her on the spot, before he even saw her face. He had intercourse with her at some time not specified in the case report. Freud noted that the Wolf Man was unusually secretive about this girl's name, which had a "motherly ring" to it—Matrona.

4. Freud states that the Wolf Man's "final choice of object," by which we presume Freud meant his wife, was determined by the same factors operating in the preceding scenes and in the Grusha episode. Freud does not give details, however, perhaps to protect the identity of the patient or out of consideration for the patient's wife.

Thus, the Wolf Man showed a pattern of sexual excitement by stimulus situations similar to that of the sight of the kneeling Grusha. The pattern is highly compatible with Freud's hunch that the boy was sexually excited when he took out his penis and urinated in front of Grusha.

The adult individual free of severe neurosis rarely shows such clear-cut manifestations of his Oedipal complex as we have seen in the Rat Man and the Wolf Man. The neurotic behaves as if he is repeating nearly the same stimulus-response patterns that were characteristic of his childhood; he seems to be *fixated* in unconscious Oedipal object relations. Many of his symptoms are manifestations of his conflictful, still-operative Oedipal wishes, as illustrated by the Rat Man's obsessive, intruding, "inappropriate" thoughts of his father's death and by the particular form of the Wolf Man's impulsive sexual behavior.

Other Evidence of the Continued Oedipal Complex The sexual and related aggressive behavior of the normal adult usually shows evidence of having *evolved from* the Oedipal complex. The exciting sexual attributes of one's spouse or adult lover are less similar to those of the Oedipal object than were the Wolf Man's; one's hostility toward one's father or everyday rivals is less intense and less tied to sexuality than in the Rat Man. In psychoanalytic terminology, the normal adult has sublimated his Oedipal complex through greater displacement, instead of remaining fixated in it.

Nevertheless, the behavior even of the person who has achieved considerable sublimation of his Oedipal complex seems to retain distinct traces of it, suggesting that the Oedipal complex may never be completely overcome. Remarkably often one discovers that a friend has found a mate who resembles his parent in some special characteristic. A man "suddenly" realizes long after he has married that his wife taught school for a few years before they met, as his mother had done before she married. Or a woman "finds" that her husband likes the outdoors, as her father did. It is as if the same process of displacement seen in neurotic patients is simply extended further.

An example from the analysis of a hysterical female patient is typical of this displacement process. (The displacement to the analyst is a characteristic event in analysis. It is part of the phenomenon Freud called *transference*. In transference, the patient reenacts in his relationship with the analyst repressed wishes and experiences involving his parents or other significant people. Thus, he "transfers" from them to his analyst.)

Each time this patient's analyst had his hair cut, she acknowledged it, even if only by remarking, with a smile, "I see you got your hair cut." There was nothing unusual about his haircuts, and none of his other patients mentioned them. This patient's interest stemmed from a favorite game she had played with her father between the ages of 5 and 10: "barbershop." She would be the barber and he the customer.

That game derived from a still more exciting activity they had shared. Regularly, until she was 6 or 7, she used to sit on the toilet and urinate while her father was shaving in the bathroom. It is presumed that she was sexually excited at that time, for the need to urinate regularly accompanied her sexual excitations in adulthood.

The displacements here are: bathroom activity with father → barber game with father → special interest in analyst's haircuts.

Figure 5-4 illustrates the way we can apply the approach-avoidance conflict paradigm to indirect manifestations of the sexual component of the unconscious Oedipal complex, such as the *sexual over-reactions* of the Wolf Man to kneeling women and the special interest of the woman just mentioned in her analyst's haircuts. Her special attentiveness to them is clearly a form of perceptual vigilance, an alertness or sensitivity to stimuli that touch upon one's inner emotional life, including unconscious conflicts.

Traces of Oedipal hostility, as well as of Oedipal sexuality, can be found in the average adult. Freud referred to a common instance of this when he said, "A physician will often . . . notice how a son's grief at the loss of his father cannot suppress his satisfaction at having at last won his freedom [1900, p. 257]." In Chapter 2 we saw just this kind of reaction by a normal person, Duane.

Freud always emphasized that another aspect of adult life provided further evidence of a still active, though sublimated, Oedipal complex: the creation and enjoyment of great myths and literary works built upon Oedipal themes. He cited, at various times, the myth of Zeus castrating his father and replacing him as ruler, Sophocles' *Oedipus Rex*, Ibsen's *Rosmersholm*, and Shakespeare's *Hamlet*. Freud ascribed Hamlet's inability to decisively avenge his father's murder to a conflict over a latent wish for his father's death. Freud reasoned that the widespread impact and appeal (as well as the creation) of such masterpieces must depend on the residual, unconscious Oedipal complex in every man.

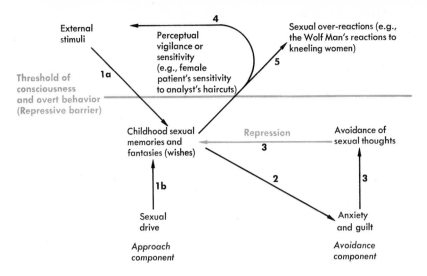

Figure 5-4 How adult manifestations of the sexual component of the unconscious Oedipal complex might result from an approach-avoidance conflict.

Most adults have repressed the unresolved residues of their childhood conflicts involving their Oedipal love. The combined action of one's repressed sexual drives and the presence of a person who resembles one's Oedipally loved parent may activate repressed childhood sexual memories and fantasies (1a and 1b). These repressed memories and fantasies will then arouse unconscious anxiety and guilt (2), which in turn motivate the intensification of their repression (3). Thus, the individual is left with enlivened memories and strong fantasies or wishes that are blocked from becoming conscious or from overt expression by a very strong repression. Such "dammed-up" sexual memories and fantasies frequently produce strange overt behavior, such as a special perceptual sensitivity to minor characteristics of other people that remind the individual of his loved parent (4), or impulsive sexual reaction to such people (5).

IS THE OEDIPAL COMPLEX UNIVERSAL?

Freud assumed that the Oedipal complex and its repression in men and women were universal phenomena. Since the relevant controlled scientific investigations have not been carried out, this must still be regarded as a tentative hypothesis. How seriously should it be taken?

The idea that the complex may be universal in Western civilization seems fairly plausible if one merely considers the great range of literary works and individual life histories in which Oedipal manifestations have been found. We have noted that such literary expressions date back to the

Greeks. As for individuals, Freud encountered the Oedipal complex in all his patients, regardless of the subculture in which they grew up. Many of his patients were reared in middle-class Viennese homes, but some were not. The Wolf Man, for example, was of a wealthy Russian family. He had spent his childhood on country estates surrounded by the opulence of the pre-revolutionary culture. Some form of the Oedipal complex is typically found by every contemporary American or European analyst in his patients, regardless of differences in subcultural origin. And we should recall the doll-play aggression study: Normal boys and girls from the contemporary Midwest displayed just those aggressive fantasies characteristically detected in the psychoanalysis of adults.

Evidence from Cultural Anthropology

The hypothesis that the Oedipal complex is universal receives additional, though indirect, support from cultural anthropology. Anthropological literature describes the widespread incidence among primitive peoples of taboos against incest and also against killing totemic animals, which are regarded as ancestors of the people. Freud reasoned (1913) that such taboos would not be required if there were not strong unconscious motivation to do the very things proscribed by them. Thus, the incest taboos indicate that strong unconscious incestuous wishes must be operative in widely scattered primitive peoples. The totemic taboos, he argued, were displacements—disguised taboos against unconscious wishes to murder the father. In short, Freud saw in the prevalence of both taboos evidence that the repressed Oedipal complex was just as active in members of these widely scattered societies as it was in his own patients.

Murdock's cross-cultural study (1949) of 250 primitive societies extended knowledge about incest taboos. Three of Murdock's findings are directly relevant to the Oedipal complex. First, in every one of the societies, incest taboos existed proscribing sexual relations between all persons of the opposite sex within the nuclear family, except of course between the parents. (In a few societies, royalty was exempted.) Second, taboos against incestuous relations with relatives outside the nuclear family tended to be less intense than taboos against incest within it. Third, Murdock noted that a "peculiar intensity and emotional quality [p. 288]" is associated with incest taboos, which he felt could be accounted for only by assuming that they were related to unconscious Oedipal conflicts.

Condominas (1957), a French anthropologist, observed at first hand those unique emotions associated with incest taboos. One day, while he was living among the Montagnards of Vietnam, disaster struck: Tieng and Aang, a man and woman of their clan, had been detected having sexual intercourse. Even though the last common ancestor of Tieng and Aang had lived 15 generations earlier, and even though both were mature adults whose mates had died, the tribesmen responded with the greatest alarm. Tieng and Aang's violation of the incest taboo was certain to bring forth calamitous events: dragons, tigers, and elephants would kill all the important members of the clan; torrential rains, landslides, and flooding from within the earth would threaten everyone's life. Drastic measures, prescribed by ritual custom, were taken to forestall the doom. Animals were sacrificed and their blood mixed and drunk, and prayers were said before an altar (Figure 5-5). Tieng and Aang had to lick excrement of pig and dog, which was painted on their chins. Finally, the community as well as the immediate families of Tieng and Aang were cleansed of evil and stain. These procedures, which occupied an entire day, relieved the distress of everyone but Tieng. His was too great: He hanged himself that night.

Anthropologists have often pointed out that prohibiting incest has many adaptive consequences: By preventing sexual rivalry it guarantees the integrity of the family unit, which is so necessary for sheer survival under primitive conditions; it prevents societies from breaking up into family-centered clans, which might happen if sexual relations and marriage within the family were permitted; it ensures greater cultural homogeneity within a society by guaranteeing that one family's skills, knowledge, and habits will be mixed with those of other families as a result of extrafamilial marriage; and so forth. The fact that incest taboos may have such adaptive consequences is regarded by some social anthropologists as an argument against connecting taboos with the Oedipal complex. Psychoanalysts argue, in turn, that if these consequences do in fact have anything to do with the existence of the taboos, they simply constitute some of society's implicit, but practical, reasons for strongly prohibiting the incestuous Oedipal wishes.

Lindzey (1967) has recently summarized evidence that inbreeding results in biological inferiority in successive generations. He proposes that in

Figure 5-5 "Early in the ceremony at riverside to expiate the incest, Aang's brother Toong-Biing prays before a small altar." (From Condominas, 1957)

its long history mankind has learned that it must prohibit inbreeding that would result from the Oedipal complex in order to remain biologically strong and to survive. He also emphasizes the rarity of any psychological phenomenon being as widespread throughout the world's many cultures as is the incest taboo. He too infers that the Oedipal complex is "universal."

Without minimizing the significance of early life experiences, Freud (1905b) believed the Oedipal complex was universal because its essential ingredients were innate. While there is a good deal of evidence that the Oedipal complex is widespread in Western civilization, and some evidence that it is manifested in many other cultures throughout the world, there is no evidence that the conflict is, or is not, innate. Its wide distribution, in the boy at least, could be the inevitable result of the close physical and emotional attachment between mother and child throughout the world and of the fact that the parent of the same sex is a real rival for the affection of the other parent. In other words, the conflict could be learned; and it could be extremely widespread because certain elemental aspects of child rearing are widespread. If child-rearing conditions do give rise to the Oedipal conflict, the conflict should be different in cultures with highly distinctive ways of caring for and socializing their children. We shall discuss this point further in Chapter 12.

Repression of the Oedipal Conflicts

Few of us, as adults, feel an erotic attachment to our parent of the opposite sex or jealous hatred for our parent of the same sex. And few of us realize that children are serious when they say they will marry Mommy or Daddy and that they are expressing genuine hostility when they push away the other parent or wish he were dead. Nor do we realize how much enjoyment children get out of pretending these things in their play. Psychoanalysts point out several reasons why the Oedipal complex seems unreal to us. First, we did not fully comprehend our own Oedipal complex when we were children. Second, what we did comprehend we energetically repressed almost as soon as we became aware of it. Third, by having gradually and unknowingly accepted our culture's prescription for our sexual and aggressive life, we have transferred most of those energies, especially the sexual, to our extrafamilial peers. Fourth, the need to keep our own Oedipal complex repressed interferes with our capacity to fully appreciate what we see in the behavior of children.

As we have noted, the fate of the Oedipal complex is repression. Why? Parents expend a great deal of effort helping their children regulate their nonincestuous sexual life, while they exert relatively little pressure, judged by external criteria, against the childhood incestuous wishes. Yet, remarkably, all of us share in "the horror of incest [Freud, 1892–99, p. 257]," and incest taboos have that "peculiar intensity and emotional quality" noted by Murdock.

The reasons the complex is repressed arise in part from the reactions of adults to manifestations of childhood sexuality. Most parents discourage whatever signs of sexual behavior they observe in their young children. And Oedipal behavior inevitably arouses jealousy in the parent of the same sex, especially since the other parent usually unwittingly reciprocates the child's attachment, if only to a slight degree. This jealousy is transmitted to the Oedipal child.

However, the repression derives not only from parental reactions but also from the psychology of the child. Psychoanalytic observations strongly suggest that neither the parents' threats of punishment or loss of love because of the child's sexual behavior nor the signs of their jealousy fully account for the repression. Parental threats seem, rather, to provide the ingredients for the child's fantasy elaboration, which occurs largely outside of awareness and in which the child's own Oedipal hostility plays a significant role. The principal evidence is that children fear a monstrous retribution, which bears no necessary relation to the actual overt behavior of the parent. The hostility that the child imagines will be vented against him appears to be proportionate to, and to derive from, his own hostility toward the hated Oedipal parent. In his fantasy the child *projects* his own intense hostility onto his parent. Fear of a largely fantasied retribution by his parents motivates the child to repress his Oedipal complex. Both boys and girls repress the Oedipal complex, and the general cause of that repression is the same, but the specific content of the fears differs in ways that we shall now discuss.

REPRESSIVE MOTIVES IN THE GIRL

The girl typically *fears that her mother hates her* for her Oedipal attachment to her father and for her rivalry. Consciously or unconsciously she expects her mother to bear a deep-seated malevolence toward her, which threatens her with the loss of her mother's love and may even cause her mother to actually abandon her or to harm her physically. The witch in the Sleeping Beauty fairy tale is a prototypic rendition of the fantasied image the young girl has of her mother, as revealed by women's memories of their childhood view of their mothers when that view is recalled in analysis.

The patient who played barber games with her father is an example.

She recalled her discomfort as a little girl when her mother combed her hair. In her subjective experience she sensed that her mother resented her blonde, curly hair and that she meanly tried to hurt her by deliberately combing her hair hard and pulling on it to straighten it out. In later years she formed a more abstract idea based on her childhood perception: She thought, in looking back, that her mother was trying then to destroy her femininity. She also feared then that her mother would destroy her in a more literal sense, for once when she was recalling those early years she dreamed of a woman who came into her analyst's office during one of her sessions. This woman, "looking daggers" and with hands outstretched, walked toward the patient as if she were about to choke her. Her associations to the woman led directly to her mother. This dream image, the memory of how her mother seemed as she combed her hair, and the more abstract idea of her mother's enmity toward her femininity are all indications of this woman's childhood conviction that her mother resented her Oedipal relationship with her father and entertained evil intentions toward her because of that relationship.

Since her childhood conception of justice was based on the talion principle— an eye for an eye—she could easily imagine that her mother was deliberately trying to hurt her when combing her hair. What more appropriate punishment situation could there be for a girl who obtained erotic pleasure from combing her beloved father's hair?

An adult woman can cope with a jealous, angry rival without sacrificing her own passionate interests. The little girl, however, cannot do so. Compared to her mother, she is weak. Also, she loves her mother, and she needs her. Thus, the possibility that her mother hates her forebodes *several* kinds of dangers, including the possibility that her mother might harm her or abandon her. To avoid those dangers she represses her Oedipal thoughts and affects and inhibits their behavioral expression.

THE CASTRATION COMPLEX IN THE BOY

The specter of an additional danger looms in the thoughts of the Oedipal boy: He fears that his penis will be cut off or damaged. Typically, he fears that his father will do this, but if his mother is dominant in the family and is more the disciplinarian, she may be the imagined perpetrator. This was so in the case of Ed, the young man described in Chapter 2. He used to dream that a witch cut off the penises of all little boys.

The danger of castration is terrifying on several counts. It threatens extreme pain and damage to the integrity of his body; the child may regard it as the equivalent of being killed. Freud speculated that man's conscious fear of death in later life was a derivative of his fear of castration. Castration also threatens to deprive the child of a highly prized part of his body, the part that he narcissistically may love most. It also threatens to turn him into a girl, with the loss of all the privileges and advantages he has been taught that men have.

How the Complex Arises

How does the fear of castration usually arise? The most meaningful data have come from psychoanalyses of boys and men, where the necessary detailed observations can be made. Freud concluded that two experiences typically antedated the appearance of castration anxiety: explicit or implicit *castration threats by the parents* and the *sight of the female genitals*, which give these threats substance and meaning. Freud's observations about Little Hans and the Wolf Man illustrate the empirical basis for his conclusion:

1. Little Hans's mother and the Wolf Man's nurses made castration threats or allusions as these boys were engaged in erotic-genital play. But no sign of castration anxiety was apparent immediately.
2. Some time later, both boys saw their sisters' genitals.
3. Following this observation, each child developed what seemed to be thinly disguised castration fears. (We shall describe some of these in a moment.)

When Little Hans saw his sister naked, he *denied the perception that she did not have a penis.* He said that she did have one but that it was small and would grow bigger. The Wolf Man also denied what he saw, for he called his sister's genitals her "front bottom."

Apparently, when they saw their sisters' genitals, both boys for the first time registered the fact that a girl does not have a penis. Yet they had to deny the reality of what they saw. Perhaps they imagined that the girls once did have penises but had lost them and that the castration threats the boys had earlier received represented a real danger. If so, the boys would be denying perceptions that aroused a distressing affect in them—castration anxiety. The paradigm would be the same as for Duane's denial of the perception of his father's dead body, which was described in Chapter 2.

If what has been said so far is valid, the subsequent anxiety of the boys should give some clue of being related to frightening thoughts of being castrated. These clues must necessarily be indirect, for castration thoughts are so disturbing that they are defensively distorted. Both boys gave such clues, and of a very similar kind.

Little Hans first developed general, free-floating anxiety, which very rapidly changed into a phobia of horses, particularly the fear that they would bite his fingers. These and other associations indicated that for Little Hans horses were displacement-substitutes for his parents and that his fear of being bitten by a horse was a disguised fear that his father would bite off or cut off his penis. Hans's fear of being bitten by a horse was derived partly from an experience he had in the country, when he heard the father of a little girl say to her "Don't put your *finger* to the white *horse* or it'll *bite* you [Freud, 1909a, p. 29]." Hans had been threatened that if he masturbated (that is, put his *finger* on his penis, as in his description of his masturbation fantasy presented on page 65), Doctor A would be called to cut off his penis. There were associative links between his father and biting horses. He used to play *biting* games with his *father*, and once when the boy and his father were talking about Hans's wish that his *father* were dead, Hans "accidentally" knocked over a toy *horse* he was playing with.

The Wolf Man gave similar indications of castration anxiety.

A picture of a wolf in a story book terrified the Wolf Man each time he saw it as a child, and a childhood nightmare was about wolves. As he later recalled this nightmare during his analysis with Freud, he pictured the scene shown in Figure 5-6. In the dream all the wolves were sitting in a tree outside his nursery window and were silently staring at him. His associations about wolves included several fairy tales in which wolves lost their tails and were also aggressors against small animals. It appeared that one of the reasons the wolves' picture and dream image frightened the boy was that they represented a disguised form of, and stimulated, both his castration fear and the fear that his father would do the castrating.

We shall mention only one of the many bits of evidence that supported this idea. In his early analytic interviews the Wolf Man used to repeat a stereotyped pattern of behavior: He would look at Freud and then turn to look at a grandfather clock in the room. The Wolf Man himself later came to realize that he had been reenacting a scene from one of the fairy tales in which a little goat had avoided being eaten by a wolf by hiding in a grandfather clock! Even as an adult, then, he was unconsciously under the influence of his childhood fantasy. The relationship between himself and Freud reminded him of the helpless little goat that was in danger of being eaten by a wolf. It was as though the Wolf Man had generalized his castration anxiety from his penis to his entire body. The wolf would get his entire body, including his penis.

Another childhood experience of the Wolf Man was an indirect manifestation of his castration anxiety. Some time after he had been threatened with castration by his nurses and had seen his sister's genitals, the idea of castration was reinforced when he was told of a female relative who had been born with six toes, only to have the extra one chopped off with an axe. The Wolf Man was almost 5 years old when he heard this news; shortly thereafter he became terrified while he was cutting on the bark of a tree with a pocket knife, and he hallucinated that his little finger was cut nearly off and was hanging by the skin.

The behavior of both boys, then, contained indirect manifestations of their castration anxiety. These indirect manifestations—which included the denial of their perceptions that girls have no penises, their animal phobias, and the hallucinatory experience of the Wolf Man—illustrate the kind of

Figure 5-6 Wolf Man's drawing, made during his analysis in adulthood with Freud, of the dream scene in his childhood nightmare. (From Freud, 1918)

clinical evidence that led Freud to the discovery of the boy's castration complex. Similar clinical data characteristically emerge in the psychoanalyses of other men, indicating that castration anxiety is not unique to Little Hans and the Wolf Man.

The reader interested in Freud's full account of Little Hans and the Wolf Man should see *Analysis of a Phobia in a Five-Year-Old Boy* (1909a) and *From the History of an Infantile Neurosis* (1918). Freud's later formulations about these two cases are contained in *Inhibitions, Symptoms, and Anxiety* (1926). The reader may also be interested in these reports for reasons going beyond what we have discussed here, particularly because they pertain to the historic controversy between Freud and Carl Gustav Jung. Jung was one of Freud's earliest colleagues, but he later formulated his own theories of depth psychology. One of the reasons he did so was his belief that many of the things patients reported as memories of sexual experiences or fantasies of childhood were really later fantasies of adolescence or adulthood. Nor did he attribute the same significance to childhood sexuality that Freud did. The patients, Jung believed, unconsciously and erroneously attributed later sexual fantasies to their childhoods. Freud wrote the report of Little Hans before the break between Jung and himself occurred during the years 1912–14. It is interesting to see that the direct observations of this small boy's behavior and fantasies were essentially identical with those recalled from childhood by adult analysands. Freud wrote the report of the Wolf Man in rebuttal of Jung's belief. For this reason, he subjected the childhood memories of the Wolf Man to what he considered to be rigorous analysis and questioning. He concluded that the crucial memories were not fantasies of later life but rather memories of actual childhood experiences or of childhood fantasies. And he remained unshaken in his belief in the reality and significance of childhood sexuality. (We have touched here on only a few aspects of Jungian depth psychology. Further discussions of it, as well as references to Jung's basic writings, are contained in Hall and Lindzey [1957] and Munroe [1955]. Both of these books also review other schools of depth psychology and "neo-Freudian" psychodynamic views. These include such systems of thought as those of Alfred Adler and Karen Horney, who were also followers of Freud who later disagreed with him on various essential postulates, and those of Harry Stack Sullivan, one of America's great psychiatrists. We shall discuss some of the views of Adler and Sullivan in the next chapter.)

An Experimental Study of Castration Anxiety

General clinical experience suggests that intense castration anxiety in childhood is often followed by a recurrence of castration anxiety in adulthood when one thinks, feels, or behaves sexually. This appeared to be the case in the example of Ed in Chapter 2. Ed used to have frank castration dreams as a boy, and as a young man his sexual behavior was followed by nightmares in which he became fatally ill or in which doctors were going to remove his genitals. As we have said earlier (page 78), Freud proposed that such a fear of having a fatal illness is a characteristic derivative of repressed castration anxiety.

Sarnoff and Corwin (1959) conducted an experiment that bears on the validity of this psychoanalytic proposition. They reasoned that if such a formulation is valid, it should be possible to demonstrate experimentally that sexual arousal will increase the fear of death in men who are characterized by high levels of castration anxiety. These psychologists recruited more than 50 college men for their experiment. They measured the subjects' preexperimental fear of death by means of a scaled questionnaire. Then they measured the degree of unconscious castration anxiety to which each person was susceptible by asking the subjects to look at one particular cartoon from the "Blacky Test" (Blum, 1949), so named because a black dog, with whom the subject identifies, is a recurrent figure in the whole series of cartoons. In the particular cartoon they used Blacky is watching a scene in which a large knife hovers above the tail of a blindfolded dog, who is unaware of the disaster about to befall him. (Compare this with the castration significance for the Wolf Man of fairy tales in which wolves lose their tails.) The subjects were asked to indicate on a scale the degree of anxiety that they imagined Blacky felt as he witnessed the threatened tail amputation. The subjects' ratings were taken as an indication of the degree of unconscious castration anxiety that the scene aroused in *them*.

A few weeks later came the experimental arousal of sexuality, followed immediately by postexperimental measurement of the intensity of fear of death. Sexual arousal was accomplished by having subjects look at and describe photographs of nude women. Immediately afterward the postexperimental measure of fear of death was obtained by readministering the original scaled questionnaire.

And now, the results. As illustrated in Figure 5-7, sexual arousal produced a significant increase in the fear of death measures in the subjects with high castration anxiety, but not in the subjects with low castration anxiety. Other subjects who were shown only magazine pictures of fully clothed fashion models, and thus were less likely to be very sexually aroused, did not show any significant difference between their two fear of death measures. These control findings make it quite probable that the change following exposure to the pictures of the nude women was in fact due to sexual arousal, not merely to looking at pictures.

The results of this study by Sarnoff and Corwin are consistent with several psychoanalytic propositions concerning castration anxiety—its existence in varying degrees in young men, its relation to sexual arousal, and its indirect manifestation in the fear of death. The study is perhaps most important in demonstrating that systematic experimentation with this aspect of psychoanalytic theory is possible.

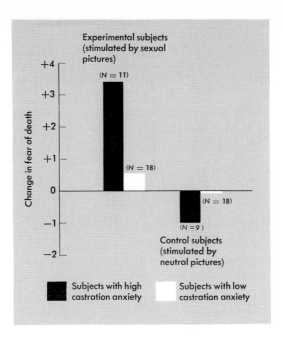

Figure 5-7   Average results of the experiment on castration anxiety in college men. (Based on data from Sarnoff & Corwin, 1959)

The subjects' fear of death was measured before and after they were either sexually aroused by pictures of nude women or presented with pictures of fully clothed women. Subjects with high castration anxiety became significantly more afraid of death after being stimulated by sexual pictures than did subjects with low castration anxiety.

THE OEDIPAL COMPLEX
AND ITS REPRESSION: A SUMMARY VIEW

Now let us return to the psychoanalytic theory of "the passing of the Oedipal complex." The typical consequence of the castration anxiety in the average young boy is assumed to be analogous to what we observed in Ed, the young man with the castration dreams. Motivated primarily by his fear of castration, the boy represses his Oedipal sexual desires and his hostile jealousy of his father. In doing so, he is behaving as if he thought he would thereby avoid the danger of castration, typically at the hands of his father. Other motives, such as the child's fear that his parents will stop loving him and will abandon him, which play the primary role in the girl, supplement the impetus for the boy's repression.

In Figure 5-8 the essential features of Oedipal conflicts are dia-

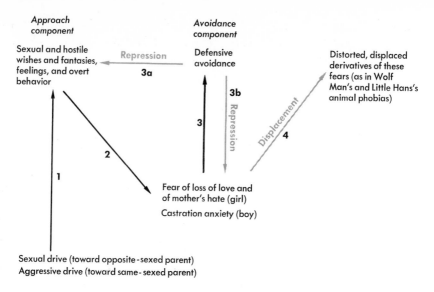

Figure 5-8   *The child's Oedipal conflicts.*

(1) *Under the pressure of his Oedipal sexual and aggressive drives, the child experiences corresponding sexual and hostile wishes, feelings, and fantasies and often engages in corresponding overt behavior (as in Little Hans, the Wolf Man, and the Rat Man when they were children). (2) Because he does such things and has such wishes, feelings, and fantasies, the child fears the loss of love of the same-sexed parent and also some form of active retaliation. (3) These fears motivate the child to engage in various defensive responses, which have the effect of reducing the fears. The child may repress his sexual and hostile wishes, fantasies, feelings, and overt behavior (3a). He may also repress the fears themselves (3b). These repressions produce a state of "dammed-up" sexual and aggressive tendencies and of "strangulated," unexpressed fears. The "dammed-up" sexual and aggressive tendencies may be expressed indirectly in the manner illustrated in Figures 15-4 and 15-5. (4) The unexpressed fears may be expressed in such distorted, disguised forms as the childhood animal phobias of the Wolf Man and Little Hans. The animals in such phobias appear to be symbolic substitutes for the feared parents, and the feared behavior of the animal appears to be a symbolic substitute for the feared retaliation by the parent. (Thus, Little Hans's fear that a horse would bite off his finger appeared to be a symbolic substitute for his fear that his father would cut off his penis.) Therefore, it is as if the child displaced his fear from his parent to the animal.*

gramed. Included in the figure are not only the repression of the sexual and hostile components (the approach component) of the conflicts but also the defensive process oriented directly against the anxieties themselves—fear of loss of love and of the mother's hate in the girl and castration anxiety in the boy. In other words, the child strives for emotional peace both by repressing his Oedipal wishes, which end in distress, and by defending against the unpleasant emotions themselves.

Aftermath of the Oedipal Conflicts

The child represses the Oedipal complex—both the sexual and the hostile conflict components—in the fifth or sixth year. But the influence of the Oedipal complex on his life obviously does not stop here. We have already seen evidence of this in our discussions of castration anxiety in college students, of incest taboos, and of the continued influence of the Oedipal complex in the life of the adult. This continual influence may be manifested in the relatively unchanged repetitions of the neurotic, such as the Wolf Man's adult sexual reactions and the Rat Man's adult death wishes for his father. Or it may be manifested in the more remote displacements of the normal individual, such as in choosing a mate who resembles the parent to some degree. Part of the significance of the repression of the Oedipal complex is that it initiates processes that continue into later life and that have the effect of freeing the person from this complex. Psychoanalytic observations and theory point to many ramifications of the repression of the Oedipal complex, however, some of which will be discussed briefly.

CHILDHOOD AMNESIA

The child's drastic repression of the Oedipal complex seems to serve as a nucleus for a widely generalized repressive process. Freud speculated that it was just such a process that caused the general amnesia almost everyone has for most events of childhood. This possibility suggests that our inability to recall much, if anything, about our childhood sexual life has an entirely different meaning from the one we customarily see in it. Rather than being a basis for refuting the reality of early sexual activities, our childhood amnesia might very well be an inevitable consequence of such activities. To be sure, the extent of childhood amnesia differs greatly from one person to another.

INFLUENCE ON THE LATENCY PERIOD

The generalized repressive process has still another consequence. It contributes to the onset and maintenance of the latency period of childhood, which separates the Oedipal and the pubertal phases of life. With the repression of the Oedipal complex, according to Freud, there is a *relative* decrease in all manifestations of childhood sexuality—pregenital and genital—and in the intensity of aggressive behavior in general. The average child becomes generally "better behaved," and, consequently, he is usually then able to participate constructively in formal schooling. While this developmental phase may also be determined in part by a decrease in the intensity of sexual and aggressive drives, it seems highly likely that the repressive process makes an important and regular contribution to it.

The clearest indications of repression are found in the exaggerated symptoms of neurosis that often appear for the first time during the latency period. It was just such a repressive process that caused Edie, the woman with the eating conflict, to change from a lively, happy, plump, feminine girl into a little spinster. Such extreme transformations in latency frequently take the form of clear-cut, severe, obsessive-compulsive neuroses in which the child strives defensively to be "very, very good": very clean, very obedient, very kind and considerate, very asexual, very moralistic, and so forth. Such a child is defending against being just the opposite because he fears the consequences of being "very, very bad." Both the Rat Man and the Wolf Man, incidentally, manifested just such neuroses, with a strong emphasis on religiosity, in their latency periods.

Recently a number of psychologists have reported that there are fewer manifestations of inhibitions in children of this age, and they suggest that the latency period may be less severe now because of more lenient handling of the child's sex behavior on the part of parents. Further studies obviously are needed on this issue.

CONTRIBUTION TO THE SUPEREGO

It is now clear that the child's repression of sexual and aggressive wishes is not an incidental aspect of personality development. It is associated with many impressive changes in the total behavior of the child. It will not be surprising, therefore, to hear that Freud attributed still another extremely important step in life largely to the repression of the Oedipal complex: the formation of the nucleus of the child's superego.

Fear of parental retribution motivates the child to repress his Oedipal complex. But the most varied kinds of psychoanalytic evidence (to which we shall refer in Chapters 10, 11, and 12) suggest that the child accomplishes that repression by internalizing a set of parental functions. (Parental functions mean here not only personality traits of the parents but also certain behavior in which every parent engages with his child. We shall mention these in a moment.) *Internalizing* connotes that he not only learns them but takes them "inside" and makes them part of himself. Foremost among these functions are the parents' own moral values in the domain of sexuality and aggression. The parents' moral values serve as internal standards of behavior with which the child struggles to comply.

If the child is to be successful in this struggle, however, the internalization of *other* parental functions must also occur: parental observation, evaluation, and moral judgment—that is, the evaluative comparison of the child's behavior against moral norms resulting in parental punishment or praise. When the latter functions have become internalized they are transformed into self-observation, self-evaluation, and self-punishment and self-approval.

The moral values and ancillary functions adopted from the parents constitute the core of the superego. While both parents are sources of such functions, the core of the child's superego consists of selective internalizations from the parent most feared in the Oedipal phase. In this sense the child is said to *identify with the aggressor* in forming his superego (A. Freud, 1936). Since the girl typically has most fear of her *mother's* retribution, the nucleus of her superego consists of her mother's values and her mother's mode of observing and judging, and punishing or approving. Since the boy typically has most fear of punishment by his *father*, the nucleus of his superego consists of his father's values, and so forth. In Chapter 10 we shall discuss identification with the aggressor in considerable detail.

Identification with a lost love object, one way people cope with grief, also contributes to the formation of the child's superego. When a child represses his Oedipal love, he is also losing a love object through his own renunciation. (We shall discuss this matter more completely in the next chapter.) He is in a psychological position analogous to the college student who still loves someone whom he has decided to stop dating. In this situation the child also internalizes some of the attributes of the parent whom he had loved in the sensual, Oedipal sense. Often these attributes are the positive ideals of that parent, which now become important ideals of the child. Even when the attributes are not parental ideals, the child may elevate them from seemingly incidental traits of the parent into major ideals or goals for himself. In this way the ideal of becoming an artist may develop in a man whose mother was only mildly interested in art. However, it is often possible in such cases to demonstrate that the "mild interest" of the parent actually derives from an intense unconscious interest that is transmitted by various slight cues to the child. We shall discuss identification with a lost love object in more detail later. The important point here is that this form of identification also contributes to the child's superego. Although it is somewhat of an oversimplification, we will say that a person's positive ideals start with his identification with the parents he loved intensely as a child and that a person's restrictive, harsh moral values start with his identification with the parent he most feared as a child. By processes like these, a person's superego usually blends the characteristics of both parents. Even so, the identification with the parent of the same sex, which is primarily identification with the aggressor, gives the superego its dominant characteristics.

Freud suggested that the degree to which parental values are internalized, and thus the extent to which a person's standards of right and wrong, good and bad, and appropriate and inappropriate are his own inner ones, depends in part on how frightened children are when they identify with their parents. No childhood anxiety, Freud reasoned, equals castration anxiety in intensity. Therefore, he concluded, *internal* moral standards are much more firmly consolidated in men than in women, while women are more likely to be concerned with *external* standards. These are provocative statements, which Freud asserted but did not document, and they have been vehemently challenged.

The results of several studies, however, are relevant, although none were concerned with testing Freud's hypothesis. Lunger and Page (1939) found that a much higher proportion of women than men worried about "not being popular socially" (71 percent versus 49 percent) and about "the possibility that no one cares for them" (32 percent versus 14 percent). Two studies in the 1950's also reported such differences. Gough (1952), whose subjects were high school and college students, found that girls were socially more sensitive and restrained than boys. The adolescent girls studied by Moss (1955) were more concerned with courtesy, neatness, and the inhibition of *public* displays of romantic and aggressive behavior than were boys. In a study of the dynamics of friendship in eighth graders (Berlin, 1966), girls were found to have greater nurturance needs and concern that their best friend would desert them for someone else than boys had. One study (Pintner & Lev, 1940), however, failed to demonstrate such differences.

The theme in most of these studies of greater concern on the part of women with external appearances, with the social effects of behavior and with being liked is consistent with Freud's view that women's standards for behavior are not as thoroughly internalized as men's. The results of the studies may also be interpreted as simply indicating greater social sensitivity in women and as not bearing on Freud's hypothesis. However one interprets the results, they do not mean that men are more "moral" than women. They do, however, imply sex differences in the extent to which one's personal standards regulate one's behavior, in the consistency with which those standards are applied in varying interpersonal contexts, and in the reasons for conforming to norms of behavior. We are speaking of average tendencies, of course; some women have a strongly internalized, severe conscience, and some men are very other-directed (Riesman, 1950).

EFFECTS DURING ADOLESCENCE

The quiescence of latency, whether it be the relative, "choppy" calm of the normal child or the ominous stillness of neurosis, comes to an end with the onset of *puberty* and the ensuing, often stormy, adolescence.

Rearousal of the Childhood
Oedipal Conflicts

Biological changes intensify the adolescent's sexual urges and his propensity for aggression. In turn, the rudimentary superego and the defenses established in latency, which constitute many of the child's character traits, are severely strained by these intensified drives. The result is a rearousal of the childhood conflicts over sexuality and aggression, as well as their displacement outside the family to peer groups and other social arenas, where the conflicts continue.

Much of the adolescent's stormy behavior is a result of the intensely renewed childhood conflicts. Thus, the adolescent girl is likely to erupt in hostile explosions with her mother, and the boy with his father, but then be on the best of terms with the parent a moment later. Manifestations of deep love for the parent of the opposite sex will oscillate with avoidance of any intimacy. Sibling rivalry and affection succeed one another in bewildering fashion. Temptations to have physical contact with a brother or sister are counteracted by prudish, standoffish reactions. Periods of ascetic abstinence separate sprees of masturbation, especially in boys. One of the major tasks the adolescent must accomplish is the further resolution of his childhood conflicts. Especially he must, and typically does, free himself from the grip of both the erotic and the hostile components of the Oedipal complex. Often, however, this freeing process is not complete until after the young adult has married and established himself in a vocation.

The Struggle with Values

Another aspect of adolescent turmoil is the young person's struggle with values—his own, his parents', and his society's. The upsurge of his drives seems to be one of the key causes of this struggle, for it puts his previously developed values to a severe test. This unstable state of affairs is further complicated by the beginnings of liberation from his childhood emotional ties to his parents, for this liberation affects his identifications with his parents as well as his drive relations with them. As he becomes somewhat estranged from his parents as real people, so too he becomes estranged from the main internal representations of them—from his superego. Until adolescence the average American and European child takes his moral standards for granted; indeed, he is hardly aware of them. But in adolescence he becomes painfully aware of them and treats them almost like objects. He "looks" at his standards and values, talks about them, likes or dislikes them, and so forth. During all this, the typical adolescent is also exposed to, becomes aware of, and is freed to experiment with an array of moral alternatives provided by his culture. Some resolution of his struggle with values is another task the adolescent must accomplish.

The two processes of adolescence we have discussed—the renewed struggle with the sexual and aggressive drives and the explorations of value systems—are obviously interrelated. We might call these major tasks, together with the establishment of an *ego identity* (discussed below), "the work of adolescence."

Sexual Identity   One outcome of these developmental processes is the determination of the *sexual identity* of the individual. While the seeds of this identity were planted in childhood in relation to the Oedipal conflict, the final outcome is not determined until the work of adolescence is completed. Nor need it be, in our society. As adolescence progresses, however, one's sexual identity is relentlessly shaped by external and internal forces. Whether one is to be a masculine man or a feminine woman, in what ways one is masculine and in what ways feminine, how comfortable and free of conflict one is with one's sex roles, the depth of intimacy one desires or tolerates—these are some of the important attributes of sexual identity. They reflect issues that must be more or less settled by the close of adolescence if one is to progress to adulthood and participate fully in marriage and parenthood.

Ego Identity   The consolidation of one's sexual identity is the central aspect of a still larger process that comes to the fore in adolescence: the crystallization of one's *ego identity* (Erikson, 1950, 1959), the definition of who and what one is. Our sexual identities, occupational or career choices, shared group identities, preferred defenses, and significant personal identifications become organized into a coherent pattern that defines each of us as a unique individual. Obviously, one's identity formation does not begin and end in adolescence. It begins with birth and ends with death. But it is typically a focal task of adolescence in our culture. During the high school and college years, the individual "decides" what kind of person he is going to be in certain crucial respects. Severe identity conflicts often arise at this time. Keniston's (1965) study of the uncommitted Ivy League college student illustrates such conflicts with concrete case material.

Those who cannot remember the past are condemned to repeat it.

GEORGE SANTAYANA. The Life of Reason

CHAPTER 6
PAINFUL EXPERIENCES AND OVER-REACTIONS OF DISTRESS

In the last two chapters we focused on childhood conflicts over sexuality and aggression, on their repression, and on the influence of such repressed conflicts on the later behavior of the adult. We discussed, for example, the childhood conflict of the Rat Man over his jealousy of his father and the way this conflict, after it became unconscious, continued to influence his behavior in sexual situations in adulthood. We also discussed the childhood sexual conflict of the Wolf Man and the way this conflict, after it became unconscious, caused him to over-react sexually in adulthood to kneeling or squatting women. Our emphasis in those chapters may have created several false impressions, such as: (1) that conflict and defense involve only inner wishes, such as sexual or aggressive ones; (2) that only sexual or aggressive over-reactions result from unconscious processes; and (3) that a person's emotional life, especially in childhood, consists only of sexual and aggressive feelings and the fears associated with them. In this chapter we shall begin to correct any such false impressions. We shall also expand on aspects of conflict and defense that we have mentioned only briefly so far. We shall do this by shifting our attention to some of the "objective" *painful experiences* nearly all children and adults undergo and by considering three of the ways such painful experiences might result in *over-reactions of distress* to innocuous stimuli. Chapters 4 and 5 have provided the background for proceeding in this way. At the same time we discuss these immediate issues, we shall be laying the foundation for further discussion in Chapters 10, 11, and 12 of the kinds of conflicts and defenses that were introduced in the preceding chapters.

We shall begin our discussion by examining major types of "objectively" unpleasant stimuli.

Six Categories
of Objectively Unpleasant Stimuli

The following set of characteristics is very useful for classifying unpleasant external situations:

1. Frustration
2. Threats to physical integrity
3. Loss of a love object
4. Separation from a protector
5. Loss of love
6. Loss of self-esteem

Most unpleasant events share the properties of two or more of these categories. The death of Duane's father represented both separation from a protecting parent and loss of a loved and loving person (as well as the realization of Duane's wish that his father would die). The danger of castration threatens not only the boy's physical integrity but also his self-esteem. Hence, the examples that we shall use to illustrate a category will be events that typically and predominantly, but not exclusively, belong to that category. The dominant features of the emotional reactions to an event will be the basis on which we shall categorize it. It should be noted at the outset that these categories may not be universal but do apply to our Western culture.

EXTREME FRUSTRATION

Frustration is an unpleasant state that can produce marked changes in behavior. These behavioral changes range from anger and aggression to regression and withdrawal. The reports of people in psychoanalysis suggest that a *sense of helplessness* is an important ingredient in the unpleasant feelings accompanying frustration. When we are frustrated, we feel helpless in the face of our *ungratified desires*. As we sense these desires becoming stronger, we feel our capacity to tolerate the mounting tension being severely strained. Our self-control seems endangered. We also feel helpless in the face of the frustrating *external obstacles*, especially those that are arbitrarily enforced. (Experimental findings that the increasing arbitrariness of frustrations imposed by other people leads to greater aggression are described in Janis, 1971, pp. 156–59.)

THREATS TO PHYSICAL INTEGRITY

Near-miss experiences that constitute threats to physical integrity include such general disasters as floods, tornadoes, and wars and such great personal disasters as a near-drowning and the stress of major surgery. (Both types of disasters are discussed at length in Janis, 1971.)

Near-misses experienced by almost all children include castration for the boy and the mother's evil, witchlike, retaliatory jealousy for the girl. While these are largely fantasy experiences, there is often some real basis for them in the signs of anger displayed by the parental rival. These experiences are very important instances of *perceived threats* to physical integrity and welfare.

LOSS OF A LOVE OBJECT

The loss of a loved person through death or a long separation is the most obvious instance of this stress. Grief—a complex blend of a painfully sad, helpless sense of loss and an anguished longing for the loved one— is the dominant emotional reaction. Even very young children are capable of complex grieving reactions, especially when they are separated from their mothers. (Chapter 10 in Janis, 1971, fully explores this and other aspects of grief.)

Loss of a love object may also occur through an undesired yet active *renunciation* by the subject or through a failure or refusal by the object to fulfill that role. Imagine an intimate, deep love relationship that has become platonic because one partner decided on moral grounds or out of fear that he must renounce the other as a lover. Each of the people has lost a love object, and each experiences something very similar to grief and bereavement. These emotions are usually so painful that the couple either become lovers again or give up even the platonic relationship.

Oedipal Renunciations

The Oedipal boy and girl, whom we discussed in Chapter 5, go through an analogous experience. They unwillingly renounce their parents as love objects, and the parents, except in rare instances, fail to fulfill the role of sexual love objects. Although the matter requires systematic research, there are reasons to believe that this childhood renunciation or imposed loss is just as painful as the more familiar adult versions.

One reason is that during the Oedipal phase—from age 3 to age 6— children long to spend every possible moment with the parent of the opposite sex, and they feel that any deprivation of this wish is a major tragedy. Little Hans, for example, showed many signs of painful longing for the close contact and the rather erotic relationship he had enjoyed with his mother (Freud, 1909a).

Second, when adults reexperience their childhood renunciations during psychoanalysis, the affects of sadness and anguished longing often become very intense.

> One woman first expressed all this in a disguised manner: in the way she experienced her relationship with her analyst. As often happens during psycho-analytic treatment, she felt that she had fallen in love with her analyst and fantasied that he was in love with her. But she also fantasied that both of them were refraining from having an affair and from eventually divorcing their spouses to marry each other out of loyalty to their spouses and on general ethical grounds. Thinking and talking about this self-denial left her tearful, filled with sadness, and overwhelmed by a hopeless yearning for what she was losing by renunciation.

Although phenomenologically it was utterly real to her, this entire experience was one of *transference love* (Freud, 1912, 1915a). In every important detail she was *repeating* love fantasies that she used to have about herself and her father (Freud, 1914b). One such fantasy had occurred on her wedding day, when she interpreted the tearful looks exchanged between herself and her father as a mutual recognition that their love for each other inevitably had to be renounced.

There is a third reason for comparing these childhood Oedipal renunciations with the loss of a loved person through death or long separation. *Identification with the lost love object* plays a major role in the subject's attempts to cope with each kind of loss. (The discussion of bereavement and mourning in Janis, 1971, pp. 183–89, applies equally well to children's struggling renunciation of their parents as love objects.) Freud often observed this process. Dora, an hysterical patient, repressed her Oedipal love for her father and later developed a nervous cough that persisted for years (Freud, 1905a). This was evidence that she had identified with him, for he had coughed persistently from tuberculosis during Dora's childhood "love affair" with him.

SEPARATION FROM A PROTECTOR

Very young children typically react with intense anxiety to being separated from their mothers. So characteristic is this reaction that it has been given a special name: *separation anxiety*. Because they are so vulnerable and helpless, young children conceive of such a separation as very dangerous and are more disturbed by it than by conditions that actually threaten their lives. During World War II, psychologists found that the youngsters of London who were separated from their mothers during the large-scale evacuation of children to the country were more emotionally disturbed than those who remained in London with their mothers, even though the latter were subjected to extensive bombings by the Germans (Pritchard & Rosenzweig, 1942; A. Freud & Burlingham, 1943). Being separated from their mothers was more real and dangerous than the possibility of their being killed, which is in any case a scarcely conceivable idea to young children.

Even brief separations from their mothers frighten young children. Sleeping alone or being left with strangers while mother goes out to shop, visit, or work are typical of such disturbing separations and bring on the normal form of childhood separation anxiety. Ordinarily, separation becomes less and less frightening as the individual grows older, but a person may experience some degree of separation anxiety at any age. The object may be a parent or a parental substitute.

LOSS OF LOVE

This type of universally experienced stress differs from grievous loss of a loved person and separation anxiety in two ways: in the kinds of situations that may produce it and in the content of the emotional experience. The impact a sibling's birth has on a young child is prototypical of this kind of experience. Commonly, the older child has been accustomed to the nearly exclusive devotion of his mother and to being the center of attention for both parents. Suddenly he finds his position usurped and his accomplishments seemingly unnoticed. In his eyes, his parents do not love him any more.

In adult life, a broad spectrum of events can produce the state and sense of loss of love:

Not being noticed by people we care about.

A decrease in their underlying emotional interest and attention.

Decreases in the amount of overt affection and care they give us.

Disapproval and punishment for an error or oversight, which are interpreted as signs of loss of love.

Outright rejection.

The state or sense of being unloved has several exceedingly unpleasant effects (though the adult victim typically tries not to show his hurt). One effect is grief. Another is frustration. The victim neither receives the love he wants nor has the satisfaction of actively loving in return. This amounts to a frustrating disruption of one of man's basic ways of relating to others, *getting and giving* (Erikson, 1950).

Self-esteem may fall painfully with a loss of love, especially in children and in "other-directed" adults, since their sense of self-worth is highly dependent on the reactions of other people to them. They may *feel* worthless, inferior, or bad and may even conclude that they *are* these things and have been ignored or rejected because of these qualities.

Rejection, punishment, and other signs of loss of love frequently arouse separation anxiety, because they stimulate fantasies that one will be abandoned and left utterly helpless if he is unloved. For example, after a teacher has criticized a student, the student may feel that the teacher will not want to supervise his work any more. An employee who has been criticized may become convinced that he is about to be fired. Children are very susceptible to such fantasies. In fact, Freud (1926) hypothesized that fear of loss of love developed out of separation anxiety through a displacement of anxiety from separation experiences to signs of loss of love.

Finally, there is loneliness. Feeling unloved cuts a man off from meaningful relations with others and leaves him feeling alienated and actually estranged. Though the exact nature of loneliness is unknown at present, it seems to blend loss of love, separation anxiety, and frustration.

In summary, the loss of love arouses varying degrees of grief and despairing longing, frustration, lowered self-esteem, separation anxiety, and loneliness.

LOSS OF SELF-ESTEEM

Rejections are not the only stimuli that lower our self-esteem. Indeed, they are not even necessary. Once we have formed our ideals, we criticize ourselves whenever we judge that we have fallen short of them. These self-criticisms can damage our self-esteem as effectively as criticisms by others. Many of these painful self-appraisals involve a comparison of ourselves with some other person whom we have taken as an ideal.

Like the other stressful experiences we have discussed, loss of self-esteem has childhood as well as adult versions. We have already discussed the narcissistic mortification experienced by most little girls when they perceive the difference between their own bodies and those of boys. Another prototypical experience of the loss of self-esteem is produced by parents' derogatory reactions to their children's strivings to be little men and women. A mother's making fun of her little daughter's physical appearance or a father's criticism of his son's handmade model airplane may severely bruise the child's self-esteem.

Another prototypical experience is familiar to most children of minority groups: the realization, provided by some form of social discrimination, that they are different from other people and are (unjustifiably) despised or regarded as inferior because of that difference.

Should any of the childhood wounds we have discussed be repeatedly and deeply inflicted, they may never heal or may lead to a badly scarred adult personality. A more or less chronically low sense of self-esteem sometimes develops because the person internalizes the attitudes that idealized people express to him about himself. Without being aware of it, he comes to regard himself as others regarded him when he was a child—that is, at that time in his life when the opinions of others really were crucial for his well-being.

The concept of self-esteem is a junction point connecting Freudian psychoanalysis with the diverging views of two other well-known theorists: Alfred Adler and Harry Stack Sullivan. Adler parted ways with Freud in 1911 largely on the theoretical grounds that a sense of inferiority, as he termed feelings of low self-esteem, was the prime mover in much human behavior, especially social behavior and neurosis. The sense of inferiority, Adler argued, caused the individual to compensate for it by engaging in various kinds of assertive or power behavior. This he termed the *masculine protest*. Such views led Adler to conclusions about any given behavior that were quite different from those reached by Freud. As Ernest Jones says in his biography of Freud, "Sexual factors, particularly those of childhood, were reduced to a minimum: a boy's incestuous desire for intimacy with his mother was interpreted as the male wish to conquer a female masquerading as sexual desire. The concepts of repression, infantile sexuality, and even that of the unconscious itself were discarded . . . [Jones, 1955, p. 131]." Adler and his followers went on to develop an independent school of thought known as *individual psychology*. It is actually a psychology that places great emphasis on social aspects of behavior.

Harry Stack Sullivan developed his views, known as the *interpersonal theory of psychiatry*, in the United States between 1925 and 1945, approximately. He too placed great emphasis on the human need for a solid sense of self-esteem and attributed many forms of interpersonal behavior to the attempt to regulate one's self-esteem by what he called *security operations* (which closely resemble what we call *defenses*). The cruel domination of a child by a mother, for example, might be the mother's attempt to make herself feel worthwhile or powerful. Usually, this viewpoint holds, people intimately involved with each other develop reciprocal security operations. Thus, the child of such a mother might very well learn to be submissive to her because she rewards such behavior. She does this, of course, to perpetuate an interpersonal relationship pattern that maintains her self-esteem. The child continues in his reciprocal behavior because his self-esteem is raised by her rewards. These remarks only touch upon a few of Sullivan's basic ideas, which are set forth in his *Conceptions of Modern Psychiatry* (1947). The surveys by Hall and Lindzey (1957) and Munroe (1955) discuss both the Adlerian and Sullivanian viewpoints in detail and contain references to the important original writings of these two men and their followers.

We have now examined the six classes of unpleasant external stimuli and the characteristic emotional reactions to them. All these emotional reactions are painful. If a person does not learn to adapt to the situations, the emotions will naturally persist and the person will then resort to defenses, to less adaptive ways of avoiding the painful emotions. Before we can discuss these defense mechanisms, however, we must deal with another issue: the arousal of unpleasant emotions by innocuous stimuli.

Transformation of Innocuous Stimuli into Noxious Stimuli

"INNOCUOUS" AND "NOXIOUS" STIMULI

No stimulus is inherently innocuous or noxious: Distress arises from the *interaction* of an external stimulus and the organism. Even elemental physical pain requires a contribution from the organism, if only in the form of pain receptors, an intact nervous system, and sensory thresholds. And an experience that most of us would find painful might be pleasant to someone else. Yet all of us in a given culture agree in considering and labeling certain stimuli "noxious" or "stressful" and certain emotional reactions to them "realistic" or "appropriate." Such labels can be used because the people in a given culture are similar physiologically and psychologically and so react in roughly the same ways to these stimuli. We call stimuli "noxious" or "stressful" when they elicit unpleasant emotions in all, or nearly all, of us. We call unpleasant emotions "realistic" or "appropriate" when all, or nearly all, of us experience them in response to the same stimuli.

The part psychology plays in determining the "appropriateness" of responses may be doubted. Are there not "objective" dangers—death or bereavement, for example—to which all people react in the same way? Consider the following historical example. During World War II, crashing on the deck of a Japanese battleship was "objectively" an extremely stressful situation for American combat pilots; fear and attempts to avoid doing so were "realistic" and "appropriate" responses. But hundreds of Japanese kamikaze pilots deliberately crashed on American ships. For them, such a death was an honorable entry to a glorious afterlife (Grinker & Speigel, 1945), not an "objective" danger. Fear would have been an inappropriate and unrealistic response. This is dramatic evidence that psychological factors, in this case internalized cultural definitions of the meaning of a "reality" event, determine and define "noxious" stimuli and "realistic" emotional distress.

Just as cultures differ from one another, so do individuals within a given culture. Most American men, for example, are only momentarily startled by the loud report of a backfiring engine. But the same stimulus may terrify a combat veteran who had once been severely wounded by an exploding shell. We shall call such inappropriate emotional responses *over-reactions of distress* to external stimuli.

What kinds of stimuli elicit such over-reactions? Why? What psychological processes transform innocuous stimuli into noxious ones?

SIMPLE CONDITIONING AND STIMULUS GENERALIZATION

The simplest types of stimuli causing over-reactions of distress are *conditioned stress stimuli* and *generalized conditioned stress stimuli*. The former are innocuous stimuli that have been associated with noxious ones; generalized conditioned stress stimuli resemble the originally innocuous, conditioned stimuli. Combat experiences often produce such conditioned and generalized stimuli, which then evoke anxiety attacks in veterans for years afterward. Actually, any stimulus situation significant for the organism, such as the six we discussed at the beginning of this chapter, can generate conditioned or generalized stimuli. If a child has been frightened by separation from his mother, merely seeing her put on her coat or hearing her say she is about to go or seeing her leave may come to frighten him. All these stimuli have been associated with her past absences and have become conditioned stimuli for him. If his own separation experiences have been unpleasant, the mere sight of another mother leaving her child may function as a generalized conditioned fear stimulus and also frighten him.

**Perpetuation
of Childhood Reactions**
Most adults outgrow the unpleasant situations of childhood. Maturation and further learning modify their original unconditioned responses, and their early conditioned emotional responses become extinguished. Obviously, a college-aged person will rarely become frightened at being separated from his mother. But in extreme cases the adult remains disturbed in essentially the same way by essentially the same childhood situations. For example, the adult may remain tied to his mother's apron strings by a separation anxiety that he was never allowed or helped to outgrow because of his mother's overprotectiveness. Or he may never have gotten over the effects of intense separation experiences. Such prolonged separation anxiety takes specific forms at various stages of life. The "school phobias," for example, are usually caused by intense separation anxiety in children of school age. A relatively undistorted fear of separation from parental protection keeps many young adults tied to the home, a family business, or the town where their parents live. Usually the separation anxiety combines with other anxieties—such as fear of parental disapproval at signs of independence—and with unconscious libidinal attachments.

The adult who was a spoiled child may still feel unloved and jealous whenever his parents pay any attention to his brother or sister. And the man who was never guided appropriately by his father along the paths of achievement may feel just as worthless when his father criticizes his present work performance as he did as a boy, when the only things his father noticed about the birdhouse he built were its imperfections.

In less extreme cases of immaturity the disturbing adult situations resemble those of childhood less closely. For example, some adults who have been able to leave their parents displace their separation anxiety to other people or even to institutions, openly experiencing anxiety at the prospect of leaving a protective employer, government bureau, university, or hospital where they have been long-term patients. Similar displacements of the sense of being unloved cause many commonplace conditions to be transformed into ones of acute distress, for example, not always being the center of attention, being appropriately criticized, seeing others being recognized for their achievements, and not being the sole concern of one's employer or spouse.

The following fairly common instance of the same general process may be less familiar. Most women outgrow their girlhood unhappiness about lacking a penis and come to enjoy their femininity and men's maleness. Some women, however, continue to experience a sense of humiliation, worthlessness, and envy of the male whenever they perceive their femaleness and the difference between men and women.

One woman, for example, told her analyst how a veil of gloom surrounded her if she happened to touch her breasts in the process of dressing, or if a man touched them. When she and her husband made love, and especially at the point of intromission, a sense of humiliation would frequently sweep over her, together with an urge to "smash" him. Another woman who also felt humiliated and hostile when she made love with her husband had the same feelings for her analyst following each analytic hour in which she referred to her clitoris. In these same interviews her free associations frequently concerned "defects" in herself and her children. She finally realized that she regarded herself as defective for having a clitoris instead of a penis.

Perceptions or thoughts about their feminine attributes and men's contrasting attributes, and indeed the situation of sexual intimacy with their husbands, devastated the self-esteem of these women. They reacted with a sense of deep humiliation, just as they had when they were little girls comparing their bodies with those of little boys. They had not developed a positive feminine identity.

The similarity between these adult situations and the comparable childhood ones is analogous to the similarity for the combat veteran between the noise of a backfiring engine and the sound of the gunshot that had severely wounded him in battle. All of them are instances of stimulus generalization and generalized responses.

The Conditioned
Response Paradigm

We have just been describing various kinds of observable relations: the close timing of unconditioned and conditioned stimuli, the similarity of certain stimuli, and the temporal relation between a stimulus and the response to it. The paradigm for these relations is presented in Figure 6-1. It states simply that

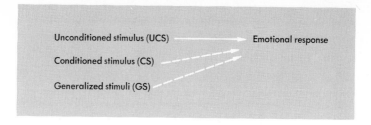

Figure 6-1   The conditioned response paradigm.

conditioned and generalized stimuli produce essentially the same emotional response that the original unconditioned stimulus produced. The dashed arrows represent learned stimulus-response relations; the solid arrow represents either innate or earlier learned relations that have become highly automatic and reflex-like. Applying this paradigm to the "over-reactions" of separation anxiety we have discussed, we get the diagram shown in Figure 6-2.

Some Unanswered Questions   Psychologists are still struggling with many of the questions implicit in these diagrams. For example, do conditioned responses result simply from the close temporal association of the unconditioned stimulus and the conditioned stimulus, as Pavlovian theory maintains? Or must there be a close temporal association of the conditioned stimulus-conditioned response sequence and drive reduction or need satisfaction, as Hullian learning theory assumes? Are more complex theories, involving cognitive concepts and language, required to explain the complex human behavior we have been describing? For example, can a mother's leave-taking preparations frighten a child who has not yet developed memory and a general capacity to anticipate the future? Does the appearance of this anticipatory anxiety reaction depend on the development of a capacity to *actively* reproduce in miniature the more intense anxieties the child experienced *passively* during past absences of the mother? A fuller discussion of such complicated issues would take us too far afield from the topic of over-reaction, but the interested reader should see Freud's monograph *Inhibitions, Symptoms, and Anxiety* (1926), Dollard and Miller's *Personality and Psychotherapy* (1950), and Hilgard and Bower's *Theories of Learning* (1966).

Another question is the nature of the internal processes mediating the over-reactions to conditioned and generalized stimuli. Some psychologists insist that psychology is a science of directly observable stimulus-response relationships and should not be concerned with this issue. Most psychologists, however, prefer to investigate the intervening mediating mechanisms as well. Some psychologists focus on the intervening physiological

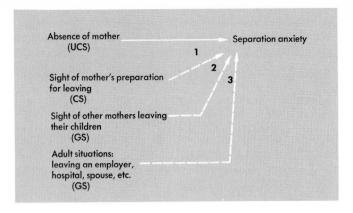

Figure 6-2 Over-reactions of separation anxiety in the child and the adult, according to the conditioned response paradigm.

The reactions produced in instances 2 and 3 are clearly over-reactions. If the reaction in 1 were intense in a very young child, or if it were present much beyond the age of 4, it too would be an over-reaction.

processes, especially brain functioning. Others focus on intervening psychological processes. Among learning theorists, Dollard and Miller, who were greatly influenced by psychoanalytic theory, have been most concerned with the mediating function of slight internal reactions, thoughts, and other intervening cognitive factors.

Every time an instance of over-reaction is observed through the microscope of the psychoanalytic technique, *it appears as if over-reactions to innocuous stimuli—conditioned, generalized, or any other kind—are mediated by memories, fantasies, wishes, and conflicts involving those stimuli.* In the rest of this chapter we shall discuss in detail the role of unconscious memories and fantasies in over-reactions.

Transformation Through Unconscious Memories: A Case of Separation Anxiety

In Chapter 1 we reviewed Freud's early work on hysteria and the role of memories of traumatic experiences. We also noted that subsequent systematic studies have demonstrated that most people selectively "forget" memories of unpleasant experiences. That is, the more unpleasant an experience is, the more likely most people are to "forget" it. Psychoanalytic case studies tell us that such "forgetting" is an active process of repression, not simply the gradual fading away of memory, and that repressed memories of unpleasant experiences often cause us to over-react with emotional distress to current events. We saw how the Wolf Man over-reacted sexually to scenes resembling those that had excited him in childhood. The process we are discussing now is analogous, but it involves distressing memories and experiences instead of, or in addition to, pleasant ones.

Memories affect everyone's reactions to external stimuli at some time or other. We may "over-react" by taking an immediate dislike to a stranger we pass on the street. Later we may realize that the person reminded us of someone else about whom we had very unpleasant memories. Some of these memories may even have spontaneously appeared in our stream of consciousness after we passed the stranger. Essentially the same phenomenon can be observed in psychoanalysis, with important differences: The process can be observed more completely there, more important over-reactions are involved, and the over-reactions may at first seem quite strange because they spring from unconscious memories.

Let us consider over-reactions of separation anxiety. In any psychoanalysis the continuity of the nearly daily analytic sessions is inevitably interrupted by holidays, vacations, trips, or illness by the person in analysis or the analyst. Many analysands react to these interruptions with separation anxiety. This in itself is evidence of an over-reaction determined by something within the analysand, for the interruptions do not inherently produce separation anxiety. Other analysands, for example, react with feelings of being unloved, or with a loss of self-esteem, or with a sense of frustration. And some are glad to be "free" for a while. When the analysand reacts with an over-reaction of separation anxiety, his thoughts at the time contain clues of the inner processes, of the activation of memories of previous separations.

THE MEMORIES
ACTIVATED BY IMMINENT SEPARATIONS

A married woman in her late twenties suffered from intense separation anxiety. Four brief separations from her analyst occurred during the first 8 months of her analysis. She reacted to three of them with a good deal of anxiety, and each time the separation from her analyst became imminent, memory fragments of previous separations, or of closely related experiences, crept into her associations. The fragments from her associations in one analytic session preceding each separation are listed below. When these occurred, they were embedded in a larger context that rationalized them and disguised their relevance to separation anxiety from the analysand. She did not realize that the current separations were activating the memories that were creeping into her associations. This process of memory activation is quite different from active, intentional recall of the past. It is an automatic, involuntary effect of current stimulation. We shall use the word "remember," in quotes, to stand for the process.

1. A Separation
of 5 Days   As she sat in the analyst's waiting room just
prior to the last session before the separation,
she had an anxiety attack. For a moment she felt disoriented spatially: The
analyst's office seemed to be on the wrong side of the waiting room, and the
windows of the waiting room seemed to be located in the wrong side of the building.
This perceptual experience was accompanied by panic.

Memory fragment 1. Shortly after describing that experience, she "remembered" an episode at college when she drank too much and was disoriented. She
did not speak of her anxiety attacks at college, which she had previously described
as having been accompanied by a similar perceptual distortion, of the walls of her
room closing in on her. But the striking similarity of those anxiety reactions and
the present one suggests that memories of her separation from home when she
went to college had also been activated but had not directly emerged into consciousness. She "remembered" being disoriented at college, but not her separation
anxiety.

Memory fragment 2. Later in the session she "remembered" a question, and
her answer, on a psychological test she had taken 2 months earlier. The question
was, "What would you do if you were *lost and alone* in the woods?" She had said
she would sit down and wait for someone to find her.

Memory fragment 3. Still later in the session, she "remembered" an episode
of a few nights before: She was *by herself* in a dark hallway in the tenement where
her apartment was. She was trying to find her way and had banged her head on
a door while searching for the light switch.

2. A Separation
of 3 Weeks   This was the first lengthy separation and occurred 4 weeks after the first one. In addition,
she was faced with the possibility of having to go with her husband to a distant
ocean resort during the interruption. If she went, she would be leaving her parents,
who lived nearby, and her home. Thus, she anticipated a double separation—from
her parents as well as from her analyst. In the end, she and her husband stayed
home; she was too frightened to leave. Two nights before this separation she had
a *nightmare,* in which her father appeared as a reassuring figure. This was a manifestation of her very intense anxiety in response to this separation and of her wish
to remain with her analyst and parents. Her associations to the nightmare included memories of previous separations, extending back to her early childhood.

Memory fragment 1. She "remembered" times several years earlier when she
had walked *alone* in a tunnel associated with the building in which her analyst's
office was located. She was scared; she always felt calmer if other people were
walking there too.

Memory fragment 2. She "remembered" a frightening scene she had observed
a year before when she and her husband had *gone away* from home to a nearby

ocean resort: The breakers had been exceptionally high, four people had been *swept away* by them and drowned, and lifeguards had been on hand to rescue people from drowning.

Memory fragment 3. Later in the hour she "remembered" a related childhood incident. Her parents had taken her to the beach for a picnic. She became *separated from them* (when they ignored her) and had tried to swim to a small island just off the shore. She was panicked by the time her mother found her on a sand bar.

Memory fragment 4. She "remembered" another traumatic separation experience in her childhood. She and her brother, she said, used to exasperate their parents by cutting up at the dinner table. On one such occasion her mother and father got up, put on their hats and coats, and walked out of the house, saying *they were leaving forever.* As she recalled this, she said, *"Just picture two little kids sitting there white with fear."*

3. A Separation of One Week

This separation occurred during the eighth month of analysis, 6 months after the preceding 3-week separation. She and her husband were about to go on a week's trip of several hundred miles, during which they would stop overnight with several different friends and relatives. She was *terrified about the sleeping arrangements* they might encounter—so much so that she was not sure she could go. This time she finally went.

Memory fragment. In associating to a dream expressing her conflict over going on this trip, an image of herself as a little girl with pigtails formed in her mind. Then she "remembered" how, as a child, she often used to be *afraid when alone in bed at night.* She would leave a hall light shining into her room when she went to bed to ease her *fear of being alone in the dark.* When the adults came to bed later, they would turn off the lights. And often she would wake up in terror, thinking that kidnappers were after her. With that, she continued to "remember," she would run and jump into bed with her big, fat grandmother. She would lie very close to her grandmother, where she would feel secure.

Her further thoughts drifted on to how she would miss sleeping in her own bed and being in her own home for a week and, later, to how comfortable she felt now in her analysis. She specified that she was no longer distressed at coming for her sessions, even at lying silently on the couch. This associative drift from the memory fragment to thoughts of feeling comfortable on the couch, where the analyst was nearby, suggested that leaving the analyst for a week was specifically reminiscent of her nighttime terrors upon being separated from her big, fat grandmother. She provided some evidence giving additional support to this inference: A short time before this separation, she dreamed of a big, cuddly, chubby, loving, and lovable cat that, according to her associations, represented her analyst.

The fact that all these memories were caused by the imminent separations is suggested by another observation: Her stream of thoughts during a "control" sample of the hours immediately following the three separations included no memories whatsoever of earlier separations.

These observations illustrate several important features about memories and their place in current behavior that are quite typically revealed by psychoanalysis. One striking feature is the abundance of memories lying ready to be activated by current stimuli. In only 150 minutes of "free-association time" (three 50-minute periods) this woman "remembered" eight clearly identifiable separation experiences. And she was not even trying to remember them. Another feature: A given stimulus may activate not just one memory but *sets of related memories.* The woman's first separation, for example, activated three memories tied together by the theme of being lost or disoriented in space. The second separation activated two memories dealing with the dangers of swimming in the ocean and the safety provided by protectors, as well as two memories sharing the theme of separation from her parents. One memory, that of being separated from her mother as she swam, was common to both sets, which hints at the intricacy of the way memory traces are organized. As we have seen, an especially important characteristic of memory sets is that they extend far into the past, back to intense emotional experiences of childhood. Thus, the observations included childhood memories of very frightening separation experiences: the time she swam off by herself, the time she thought her parents were abandoning her, and the nightmares she had when she slept alone.

COVARIATIONS IN SEPARATION STIMULI, MEMORIES, AND ANXIETY REACTIONS

The abundance of memories, their organization into sets, and their extension back to childhood do not shed much light on the process of over-reaction per se. Another phenomenon illustrated by the observations does exactly that: the covariation in the three variables—the current separation stimuli, the nature of the memories, and the current separation reactions.

Let us consider first the covariation on the dimension of sheer *intensity.* As the intensity of the current separation stimulus increased, so did the intensity of the anxiety in the "remembered" experiences, and so did the intensity of the current separation anxiety. *The three separations can easily be ordered into different degrees of intensity.* The *most intense* separations were the second and third ones. The second was to be a long one, and the distance from home and the analyst was to be considerable. The third was to take her a considerable distance away too, but its intensity also stemmed from the subjective meaning of the analytic relationship, which by now had taken on a special quality for her that had not been present earlier. In contrast, the first separation was of *moderate intensity.* While it was nearly as long as the last one, she would not be leaving home and she did not perceive the analyst as going far away. Nor had her relationship to her analyst yet taken on quite as special and personal a meaning for her. There was another very brief separation of 2 days during the period we have studied, and it was the least frightening of all. *The intensity of the "remembered" anxiety closely parallels the severity of the current separations and the intensity of the current anxiety reactions.*

Equally important, and nearly as clear-cut, are the covariations in the qualitative or substantive *content* of the current stimuli, of the memories, and of the current reactions. By contrasting the first and last separations, we can demonstrate these phenomena most fully. The first separation occurred one month after this woman had started her daily analytic sessions. Her relationship to the analyst was more impersonal than personal, so the separation could only be somewhat impersonal. And, in fact, she voiced no such personal feelings as she did later. The same impersonal quality permeated her memories. She "remembered," for example, the question about being "lost and alone in the woods" and the experience of being by herself in a dark hallway. And she "remembered" being slightly disoriented when somewhat tipsy in college. There were no references to people, except to the "someone" who would find her waiting in the woods. Her anxiety reaction, too, bore this stamp of her being lost and disoriented in an impersonal world: As she sat in the waiting room, her orientation in space seemed out of kilter, not her relationship with the analyst. The match, or fit, between the quality of this separation, her memories, and her anxiety reaction is impressive.

Now let us look closely at the last separation, which had a much more personal and special meaning for her. Instead of being separated from *an* analyst with *a* couch in *an* office in a large building, she was about to be separated from a very *real*, warm *person*, toward whom she had all the feelings expressed in the dream of the big fat cat. And now *the couch* was a place on which she could lie quietly and feel safe and at ease. What she now "remembered" were the nightmares she used to have as a child when sleeping alone in the dark and the wonderful safe feeling that would come over her as she ran and climbed into bed with her big, fat grandmother. Further, the specific content of her intense anxiety about the separation shows the imprint of these memories, for what she feared was that the strange bedrooms in which she would be sleeping while she was away would be so located in the houses that she would not be able to get out of them easily and rapidly in the middle of the night. Here again the meaning of the current separation, the content of her memories, and the content of her current anxiety are strikingly similar.

Finally, our brief description of the second separation suggests that the same "good fit" existed there as well.

MEMORIES AS MEDIATORS IN OVER-REACTIONS

What does the precise covariation in the nature of the current separation stimuli, of the memories, and of the anticipatory reactions to the current separations tell us about over-reactions? It very strongly suggests that the memories mediate the over-reactions. *Innocuous conditioned and generalized emotional stimuli appear to activate memories of past emotional experiences, which appear, in turn, to determine the intensity and content of the over-reactions.* Very often these memories emerge from repression only during free association. Even if they have not been repressed, the individual is usually not aware of their influence on his over-reaction. The woman, for example, was not aware that her memories of her nighttime terrors in childhood played any part in her fears about the sleeping accommodations she would encounter during her separation from the security of her analyst's couch. Nor was she aware of all the details of the covariations we have described. In other words, the mediation by memories is an unconscious process, and usually the memories themselves are unconscious.

Memories may mediate any kind of over-reaction; we have merely chosen to illustrate the process in detail for over-reactions of separation anxiety.

If we incorporate what we have inferred about memories into Figure 6-1, we get the scheme shown in Figure 6-3. This new diagram places the conditioned and generalized stimuli and the over-reaction above the "threshold of consciousness and overt behavior (repressive barrier)" because those variables are consciously experienced or overtly displayed by the subject. They are also apparent to the outside observer. We have placed the memories at and below the threshold of consciousness because they are not ordinarily conscious to the subject and he is not aware of the important part they play in his experience and behavior. The threshold of consciousness in instances like these is different from the ordinary sensory thresholds, which may be passed simply by increasing the intensity of a stimulus—as when we notice a sound simply because it becomes louder. Instead the threshold of consciousness in such instances is determined largely by the active repression of the crucial memories. (Thus, the threshold may be termed the "repressive barrier.") When the repressive efforts are decreased, as during free association, the memories emerge into consciousness. The case material presented above illustrated these aspects of Figure 6-3. The woman was conscious of the fact that the separations were imminent, and she consciously experienced her anxiety reaction. Any outside observer would also have been aware of these matters. But it was only during the process of free association that the memories emerged into consciousness.

Figure 6-3   The memory mediation of emotional over-reactions to relatively innocuous conditioned and generalized stimuli.

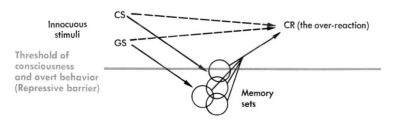

The diagram shows memory *sets*, and it depicts them as *intersecting*. We illustrated these characteristics of memory organization in the case material. The diagram also portrays the memory sets as being at varying depths below the threshold of consciousness. This represents the fact that some memories appear to be more strongly repressed than others. The woman, for example, readily "remembered" the test question about being lost and alone in the woods. In marked contrast, however, the memory of her parents' pretended abandonment, which left "two little kids sitting there white with fear," was so strongly repressed that it first found indirect expression in a nightmare and then slowly emerged in her associations to the dream.

The dashed arrows in the diagram represent the direct causal relationship that the "purest" stimulus-response psychologist would infer. The solid arrows represent some of the relationships that the psychoanalyst would infer. He believes that unconscious, repressed memories mediate many over-reactions of distress to innocuous stimuli. The precise nature of the memories appears to determine the nature of the over-reaction—the kind and intensity of the felt emotion and the nature of the accompanying thoughts. In our example, the observations of the covariation in the current separation stimuli, in the woman's memories, and in her concurrent anxiety reaction illustrate the basis for these psychoanalytic inferences.

One final comment about Figure 6-3: It does not portray everything we observed in the case material dealing with separation anxiety. It does not show, for example, the changing feelings of the woman for her analyst or her conflicts over those feelings. The presence of such conflicts appeared to influence what the meaning of the various separations was for her and which memories were activated. But the figure does diagram what appears to be the essential process in many over-reactions of distress: the relatively direct activation of repressed memories of painful experiences.

We shall now discuss the way in which unconscious fantasies of painful experiences often produce over-reactions of distress.

Transformation
Through Unconscious Fantasies

INFLUENCE OF CONSCIOUS FANTASIES ON BEHAVIOR

A normal person walking down a dimly lit street may be preoccupied with fearful fantasies that a robber or a "sex maniac" might be lurking in the darkness. Under these circumstances the person may freeze in terror at the mere sight of the moving shadows of swaying trees. A student's fantasies of how poorly written his last essay was and of how displeased his teacher must be with it can transform the teacher's minor criticisms into very harsh ones. A surgical patient may panic before her operation because she suddenly fantasies that her surgeon will fiendishly mutilate her. (Such cases are described in Janis, 1971, pp. 101–02.)

Murray (1933) conducted an experiment with 11-year-old girls that showed how fantasies can influence reactions to external stimuli. When the girls were in a relaxed state of mind, Murray asked them to look at some photographs of strange men and to rate how malicious the faces appeared to them. Then he had the girls play a game of "murder." Playing games is a special form of fantasy activity for children, and doing so stimulates still further fantasies. After the game the girls rated the faces as much more malicious. The child who had been most frightened by the game woke up the next morning screaming with fear, saying she had seen a "bad man" coming into her room. In the confused state of awakening she falsely perceived the external world to be in line with the scary fantasies of the preceding night.

These girls took their perceptions of men's faces as representations of *reality*, and the surgical patient was convinced that her perception of her doctor also reflected a real situation. Why? Basically because they did not know that they had distorted their perceptions. External stimuli and internal mental and emotional processes, operating *automatically and unconsciously*, combined to produce their perceptions. And they took their perceptions for reality, regardless of their objective validity. They were merely doing what all of us do when we dream and accept the wildest perceptions arising almost completely from our fantasies as absolutely real. And they were doing what many of us do to a lesser extent in our waking life, when we see things the way we need to or want to.

MASS FANTASIES IN THE IVY LEAGUE

A good example of seeing things the way we want to—or living in a fantasy world—was provided by Hastorf and Cantril (1954). Following a bitterly fought game between the Princeton and Dartmouth football teams, the two psychologists made a survey of students at both schools who had attended the game. It turned out that the two groups "saw" the game quite differently: The Princeton students were nearly unanimous in seeing it as "rough and dirty" and the Dartmouth team as much "dirtier" players than their own. Most of the Dartmouth students thought the game had been "rough and dirty," more than one-third of them thought it had been "rough and fair," and one-tenth of them thought it had been "clean and fair." They did not think the Dartmouth players had been "dirtier" than the Princeton players. Judging from the objective evidence—the incidence of serious injury on both sides and the official penalty statistics—both teams played a rough game, and about equally so.

This episode involved conscious fantasies. Unconscious fantasies can have analogous effects on behavior.

A MARITAL RELATIONSHIP
BEDEVILED BY UNCONSCIOUS FANTASIES

Situations that directly arouse heterosexual wishes and sensations very commonly end up producing conscious experiences of anxiety, shame and humiliation, or guilt. The role of unconscious fantasies and conflict in such instances is especially clear when the persons involved are married adults with no external, realistic reason for not enjoying sexuality. Again, the unconscious conflicts often date from childhood. They are usually Oedipal, but frequently they involve conflictful incestuous fantasies about brothers or sisters.

Ed, the young man with castration dreams who was described in Chapter 2, had attacks of anxiety and guilt and occasional castration dreams when he and his wife made love. One reason he responded this way was that *any* sexual arousal and gratification were by now adequate activators of his unconscious castration anxiety. But there was another particularly important reason: Ed had conflictful incestuous fantasies as well.

As a boy Ed had loved one of his sisters dearly. He had frequently played sexual games with this sister, and he had been terrified that his mother would cut off his penis if she ever found out. This was one reason he had castration dreams at the age of 7. His boyhood fear manifested itself in yet another way during this period of his incestuous play with his sister: Once when he was being examined by his doctor, he became so frightened that he doubled up his knees over his abdomen so that she would not be able to examine his scrotum and groin. It seemed that he was afraid that the doctor would be able to divine what had happened between him and his sister and would then tell his mother, whereupon the two would castrate him. This boyhood castration fantasy caused Ed to inhibit his sexual play with his sister and to repress his love for her. The fantasy was also recorded in Ed's memory just as though it were an objectively real experience, and the unconscious memory of this fantasy experience continued to affect his adult behavior. Its influence can be detected in Ed's castration dreams as an adult, which were cited in Chapter 2: There too, doctors were castrators.

Ed's early experiences with his sister had a significance transcending the arousal of castration anxiety. His erotically toned attachment to her served as a model for his later relationships with women. Eventually, as the Wolf Man had done, Ed "just happened" to marry a woman who resembled his childhood incestuous love object and substituted for her. There were several details—such as age, intellectual interests, and emotional attitudes—in which the two women resembled each other, but they were insignificant compared to one major attribute. The woman came from a cultural background that was despised by Ed's parents. His marriage to her was a tabooed act in their eyes, and to some extent in his own. It was in being a "tabooed female" that his wife most clearly resembled his sister.

There was a good deal of other evidence that his wife represented his sister. For example, once, when his sexual conflicts were prominent, Ed dreamed he saw a brother and a sister sitting in front of a television set and thought to himself that they were emotionally disturbed. Earlier that night he and his wife actually had sat in the front row of a theater watching a sensuous play. Ed had become sexually excited by the play and had felt guilty about it. When the analyst pointed out the similarity between the real scene with his wife and the dream scene, Ed realized that recently he had been thinking that living with his wife was like living with a sister. Later he commented that all his wife did when he was home in the evening was watch television. During other periods in his analysis, Ed found that for several days in a row his sister's name would come to the tip of his tongue in place of his wife's. And visits with his sister intensified his anxiety over his sexual intimacy with his wife. It is reasonable to conclude that his wife was a "generalized sister stimulus."

Making love with his wife, then, often made Ed feel tense, uneasy, and sweaty because it activated conflicting unconscious fantasies that resembled the conscious sexual conflict of his childhood. Sexual intimacy with a woman who resembled his sister stimulated repressed incestuous fantasies and, in turn, his unconscious castration fantasies. His adult conscious experience of anxiety was simply *the emotional component of these castration fantasies stripped of the castration thoughts themselves.* These he continued to repress, but they manifested themselves in his castration dreams. Such *isolation* of affective and ideational components—a particular defense mechanism, which we shall discuss further in Chapter 11—is a common mechanism in over-reaction.

Ed's anxiety motivated him to avoid sexual intimacy with his wife until his own sexual needs, his wife's demands, or his "need to be masculine" became imperative.

If we incorporate what we have inferred about Ed's unconscious fantasies into Figure 6-1, we get the scheme shown in Figure 6-4. The clinical data strongly suggest that the over-reaction, though it appears to be directly elicited by the generalized stimulus, is actually mediated by the unconscious fantasies. The dashed and solid arrows and the "threshold of consciousness and overt behavior (repressive barrier)" shown in Figure 6-4 have the same significance as those of Figure 6-3.

Over-reactions to many different kinds of stimuli are mediated by intervening unconscious sexual fantasies and conflicts in essentially the same way as in the case of Ed. Edie's fear of eating, which we discussed in Chapters 2 and 3, is another example. The opportunity to dine with an attractive date thrills nearly every young woman. Yet this stimulus situation frightened Edie because of the unconscious sexual-oral fantasies it triggered. Casual contact of her breasts with her hand or a piece of her clothing rarely brings about a feeling of depression in a woman. But we saw earlier in this chapter that this can happen if this stimulus activates an unconscious fantasy that to be a woman is to be an inferior human being. Walking down the street to the grocery store in broad daylight frightens some women so much that they are unable to continue once they have started, if indeed

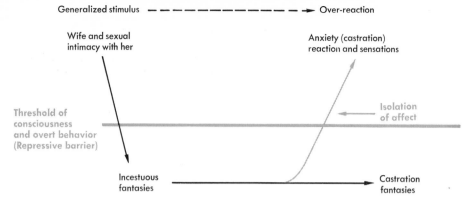

Figure 6-4 The mediation of an emotional over-reaction to a generalized stimulus through the activation of unconscious fantasies.

they are even able to leave their doorstep. Very commonly, unconscious wishful fantasies of exciting some man into picking them up are stimulated by this "street-walking." And these fantasies, in turn, arouse frightening fantasies of various kinds stemming from childhood. As with Ed, however, only the emotional component of these fantasies may become conscious and overt and thus result in over-reactions of distress.

In the next chapter we shall discuss how somewhat different processes also produce such over-reactions.

The Captain was a tall man of about forty, grey at the temples. He had a handsome, finely-knit figure, and was one of the best horsemen in the West.

He had never married . . . .

To his orderly he was at first cold and just and indifferent . . . . Then the change gradually came.

The orderly was a youth of about twenty-two, of medium height, and well built. He had strong, heavy limbs, was swarthy, with a soft, black, young moustache. There was something altogether warm and young about him. . . .

. . . He could not get away from the sense of the youth's person. . . . It was like a warm flame upon the older man's tense, rigid body, that had become almost unliving, fixed. . . . And this irritated the Prussian. He did not choose to be touched into life by his servant. . . . He now very rarely looked direct at his orderly.

. . .

In spite of himself, the Captain could not regain his neutrality of feeling towards his orderly. . . . Sometimes he flew into a rage with the young soldier, and bullied him.

. . .

At last he slung the end of a belt in his servant's face. . . .

. . . His own nerves must be going to pieces. He went away for some days with a woman.

It was a mockery of pleasure. He simply did not want the woman. But he stayed on for his time. At the end of it, he came back in an agony of irritation, torment, and misery. He rode all the evening, then came straight in to supper.

. . .

The orderly took his hands full of dishes. . . . As he was crouching to set down the dishes, he was pitched forward by a kick from behind. . . . And as he was rising he was kicked heavily again and again.

. . .

The officer, left alone, held himself rigid, to prevent himself from thinking. . . . He stood there for an hour motionless, a chaos of sensations, but rigid with a will to keep blank his consciousness, to prevent his mind grasping.

D . H . L A W R E N C E . The Prussian Officer

CHAPTER 7
PROJECTION, OVER-REACTIONS, AND UNCONSCIOUS HOMOSEXUAL CONFLICTS

With the keen eye and sensitive skill of the artist, D. H. Lawrence has portrayed the Prussian officer's agonized attempts to cope with his conscious attraction to his orderly. Each reaction —his reluctance to look at the orderly, his episodes of increasing conscious hatred of him, his flight into heterosexuality, and his final supreme struggle to rid his mind of all thoughts and feelings— was part of a defensive effort to ward off homosexual feelings and the inner distress they evoked.

Suppose the Prussian officer had succeeded in obliterating this homosexual conflict from his consciousness. By this repression he would have achieved relief from the conscious misery of frustrated desires and of the shame, guilt, and self-criticism those desires provoked. But the repression would have left him with an unconscious homosexual conflict. If this unconscious conflict were to be intensified in the future, it might again become conscious. Suppose the officer was later faced with the danger of such a rupture of his repressive barrier as he was becoming acquainted with a new orderly. He might then resort to another defense that could help to maintain his repression. He might perceive this orderly as being attracted to him, rather than himself as being attracted to the orderly. The officer would then have been using a defense mechanism called *projection*. In this mechanism the person protects himself from becoming aware of repressed impulses, feelings, and thoughts by attributing them to others. If he had projected his homosexual wishes onto his orderly, the officer could have remained unaware of his own homosexual wishes and thus could have protected himself from the torment those wishes caused him.

Projection of unconscious wishes causes one to live in a perceptually distorted world. The projectively transformed people now evoke in the subject all the unpleasant emotional reactions his own wishes would evoke if they were to become conscious or to be expressed in overt behavior. At other times the subject may project his negative reactions to his own wishes and thus be confronted with projectively created people who seem to view him just as negatively as he unconsciously views himself.

Thus, the projective distortion of reality is another way in which unconscious conflicts cause over-reactions of distress. It was primarily in attempting to understand homosexual conflicts that Freud discovered projective patterns. Hence we shall illustrate the two patterns described in the paragraph above with two examples of over-reactions based on homosexual conflicts.

Male Companionship Spoiled by an Unconscious Conflict

PROJECTION OF UNCONSCIOUS HOMOSEXUAL WISHES

Ray, a young, married attorney, went camping with his family. His long-standing goal had been to climb a high mountain in the area. Although Ray was not a sociable person, he did manage to seek out and find another camper who appeared to be an ideal companion for the difficult overnight climb: a congenial young doctor whose family, like Ray's, did not relish the hike. On the eve of the climb the two men sat by the fire, talking over their final plans. Suddenly the doctor stood up, adjusted his underwear, and scratched his groin, all the while smiling at Ray. An alarming thought struck Ray: "He's a homosexual." Ray suddenly saw standing before him a man who was excited at the prospect of spending a night in a lean-to on the trail with him and who was crudely but seductively hinting at what he had in mind. Ray now felt only scorn and contempt for the doctor, and making many excuses the next day, he set off on the hike alone.

Ray's perception of the doctor that night might conceivably have been correct, but he certainly lacked sufficient evidence for the sense of conviction he had. When he recounted this episode in analysis and later reconsidered it, Ray was not even sure that the man's "smile" had not really been a grimace. And the scratching was not so unusual, especially since no women were present. Many relevant thoughts were stimulated by his recounting of this episode in his analysis, so we can reconstruct what probably happened. Ray's behavior was an over-reaction to an ordinary stimulus situation that had triggered an unconscious conflict in him.

In childhood Ray had occasionally initiated and participated in homosexual play, as many a boy does. Usually it occurred with friends but occasionally with new buddies with whom he wanted to develop a close relationship. For example, at the age of 7, Ray moved into a new neighborhood. The boys there played "soldiers," using homemade tents in their backyards. One boy and Ray had "played with each other" in their tent. Ray's last overt homosexual behavior had occurred when he was 13. He and a friend had shared a bed in a bunkhouse on an overnight Boy Scout hike. Ray became excited and masturbated his friend. This boy acquiesced to Ray's masturbating him until he had an orgasm but did not reciprocate in any other way. Ray then disappointedly masturbated himself and fell asleep. To his great shame, a fellow scout taunted him the next day by saying that he had overheard the activity of the night before. From this moment his homosexuality became a source of greatly increased conflict for him. He first consciously suppressed it and later unconsciously repressed it. In fact, he went on to achieve a fairly satisfactory heterosexual adjustment, although he was occasionally preoccupied with homosexual fantasies, fears, and suspicions about himself as well as others. But his heterosexual life and his defenses against his homosexual inclinations maintained those inclinations in a latent, but not dormant, state.

The hiking situation with the doctor disturbed this balance. In its budding intimacy and the details of the physical setting—the tents, the outdoors, sleeping in the lean-to—the situation with the doctor was very similar to those of the "tent game" and the Boy Scout hike. It was a generalized stimulus that, together with Ray's latent homosexual wishes, activated memories of those experiences and the fantasy of repeating them. But these memories and wishful fantasies as to what might happen if he and the doctor were to camp out overnight in a lean-to could not become conscious, for they were in direct conflict with Ray's adult masculine values and superego, and they were opposed by self-scorn and self-condemnation. Yet there was a very real danger that the memories and fantasies would become conscious, for Ray's homosexual desires were intensified. This was made perfectly clear by the excitement (warmth in his genitals, for example) that accompanied the fantasies when they were expressed in his analysis. Some defensive effort was necessary, beyond his customary repression, so Ray's unconscious solution was to project his unconscious homosexual wishes and thoughts onto the young doctor. The doctor now evoked the critical, scornful emotional attitudes Ray had about his own homosexuality. That is, Ray displaced these attitudes from himself to the doctor. He actively avoided the opportunity for enjoyable companionship. In avoiding intimacy with the doctor Ray removed himself from the stimulus situation that had upset the original equilibrium between his homosexual wishes and his opposing masculine values. Figure 7-1 schematizes this process.

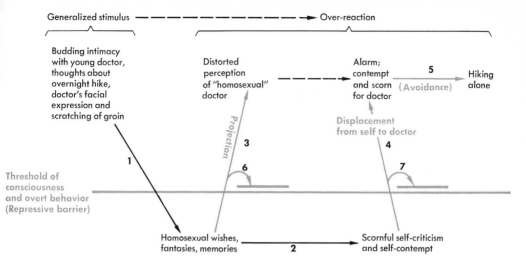

Figure 7-1   Ray's over-reaction to the prospect of hiking in the mountains with a young doctor.

The "threshold of consciousness and overt behavior" distinguishes between those aspects of Ray's behavior that were conscious or overt (above the line) and those that were unconscious (below the line). Since it is determined largely by the active resistance of repression, the threshold is also termed a "repressive barrier." The dashed arrows indicate the apparent stimulus-response relationships. The solid arrows represent the causal relationships inferred from clinical evidence to be the actually important ones. (1) The interaction between Ray and the doctor stimulated Ray's unconscious homosexual wishes, fantasies, and memories. (2) These, in turn, evoked unconscious self-criticism and self-contempt. At this point Ray's unconscious homosexual conflict was so intensified that it could have become conscious. (3) But Ray projected his homosexual wishes onto the doctor and (4) displaced his self-criticism and self-contempt to the doctor. (5) As a result, he hiked alone. By hiking alone Ray avoided further stimulation of his unconscious conflict. By projecting his homosexual wishes and displacing his self-criticism and self-contempt he reinforced the repressive barrier. This is represented by the curved arrows and the double line (6 and 7). (These reinforcements consist of the distorted perception and the displaced criticisms themselves, not of the acts of projection and displacement. For example, the thought "He's a homosexual" prevents the subject's own homosexual wishes from coming into his consciousness.)

PROJECTION OF NEGATIVE REACTIONS
TO UNCONSCIOUS HOMOSEXUAL WISHES

In the episode in the mountains Ray projected his homosexual wishful thoughts to prevent them from agitating his conscience into such intense self-criticism and self-condemnation that he would have felt worthless. At other times he created a dangerous reality out of very ordinary situations by projecting the unconscious self-criticisms and self-condemnations. Some of Ray's lunchtime experiences illustrate this point.

As one might expect, Ray did not enjoy easy, comfortable relationships with men. He was a "loner." Habitually, for example, he ate lunch by himself at his desk instead of making his lunch hour an occasion for comradeship. To ease his loneliness, he would occasionally go to a nearby businessmen's restaurant, where at least there would be other men present. Every once in a while, however, something happened to spoil these ventures. When he would start to open the door of one of these restaurants he would look in at the men already there and be seized with the thought, "I can't go in there. They will all look at me and think to themselves, 'Look at that fellow. He looks like a woman. He must be a fairy.'" Feeling sickened and worthless, Ray would turn away. (Incidentally, Ray's appearance was quite masculine.) One day this experience was repeated every place he went until his lunch hour was gone, and he still had not eaten.

When Ray was discussing this episode in his analysis, his thoughts drifted to a memory of an experience he had had in late adolescence. He was attending an out-of-town convention and had gone to a restaurant. He asked the waitress for directions to the house where he was to be quartered. In a few minutes, a man came to his table and said that he had overheard Ray's question and offered to give him a lift. On the way this man told Ray that he was an overt homosexual and tried to seduce him. Although he did not succumb, Ray had difficulty falling asleep that night and then had a disturbing dream with homosexual overtones. When this dream woke him up, he was not sure for a moment whether or not he actually had refused the man's advances the night before.

Shortly after recalling this experience, Ray "remembered" that the Boy Scout hike when he was 13 had occurred in winter and that the bunks had been set up in a large, heated mess hall. Thus, that homosexual experience had involved an eating place. The businessmen's restaurant can be regarded as a generalized stimulus similar to these earlier eating places.

From all we know about Ray, it is possible to reconstruct the chain of events resulting in that intensely unpleasant experience at the door of the restaurant. Although his isolation from male company was caused by his unconscious conflict over homosexuality, the loneliness it produced only intensified this conflict. Eating in a businessmen's restaurant could have been a good solution, relieving his loneliness and providing a sublimated gratification of his homosexual longings. But the combined action of his unconscious wishes and the generalized stimulus—the sight of the restaurant —activated those two unconscious memories of homosexual experiences and

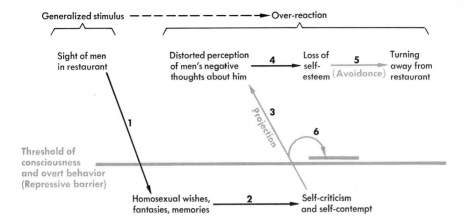

Figure 7-2   Ray's over-reaction at the restaurant door.

*The dashed arrow indicates the apparent stimulus-response re-
lationship. The solid arrows represent the causal relationships
inferred from clinical evidence to be the actually important ones.
(1) The sight of the men in the restaurant stimulated Ray's unconscious homosexual wishes, fantasies, and memories. (2) These,
in turn, evoked unconscious self-criticism and self-contempt. At
this point Ray's unconscious conflict might have become conscious. (3) But Ray projected his self-criticism and self-contempt
onto the men in the restaurant. Now he saw them as judging him
harshly and negatively. (4) This distorted perception lowered his
self-esteem and (5) caused him to turn away from the restaurant.
By doing this he avoided a situation that stimulated his unconscious conflict. The projection of his self-criticism reinforced the
repressive barrier. This is represented by the curved arrow and the
double line (6). (The distorted perception prevented his repressed
self-criticism from becoming conscious.)*

fantasies of doing something similar now. These in turn instigated unconscious, harsh, negative self-criticism, which he projected onto the men eating
in the restaurant. Having done so, but without realizing it, Ray could only
feel inferior and worthless and turn away from the door. This experience
was very painful. But awareness of his unconscious conflict would have been
more painful. The projection and the reaction to the "reality" constructed
by it prevented this awareness. Figure 7-2 represents the main aspects of
our reconstruction.

PARANOIAC PROJECTIONS OF JUDGE SCHREBER

The episodes in the mountains and at the restaurant door illustrate some common causes of social isolation among men. The former
involved projection of unconscious homosexual wishes and displacement of

the self-criticism prompted by those wishes; the latter involved projection of the unconscious self-criticism. Frequently the defensive pattern also includes a defensive hatred by the subject of the man toward whom he is attracted, which helps to keep his desire for contact with the other man out of consciousness. The Prussian officer in Lawrence's story reacted this way. The reactive hatred is often repressed and projected. Projection of the hatred occasionally leads to frankly paranoid reactions toward one's fellow men and an eventual withdrawal from them.

When Freud analyzed Judge Schreber's memoirs (1911), which we mentioned in Chapter 4, he discovered essentially the same basic pattern illustrated by Ray's experience.

> At one time or another Schreber projected his unconscious homosexual wishes, his unconscious defensive hatred, and his unconscious self-criticism. But he differed from Ray in two very important ways: Schreber projected continually and his capacity to test the reality of his projective perceptions was severely impaired, whereas Ray seldom projected and his sense of reality was largely intact. As a result, Schreber lived in a delusional and hallucinatory world, a condition that is designated as a psychosis. In his untested, projected reality, God loved him and wanted to copulate with him (projected homosexual wishes); doctors were intent on persecuting him and emasculating him (projected defensive hatred for man and projected wish to be a woman); and, in his auditory hallucinations, he heard derogatory accusations about himself (projected self-criticism). In the latter, he heard mocking and jeering voices say such things as "*Miss* Schreber" and "so this sets up to have been a (Judge), this person who lets himself be f——d!" and "Don't you feel ashamed in front of your wife [Freud, 1911, p. 20]."

Incidentally, these auditory hallucinations of Schreber are of great historical significance to psychology, for they stimulated Freud's concept of the superego. Freud conjectured that they were created by the distorted externalization of processes operating within us all the time, whether we are aware of them or not (1914a). These are the processes of self-observation, self-evaluation, and self-approval or self-criticism—many of the processes fused in the concept of conscience. Freud saw the similarity between these and comparable parental functions of watching over, evaluating, and praising or scolding the child. He reasoned that these parental functions were internalized along with the parents' values in the course of the child's growing up. Here was the kernel of his later theory (Freud, 1923, 1933) of superego content, function, and development: moral values, self-observation and self-assessment, and the resulting self-approval or self-criticism—all developed by identification with the parents.

Experimental Studies
of Projection and Paranoia

Several psychologists have systematically or experimentally investigated some of the behavioral mechanisms that we have been discussing and that Freud originally inferred from his clinical observations. One question that has been investigated is whether the basic phenomenon of projection can be demonstrated by methods more "rigorous" than clinical observation. This is an extremely difficult question, but some suggestively affirmative results have been obtained.

PROJECTION ALONG FRATERNITY ROW

A study by Robert Sears (1936) illustrates both the suggestive findings and the difficulties. Sears asked members of college fraternities to rate themselves and their fraternity brothers on the traits of *stinginess*, *obstinacy*, *disorderliness*, and *bashfulness*. The extent to which a person actually manifested each of these traits was estimated by averaging the ratings all his friends gave him for that trait. Each person's self-awareness was determined by comparing his self-rating with the average of the ratings others made of him. A person who rated himself low in stinginess while

Figure 7-3 *Average trait scores assigned to fraternity brothers by subjects high in the traits and with or without insight about themselves. (Based on data from R. Sears, 1936. In this figure Sears's data have been changed to comparable scores that equal his average ratings.)*

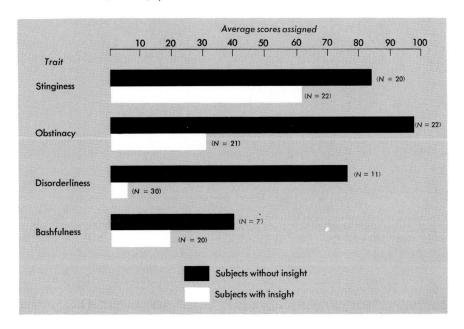

being rated high by his fraternity brothers, for example, possessed little awareness of his own tendency to be stingy. If projection occurs, those students high in a presumably "undesirable" trait but unaware of being so should attribute more of that trait to other students than would those who were high in the trait and aware of it.

The key results are shown in Figure 7-3, which contains averages of the rating scores assigned to their friends by subjects who lacked insight into themselves and by subjects who had this insight. Those subjects who were stingy but did not realize it rated their fraternity brothers as being more stingy than did those subjects who were stingy and knew they were; and so on for the other traits. These subjects were acting somewhat like Ray did in the episode in the mountains and then later in psychoanalysis. When the traits he felt were contemptible (latent homosexual inclinations) were stimulated to a "high" level and he was not aware of it, he thought his friend was homosexual. But when he became aware that he himself had been homosexually aroused, he was no longer certain that his friend had been.

Another finding of Sears illustrates some of the difficulties of validating psychoanalytic hypotheses by simple rigorous methods. The students attributed "good" qualities to their friends just as readily as they did "bad" qualities. The "good" traits of generosity, flexibility, and orderliness, for example, were attributed in the same way as their "bad" counterparts. These findings would not have been expected on the basis of general psychoanalytic theory about projection, which emphasizes its defensive function. There would be no defensive gain in projecting "good" traits. It is possible, however, that these results could be produced by man's general tendency to conceive of the world as a reflection of his own nature, as it is assumed people do during projective testing, and this might offer a simpler explanation. But it is possible that both tendencies entered in: Sears's subjects may have *defensively projected* their "undesirable" traits and also indulged in the more general *nondefensive attribution* of desirable characteristics. (See Holt [1951] for another study and further discussion of this issue.) One way of testing whether both tendencies were involved would be to see how upset subjects become as you "undo" these two kinds of projections. They should be much more upset when the presumably defensive projections are interfered with than when the presumably more general, nondefensive tendency to attribute one's own qualities to others is interfered with. But this type of experiment has not yet been carried out, perhaps because it is too difficult to find an appropriate and ethically justified situation for such interference.

HOMOSEXUAL CONFLICTS IN PARANOID MEN

Another group of studies has been concerned with the proposition that paranoid men—that is, men who project hatred extensively—do in fact have homosexual conflicts. Zamansky (1958) showed paired pictures of men and women to male paranoid schizophrenics and to a control group of male nonparanoid schizophrenics and measured the amount of time the subjects looked at the male picture and at the female picture of each pair of pictures. The paranoid men spent much more time looking at the pictures of men than at those of women. The nonparanoid men looked longer at the female pictures. Sternlaff (1964) obtained similar results when he presented pictures of men or women singly to male paranoid schizophrenics and to psychotically depressed men. In addition, Sternlaff fused his pictures of men and women, making a series of ambiguous pictures. The paranoid men perceived more of these as pictures of men than did the depressed men.

Wolowitz (1965) also showed single pictures of men and women to paranoid schizophrenic men and to nonparanoid schizophrenic men. His pictures, however, were graded for the "powerfulness" of the faces in them. Both the male and female faces ranged from weak, ineffectual-looking ones to powerful or potent ones. And instead of measuring the amount of time the subjects looked at these faces, Wolowitz measured the distance at which the subjects placed the pictures from their eyes by asking them to slide each picture back and forth in a specially designed viewing box until it "looked best." The paranoid men, when compared with the nonparanoid men, placed the male faces farther away than the female faces. This difference was not quite statistically significant when the "power" factor was disregarded. However, there was a significant effect of the power factor. The more "powerful" the faces of the men in the pictures, the farther away from themselves the paranoid men placed them. They did not respond this way to differences in the women's faces, however. But the nonparanoid men did, and, at the same time, they were unaffected by the power factor in the men's faces.

Here, then, are three experiments in which pictures of men produced special reactions in paranoid schizophrenic men, just as one would expect if these pictures activated an unconscious homosexual conflict in these men. In Wolowitz's study the paranoid subjects apparently felt less threatened by the male pictures if they moved the pictures slightly away from themselves, and this was increasingly so the more "powerful-looking" the faces were in the pictures. We cannot be sure, however, why the more powerful faces were more threatening. Perhaps they were more attractive and hence more conflictful, or perhaps they could more easily be projectively distorted into critical or persecutory images. Perhaps the reason differed for different subjects. Only the study of each subject in depth would enable us to answer this kind of question.

The paranoid men's selective perception of ambiguous figures and their preference for looking at the pictures of men in Sternlaff's and Zamansky's experiments could also have resulted from two different consequences of the unconscious homosexual conflict we have assumed was triggered by the pictures. On the one hand, seeing male figures in ambiguous pictures could have been wish-fulfilling perceptions, and looking at pictures of men could have been pleasing because of unconscious attraction to them. In principle, such behavior would be no different from that shown by hungry subjects in other perception experiments. Several investigators, for example, have shown that normal people, when hungry, will see more food-related things in ambiguous pictures than will people who are not hungry (Sanford, 1936, 1937; Levine, Chein, & Murphy, 1942; McClelland & Atkinson, 1948).

On the other hand, the paranoid men tested by Sternlaff and Zamansky could have been especially attentive to male pictures because of the anxiety and guilt components of the conflict. In this respect they would be showing the same general kind of perceptual vigilance for unpleasant stimuli shown by people under stress.

The fact that several explanations are possible is not unusual in science. And people, after all, regularly do the same thing for different reasons. But much of the uncertainty in experiments such as those we have been discussing might be eliminated through more intensive observation and measurement of other details of behavior, such as muscle tension, autonomic responses, and free associations. For the time being, we can either leave the question about Sternlaff's and Zamansky's results open or attribute them to the aversive component of the homosexual conflict, which seemed to account for Wolowitz's findings. Regardless of all these details, however, the results of the three experiments fit very well with Freud's hypothesis of the significance of unconscious homosexual conflicts in paranoia and with the clinically based explanations of "over-reactions" such as Ray's. The special responsiveness to men's pictures resembles Ray's sensitivity to men in the real-life episodes in the mountains and at the restaurant door.

Oh, what may man within him hide,
Though angel on the outward side!

WILLIAM SHAKESPEARE. Measure for Measure

CHAPTER 8
OVER-REACTIONS AND UNCONSCIOUS CONFLICTS ABOUT AGGRESSION

One major theme unites this chapter with the preceding two and with the following one: *Any unconscious conflict has the potential of producing a distressing over-reaction.* In Chapter 6 we saw how a young woman over-reacted with intense anxiety at the prospect of separations from her analyst; her separation anxiety was produced by the activation of unconscious memories of childhood separation experiences. In the same chapter we saw how Ed's unconscious castration and incestuous fantasies were responsible for his over-reaction (intense castration anxiety) to sexual intimacy with his wife. In Chapter 7 we saw how Ray's unconscious homosexual conflicts triggered such over-reactions as his alarming, distorted perception of and scorn for his proposed hiking companion and his turning away from businessmen's restaurants in a state of extremely low self-esteem. In this chapter we shall discuss certain over-reactions resulting from unconscious conflicts over aggression. In the next chapter we shall conclude our focused discussion of over-reactions with an examination of the distress caused by interference with defenses and with other controls over unconscious processes.

Conflicts over aggression produce a variety of over-reactions: in one instance, an excessive anger far out of proportion to the ostensible provocation; in another instance, too little aggression, or even excessive affection, when there is every reason for anger; in another, very unpleasant emotional experiences such as guilt, anxiety, or depression. The case study that is the heart of this chapter provides a striking example of this last kind of over-reaction, on which we are focusing in this chapter: a severe depression that was precipitated by the loss of a pet. The case study also illustrates all of the other over-reactions that arise from unconscious conflicts over aggression, except excessive anger. However, we have already seen examples of this: Duane's reaction to his father's death, discussed in Chapter 2, and the dreams of the death of the same-sexed parent and the Rat Man's hostility, discussed in Chapter 5. To dream wishfully for the death of one's parent and to feel even fleeting pleasure when this actually happens are both excessive reactions. And so is the gleeful contemplation of killing one's father, such as the Rat Man experienced when he had sexual intercourse for the first time. Such intensely hostile thoughts accompanied by malicious pleasure are obviously not commensurate with anything parents do. Instead, they are caused by the unconscious, hostile component of the Oedipal complex.

A common instance of the over-reaction of excessive anger is the displacement of inhibited aggression resulting from frustration. Scapegoating and other everyday incidents of excessive anger arise in this way. This is often what causes a man to shout angrily at his wife and children after an irritating day at the office. All day he has been inhibiting the anger provoked by one frustration after another, and now he takes it out on his family at the slightest provocation. Frequently an individual realizes later what has happened in such incidents, but the scapegoating represented by social prejudice, such as anti-Semitism, remains largely unconscious.

Now we shall turn to the other over-reactions produced by unconscious conflict over aggression. Most of what follows is based on a clinical paper by a famous psychoanalyst, Helene Deutsch. Her report (1965) deals with the life history of an unmarried woman who became so severely depressed in her late forties that she was hospitalized and treated with psychoanalytic therapy by Deutsch. As will become apparent, this case study is instructive on many counts and reveals in extreme form some of the psychological mechanisms that occur in normal persons when they become temporarily depressed.

An Example of Over-Reactions
to a Minor Loss

At the time Miss Eaton (our name for this patient) started treatment with Deutsch, she suffered from three kinds of symptoms: (1) She was *deeply depressed*; (2) she had *frightening delusions* that people were going to throw her naked into the street and leave here there to die; (3) her thoughts were replete with *self-accusations* that she deserved this horrible fate, though the only transgressions she could cite to justify such thoughts were trivial. One of Deutsch's first discoveries was the immediate cause of her patient's condition: the death, 3 years earlier, of her pet dog. At the time, her dog had been her constant and closest friend, perhaps her only friend. Even so, her reaction was clearly excessive.

During treatment, it became obvious that an unconscious conflict over aggression was the primary cause of this and other over-reactions Miss Eaton had experienced from childhood on. We shall describe all of these over-reactions, because each sheds light on the others and because they illustrate a variety of emotional reactions produced by variations on the same theme: *an unconscious struggle against hatred for her sister* that, like other conflicts we have examined, arose in childhood. In this account the formulation of some of Deutsch's observations has been changed slightly, and aspects of Miss Eaton's emotional life not essential for our purposes have been omitted. But Deutsch's empirical observations and basic formulations have not been altered.

Miss Eaton's struggles began when she was 8 years old, with the birth of her "very beautiful and talented" sister. For a few years she was intensely and openly jealous of her sister. She hated her and wished she were dead. Exactly why her sibling rivalry was so intense is not reported, but her having been an only child for so long may have been an important factor. Perhaps, too, her parents had wanted another child for some time and now doted over the new baby at Miss Eaton's expense. In any case, the inappropriate emotional reactions with which we are concerned proceed from the basis of Miss Eaton's jealous hatred of her sister.

Adolescent Defense
Against Sibling Rivalry

The first inappropriate emotional reactions appeared a few years after her sister's birth. When Miss Eaton was 12 her mother died. She now began to respond to her 4-year-old sister with excessive love and tenderness. This dramatic change did not come about because her sister ceased being a rival, nor because her jealousy had vanished; it occurred primarily because her jealousy was banished from consciousness and overt behavior. Indeed, the primary reason for this excessive love was that it helped her to repress her hatred and the guilt and anxiety the hatred provoked in her. An attitude of this kind—one that is the direct opposite of how one really feels about a person—is a specific defense mechanism called *reversal of affect*. Miss Eaton's loving thoughts, actions, and feelings crowded hating thoughts, actions, and feelings out of consciousness and overt behavior. And, of course, she now had no rational reason to feel guilty. It is quite likely that this reversal also served two other important functions dealing with the two sides of her feeling about her mother.

(1) The reversal relieved her pain at losing her *beloved* mother by enabling her to *identify* with her mother. In loving and caring for her little sister, she no doubt fantasied that she was in fact her mother. Identification with the lost object, as noted earlier, is one major defense against grief. (2) The reversal, again by enabling her to identify with and "replace" her mother, fulfilled her unconscious Oedipal wishes. She was now the little woman of the house.

Development
of an Obsessional Symptom

A balanced situation such as this one rarely lasts forever; sooner or later unconscious conflicts erupt. This happened when Miss Eaton was 18, while she was still living with her father and her sister, who was 10 years old at the time. Miss Eaton now became obsessed with the frightening thought that something harmful might happen to her little sister unless she repeated all her actions a number of times. As long as Miss Eaton did this she felt at ease and was certain that she was protecting her sister from an evil fate.

What was happening here? Many actions Miss Eaton performed were stimuli to which she responded with the unrealistic fear that something harmful might now happen to her sister; this fear could be reduced if she then repeated the action a magical number of times. Here was inappropriate behavior compounded: an unrealistic fear in response to the most innocuous stimulus, followed by nonsensical, superstitious behavior. Such experiences are classical obsessive-compulsive symptoms. ("Obsessive" refers here to the *thoughts* that evil would come to her sister and to her *lack of control* over these thoughts. They would suddenly intrude into her consciousness, and, once there, would preoccupy her. "Compulsive" refers here to the ritualized *acts* and to the fact that she felt *compelled to perform* them. Such symptoms occasionally occur in normal persons and evidently have the same psychological basis as when they appear in such a severe or persistent form that the person is regarded as suffering from an obsessional neurosis.) Symptoms like these are frequently found to be caused by unconscious conflicts over aggression. The basic fact was that her sister was not in any real danger. Only Miss Eaton entertained evil wishes for her; only Miss Eaton knew of these wishes; only Miss Eaton felt frightened and guilty because of them; and only Miss Eaton had to be relieved of this fear and guilt. All this was true with one qualification: We have been describing her unconscious conflict. Her conscious experience and behavior consisted of *derivatives* of this unconscious conflict and the defense known as *undoing*, which consisted of her repetitious, protective actions. We shall refer to these again in a moment.

For some reason not specified in the case report, the balance Miss Eaton had achieved between her hatred for her sister and the defenses against it was disturbed at this time. Possibly something happened that intensified her hatred. Perhaps there was a weakening of her reversal of hate into love. Perhaps both these things happened. Whatever the reason, this disturbance caused both components of her unconscious conflict—both her hatred and her guilt and anxiety—to become conscious in an indirect way. Minor, everyday actions were now expressions of her hatred, and her unconscious guilt and fears were now expressed in the vague conscious sense that these actions would somehow result in great harm to her sister. By repeating these actions, Miss Eaton was attempting to undo any possible effect of her unconscious hatred. She was engaging in superstitious behavior.

OBSESSIONAL SYMPTOMS
AND THE DEFENSE OF UNDOING: THE RAT MAN

In his clinical paper about the Rat Man (1909b) Freud reported some cogent illustrations of obsessional derivatives and the defense mechanism of *undoing*.

The Rat Man was very much in love with an attractive young woman, but like all people afflicted with severe obsessional neuroses, he hated her as much as he loved her. Naturally this hatred was a source of conflict for him, because it produced distressful emotions (anxiety and guilt in his case). The hatred, as part of such a conflict, was largely unconscious. As was true of Miss Eaton, a broad range of the Rat Man's daily activity was invaded by his unconscious conflict. One summer he and the young woman were staying at the same resort. Once, when they were out boating and a strong breeze was blowing, a command popped into his conscious thoughts that "nothing must happen to her." And because the sentence was completed in his unconscious thoughts with the words "for which [I] might be to blame [p. 189]," he forced her to put on his cap. Another time, they were together during a thunderstorm. He was compelled to count to 40 or 50 between each lightning flash and thunderclap to protect her from being harmed.

The day she was to leave the resort, he was out walking a few hours before her departure. As he was walking along, his foot knocked "accidentally" against a stone in the road. He picked up the stone and put it off the road, but after walking on for a short while he returned and put the stone back in the middle of the road.

Why did he act so oddly? When he kicked the stone, he immediately thought that the carriage in which his friend would be leaving would hit the stone and overturn. So he put it off the road. But then he thought this was a foolish idea, so he put the stone back. His kicking against the stone and the thoughts that followed it were derivations of his repressed hate and his unconscious guilt; his removal of the stone was an *undoing*, which undid the danger and wish of the first act and thus reduced his guilt and anxiety; but then his unconscious hate drove him to put the stone back in the road. Of course, he *rationalized* this latter action, ascribing it to a thought acceptable to his conscious image of himself (that he was not a foolish man), rather than to his repressed hate, which was intolerable to his conscious self. His behavioral oscillation with the stone is a classic example of the oscillation of approach-avoidance conflicts, which was mentioned in Chapter 2. The Rat Man's "goal" here was expression of his hatred. The approach drive was his hatred itself; the avoidance drive consisted of the guilt and anxiety that hatred produced.

The same basic phenomenon had a drastic effect on his nightly prayers, only here the unconscious hatred was very directly expressed. Although he consciously wanted to pray, "May God protect her," his unconscious hostility would cause him to make a slip of the tongue and say, "May God *not* protect her." Naturally, this curse against his loved one would arouse the most intense guilt in him. Thus he would try to repeat the prayer very rapidly so that the "not" could not slip into it. He might have to repeat it several times before an uncontaminated version would come from his lips. At other times he tried to shorten his prayers to prevent this kind of thing. Finally he was driven to replacing ordinary prayers with a nonsense word made up of the initial letters and syllables of his favorite prayer phrases, to which he added "amen." And he uttered this "prayer" as rapidly as possible. But even this defensive effort was unsuccessful. His unconscious wish to curse his loved one caused him to select such letters and syllables that the total "nonsense" word now contained her name and the word *semen*. Without realizing it, he still insulted her, expressing at the same time a sexual wish. It is not surprising that he often had to spend several hours praying and finally gave it up entirely—a striking case of unconscious conflicts over aggression transforming an innocuous situation into a most unpleasant one.

When we discussed Miss Eaton's repetitious actions, we did not specify their nature. It is possible that they followed the same pattern as the repetitive prayers of the Rat Man; that is, the first occurrence of the actions may have been "spoiled" by some expression in them of her unconscious anger at her sister, and the repetitions of the actions may have been attempts to perform those actions "perfectly," without having them "spoiled" in this way. But the symptoms are not described in sufficient detail in the case report to draw any such inference.

Although Miss Eaton's obsessional behavior appears to have been less severe than the Rat Man's, it did persist for the next 20 years or so. Yet because she so successfully concealed it, no one but herself knew about it until she confessed it to her psychoanalyst.

Altruistic Surrender in Adulthood

We shall now return to the case study of Miss Eaton, because the later events in her life help to illuminate several additional psychological mechanisms.

When she was 21, her father died, leaving his two daughters poor and virtually alone in the world. Miss Eaton had seriously hoped to pursue a writing career, but she now had to postpone that goal in order to support herself and her younger sister. It is easy to imagine how severe was the internal conflict with which she now struggled: She must set aside all her own interests and hopes and take a safe, steady job in order to care for a little sister she had hated from the day she was born. Miss Eaton, showing the strength of many "neurotics," did what she had to do and mothered her sister into young womanhood. She took a menial job as a typist, masochistically subjecting herself to a humdrum career. She bestowed on her sister even more tenderness and loving care than before.

Indeed, this reversal of feelings became a *general character trait* of kindliness. When this further development of a reversal occurs, the defense is called a *reaction formation* (see Chapter 11). Miss Eaton also fostered her *sister's* ambitions to become a writer. She was able to do this because in her unconscious fantasy life she and her sister were the same person: She had achieved a *projective identification* with her sister. She would become a writer through her sister's achievements, just as many parents fulfill their own thwarted desires through their children's accomplishments. By means of three defenses—a projective identification, a masochistic turning of her hatred for her sister against herself by working at menial jobs, and a reaction formation—she was able to contain her aggressive response to the frustration she had to endure.

Anna Freud (1936) pointed out that the general behavior pattern based on projective identification, which she called *altruistic surrender,* has an important adaptive function as well as a defensive one: It enables the individual to maintain a meaningful emotional relationship with another person where this might not otherwise have been possible. The altruistic surrender enabled Miss Eaton to live relatively happily with her sister for the next 25 years, first raising her and then supporting her so that she might develop her writing talents. And she came to love her sister in a quite genuine way, while still hating her so much that her relationship remained basically *ambivalent.*

Incubation and Triggering
of the Severe Depression

The years passed, but Miss Eaton's sister did not become a successful writer. Perhaps Miss Eaton could have tolerated this disappointment, but then something even more drastic happened. Unexpectedly, her sister, who was then about 37, married and moved to a distant country. At first Miss Eaton repressed her intense feelings. Instead of becoming angry or depressed, she "bore the parting with quiet dignity, even appeared to be pleased at her sister's happiness, and remained behind alone [Deutsch, 1965, p. 148]." *Soon she obtained a small dog, which substituted emotionally for her sister.* For more than a year they were constant, close companions. Then one day the dog was lost. Miss Eaton became severely depressed and began to experience the persecutory ideas and self-accusations mentioned earlier.

The loss of the dog was a symbolic repetition of the loss of her sister. Miss Eaton's over-reaction to the loss of the dog was mediated by all the feelings and wishes she had repressed when her sister abandoned her. Her depression was primarily a displacement of all her repressed grief over the loss of her sister. It would be quite understandable if Miss Eaton had now become very angry at her sister for deserting her. But she didn't—because she couldn't. And not because she wasn't angry, as Deutsch's report, here quoted, shows:

> In the further course of the treatment the patient's so reasonable attitude at the separation from the sister was soon succeeded by bitter reproach against the ungrateful one, by the return of the most intensive sadistic vindictiveness against the once-hated, afterward loved, and finally so faithless sister.
> What had this sister done to her? For the sake of a strange man she had betrayed her self-sacrificing love and ruthlessly left her to a life of loneliness. This was the thanks she got for having reached the little orphan a helping hand at the time when she was completely helpless. The clearer the picture of her own loss became in the analysis, the louder grew her reproaches against the sister until they took the form of wishing her to be thrown out into the street, where she would have landed in any case if she had not had mercy on her [Deutsch, 1965, pp. 148–49].

Miss Eaton could not tolerate consciously thinking, feeling, or expressing her rage until her treatment enabled her to feel less guilty about it. Instead she repressed it. The loss of her dog, however, was like putting a match to a fuse on a bomb: It threatened an explosion of her unconscious rage. New and renewed defenses were now necessary.

Miss Eaton's new defense was *projection* of her hatred, which contributed to the production of her persecutory delusions: Others might throw her into the street to starve, as she unconsciously wished she had done to her sister. Her renewed defense was a further *turning of the hatred against herself,* which helps to account for her self-reproaches. The critical evidence that these two processes took place is the observation that the content of her persecutory ideas (delusions) and self-reproaches was identical with the content of her furious wishes and thoughts about her sister. Only the subject and the object of these wishes were changed. These were, of course, drastic changes that transformed an easily understandable over-reaction of depression into a bizarre, delusional one.

How were the changes brought about? By the combined action of the defenses and the preexisting identification with her sister. We can best appreciate what happened by recalling that in her unconscious thinking she was, to a significant degree, her sister. Thus she was a potential target of her own hatred. When she then projected onto others her wish to throw her sister into the street, she (now identifying with her sister) became the object of these "others," these projectively created tormentors. She did not project her reproaches against her sister. They were directed against herself. Something else was also involved in the production of her self-reproaches: Her hatred for her sister was first transformed into self-criticism and guilt. In Miss Eaton's case the empirical basis for these concepts is the moralistic, judgmental quality of her self-criticisms. They were self-*accusations* and self-*reproaches* accompanied by a sense of being a guilty, worthless person, deserving of punishment. In short, the stamp of conscience was plain. In fact, the self-reproaches of extremely depressed and delusional patients, such as Miss Eaton, formed the second major empirical basis for Freud's concept of the superego (1917). The first, noted earlier, was the observation of the critical, derogatory nature of Judge Schreber's auditory hallucinations.

This discussion of Miss Eaton's over-reaction to the loss of her dog concludes our discussion of her lifelong struggle with her hatred for her sister. It is also our last example of over-reactions mediated by unconscious conflicts over aggression.

Other Unconscious Conflicts

Unconscious conflicts over aggression mediate over-reactions to just as broad a range of stimuli as do sexual conflicts. The episodes in Miss Eaton's life and the obsessive activities of the Rat Man give a sense of this range. Many other examples could be cited, some of which may occur temporarily in very mild form in normal persons who ordinarily are free from neurotic symptoms: the mother who is afraid to use a butcher knife in the kitchen because she unconsciously fears she will kill her child with it; the man who panics as he drives his automobile because his unconscious urge to run over pedestrians is so strong; the brilliant scientist or student who becomes very anxious or guilty as he writes a paper because he fantasies that his considered evaluation of another man's ideas will destroy that person's scholarly status.

Most of our examples of over-reactions based on unconscious conflicts have involved aggression and genital sexuality. *Any* conflicted wish, however, may mediate an over-reaction to an innocuous stimulus, for linked to any such wish is the unpleasant emotion that either forms the main ingredient of the over-reaction or leads indirectly to it. Since many children in our culture are punished severely for enjoying their oral and anal activity and their voyeuristic and exhibitionistic tendencies, they develop conflicts over such wishes that may lead to over-reactions. Thus, the act of defecating or the sight of a speck of dirt may upset the person who has repressed his anal eroticism and his wishes to be messy. A person driven by strong but conflicted voyeuristic desires may be unable to look at the person he is talking to; a person with an unconscious conflict over oral eroticism may become very uneasy as he watches a diner smacking his lips out of sheer pleasure at the taste of his food; and so on. The theme announced at the beginning of this chapter also concludes it: Any unconscious conflict has the potential of producing a distressing over-reaction.

I lost all sense of the place in which I had gone to sleep, and when I awoke at midnight, not knowing where I was, I could not be sure at first who I was; I had only the most rudimentary sense of existence . . . and out of a half-visualized succession of oil lamps, followed by shirts with turned-down collars, [I] would put together by degrees the component parts of my ego.

MARCEL PROUST. Swann's Way

CHAPTER 9
INTERFERENCE WITH DEFENSES AND REALITY CONTACT

In the discussion of over-reactions in Chapters 6, 7, and 8, we emphasized one general mechanism: that in which an objectively innocuous external stimulus situation has influenced unconscious processes in such a way that they have burst into consciousness, even though frequently disguised. Thus, we first discussed the way in which innocuous stimuli (such as a brief separation from the analyst) may activate repressed unpleasant memories and thereby result in over-reaction (such as acute separation anxiety). This process of memory activation appears to be analogous to the arousal of a person who is half-asleep. Then we discussed the way in which innocuous, or even very pleasant, stimulus situations (such as approaching a restaurant door or making love with one's wife) may similarly activate the approach component of an unconscious conflict—the wish or impulse and relevant memories and fantasies (such as repressed homosexual wishes or repressed incestuous wishes and fantasies). Sometimes the external stimulus functions more like a triggering device that fires a loaded gun or like a puff of air that causes a smoldering fire to burst suddenly into flames. This appeared to be the case when the loss of her little dog triggered Miss Eaton's repressed hatred for her sister, who had deserted her. In either case, as we saw, the intensification of the approach component arouses some kind of aversive unpleasant emotion, such as Ed's unconscious castration anxiety, Ray's unconscious self-contempt when he was at the restaurant door, or Miss Eaton's intense unconscious guilt. Sometimes these emotions become conscious and constitute the over-reaction, as in Ed's anxiety when he made love with his wife or Ray's loss of self-esteem or Miss Eaton's unrealistic feelings of guilt. But they may also motivate such defensive actions as phobic avoidance, projection, identification, undoing, turning of aggression against oneself, and reaction formation, all of which have been illustrated in the last few chapters. Sometimes these defenses contribute very significantly to the distress of the over-reaction, as they did when Miss Eaton's projection of her self-criticism, turning her aggression against herself, and identification with her sister combined to produce her terrifying delusion that other people were going to throw her into the street naked to starve. While the defenses do not always eliminate unpleasant emotional experiences, they do minimize the intensity of these experiences. That is why they are learned in the first place, and that is why they persist.

It follows that any stimulus situation that interferes with the operation of defenses will produce the very emotional experience that the defense normally prevents. In this chapter we shall discuss two such situations. One is the *interference with defenses*. The other is the *interference with contact with reality*. As we shall see, the latter situation can be very unpleasant, because it results in a marked change in defense effectiveness and in many of the other ways people control the expression of their unconscious wishes and thoughts.

Interference with Defenses

Forcing or persuading an individual to give up his defenses only makes him miserable. If Miss Eaton's father, for example, had coerced her into stopping her ritualized repetitions, she would only have suffered greater anxiety. If a boy has developed a hand-washing compulsion that relieves his guilt over masturbating, any attempts by his parents to stop him—reasoning, pleading, threatening, or hiding the soap—will only leave him intensely guilty. Unless his guilt is resolved, it will drive him to secretive hand-washing or to some other defensive action.

Psychotherapy has identical effects if the therapist resorts to the same tactics.

One "victim" of such a strategy was a man in his early twenties. He was a passive, dependent person, afraid to function away from the protective security of his parents. Since he became very frightened at being away from home, for example, he was not able to hold a steady job. He finally learned that he could venture outdoors if he had enough to drink. Drinking, then, was his defense; it was motivated by his anxiety, and it relieved that anxiety. But, of course, this was a maladaptive defense, which led his family physician to refer him to a mental health clinic.

He came quite regularly for psychotherapy interviews for several months without improving. Always arriving slightly intoxicated, he passed most of the time talking about that fact: apologizing for it, berating himself for it, complaining that he could not do otherwise, and so forth. The well-meaning but inexperienced therapist impatiently concluded that psychotherapy would be worthless if the man could not come sober, whereas if he did come sober his underlying anxieties and conflicts might become so uncomfortable that they would properly become the focus of attention. Accordingly, the therapist abruptly suggested one day that at the next interview the young man would start a new conditioned response treatment. The treatment, he explained, consisted of ingesting a chemical together with a drink of whiskey. The chemical would make him violently sick to his stomach. After one, two, or three such experiences the sight of a glass or even the thought of taking a drink would nauseate him. Soon the young man would be coming for his interviews completely sober, and they could then get down to what was really troubling him. The young man agreed to all of this. But he did not show up the next time. He later sent word to the clinic that he had gotten a job that did not allow him time off for his interviews. And, anyway, he felt he could get along without more psychotherapy.

Five years later he reappeared at the clinic and was interviewed by the same therapist. The patient explained that for the last three years he had been in a state hospital, where he had voluntarily gone, hoping to get over his anxiety and drinking. Both had actually increased after the earlier efforts at psychotherapy. Now he was trying life again outside the hospital and in coming to the clinic was following the advice of his doctor at the hospital. He had broken off his earlier psychotherapy, he explained, because he had been frightened by the therapist's plans to stop his drinking and make him talk about his emotional problems. The threatened premature and forcible interference with his defense had mobilized the very anxiety he was trying to relieve himself of by drinking. His psychotherapy was transformed into a noxious situation, to which he over-reacted with anxiety and flight.

This is a typical clinical experience when techniques are used that do nothing more than forcibly interfere with defenses and leave the underlying conflict unresolved. Even when a "cure" has apparently been achieved, it is likely that the old symptoms will reappear or that new ones will arise. As we pointed out earlier, this was the main reason Freud abandoned the use of direct hypnotic suggestion.

The reader who is familiar with behavior therapy derived from conditioned response theory and laboratory experiments may wonder how much of what we have just asserted applies to behavior therapy. We are, frankly, uncertain, and prefer to leave this issue open for careful investigation in the future. It should be noted, however, that behavior therapy as formulated by Wolpe and his followers attempts to reduce the anxiety behind symptoms and not simply to abolish the symptoms. Nor do experienced behavior therapists deal with their patients as abruptly and impatiently as the therapist did in the instance we have discussed.

THE NEGATIVE THERAPEUTIC REACTION

Effective psychoanalytic psychotherapy includes interference with defenses, but in a quite different way from the procedure described above. Rather than blocking them, the therapist strives to identify what defenses a person uses, what kind of distressing affect motivates them, and what "approach" tendencies are eliciting this distressing affect. He also helps the patient work through the developmental history of the conflict. As the patient becomes aware of his defenses, they become less automatic and less effective. He begins consciously to experience the unpleasant emotions—for example, anxiety, guilt, shame, and disgust—that had been motivating the defenses and to recall and reexperience the childhood situations in which his conflicts developed. All of this can be very unpleasant and disturbing, even to the point where the patient consciously suffers more than he did before treatment started. But the patient is usually "getting better"—he is enjoying life more and functioning better than he did when he suffered less, before treatment started. This paradox is part of what is referred to by the term "negative therapeutic reaction."

The negative therapeutic reaction includes another seeming paradox. As the person becomes aware of the nature of his conflicts and their past history, he indulges more in the approach components of his conflicts because the intensity of the competing aversive emotional reactions eventually decreases. Yet he experiences greater emotional distress than he did before treatment started! If one follows Miller's reasoning, it becomes clear that this *must* happen, according to the dynamics of approach-avoidance conflicts (Miller, 1944; Dollard & Miller, 1950).

Let us take a specific example of a man with a sexual conflict and follow Miller's argument with the aid of part A of Figure 9-1. The approach and avoidance gradients in part A of the figure represent the strengths of this man's tendencies to approach and to avoid a certain woman, and these are motivated, respectively, by his sexual desires and by his sexual anxiety or guilt. As we saw in Chapter 2, the avoidance gradient is steeper than the approach gradient. Thus, at any point beyond the intersection of the two gradients, avoidance is stronger than approach, and the person will retreat from the goal. The point of intersection of the approach and avoidance gradients represents how close the man gets to the goal of complete psychological and physical intimacy with the woman. In other words, the closest a person in an approach-avoidance conflict will get to the goal is the point of intersection of the approach and avoidance gradients. The man's situation at the outset of treatment is represented by the combination of the "approach" gradient and the "strong avoidance" gradient. That is, he desires intimacy, but his opposing anxiety is so strong that he cannot come closer to her than the idle talking stage (intersection 1). After many weeks of psy-

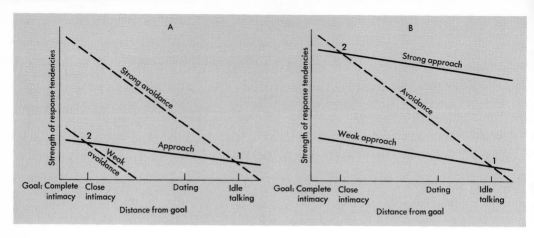

Figure 9-1   *Effects of changing the strengths of avoidance and approach gradients. (Adapted from Miller, 1944)*

Part A demonstrates that, within the limits in which the two gradients cross, decreasing the strength of the avoidance gradient moves the intersection closer to the goal and at the same time raises the height of the intersection. Thus, decreasing the strength of the avoidance gradient has the paradoxical effect that the man will engage in more intimate sexual behavior than formerly and at the same time will experience greater anxiety and conflict over doing so than he did when the avoidance gradient was higher. Part B demonstrates that increasing the strength of the approach gradient also moves the intersection closer to the goal and, in addition, places it higher on the avoidance gradient. Thus, decreasing the avoidance gradient results in less intense conflict and avoidance at intersection 2 than does increasing the approach gradient. This difference is reflected in the difference in the heights of intersections 2 in the two diagrams.

chotherapy he may be in the dynamic situation represented by the "approach" and the "weak avoidance" gradients. That is, his underlying anxiety may now be sufficiently reduced so that he can not only date but also be somewhat intimate with the woman (intersection 2). (Miller assumes that such reductions in anxiety lower the overall height of the entire avoidance gradient.) Yet he will be experiencing greater anxiety at this point than he did earlier, when he could only engage in idle talking with her. (That is, the point on the "weak avoidance" curve at intersection 2 is higher than the point on the "strong avoidance" curve at intersection 1.) He can come closer to her, but he experiences greater conflict—greater desires *and* greater anxiety—than he did earlier. His torment is greater but also more pleasurable. The hopeful outcome, of course, is a further weakening of the avoidance gradient through the combined action of more therapeutic self-exploration, learning from the actual experiences of increasing intimacy that his anxieties are groundless, and outright extinction of his anxieties.

Freud and other psychoanalysts gradually learned empirically that the most effective way to resolve conflicts was to follow the detour just described—to "analyze the defenses" first. It might seem more expedient to start by interpreting the unconscious wishes and actively urging a person to gratify them in spite of his conflicts over them. Indeed, Freud often did this early in his career. But this direct method leads to such great conflict that it is doomed to failure. Part B of Figure 9-1 may explain why this is so. This direct method leaves the strength of the avoidance motives and responses unchanged; its only effect is to increase the strength of the approach drives and responses. A comparison of the two intersections within part B shows that this method will cause the person to experience very great anxiety—and he will still not reach the goal. Comparing the strengths of the avoidance tendencies at intersection 2 of both parts A and B makes it clear that the first method—decreasing the defenses and their underlying avoidance motives—brings the person just as close to the goal, with less intense anxiety and conflict. Being less miserable, he is less likely to flee therapy and can more easily progress in unlearning his irrational anxieties. Throwing people into deep water is not a very good way to help them learn to swim; most of them will have to be rescued and will refuse to try again. Increasing the approach gradient is simply a way of trying to overpower one's defenses. The result is the same as any other direct interference with defenses—an over-reaction of anxiety or renewed defensive efforts.

A complete discussion of the negative therapeutic reaction would lead us into the masochistic gratification of an unconscious need for punishment and suffering many people obtain from their neuroses, and their resulting negative reactions to what seems to be technically correct therapy. But we have been mainly interested here in those aversive events in therapy that are related to the direct interference with defenses.

Interference with Reality Contact

Imagine yourself floating in a balloon at 60,000 feet or lying in bed, halfway between wakefulness and sleep. Or picture yourself suspended for hours in a tank of water maintained at the same temperature as your body. The light level is constant, and no noise reaches you. You are alone, attached to the outside world by an oxygen line and a microphone cable over which you can report how you feel. All these situations represent an *interference with reality contact*: an absence of direct human contact and a marked decrement in sensory stimulation. Furthermore, the small amount of sensory input that exists is monotonously constant and of very low intensity.

Many people—among them Arctic explorers, astronauts, prison wardens and inmates familiar with solitary confinement, physicians caring for patients isolated in hospital beds, and psychotherapists—have long known that *sensory deprivation*, or *interference with reality contact*, has marked effects on behavior.

The pioneering experimental investigations started in 1951, when Hebb, Bexton, Heron, and Scott paid college students to spend time in a condition of sensory deprivation (Bexton, Heron, & Scott, 1954). The subjects lay on comfortable beds in a lighted, semisoundproof chamber (see Figure 9-2). They wore translucent goggles, which passed a uniform, diffuse light to their eyes but prevented patterned *vision;* cotton gloves and long cardboard cuffs decreased their *tactile perception. Auditory perception* was reduced by means of the semisoundproofing, by a U-shaped foam rubber pillow, and by the masking noise of the air-conditioning equipment. *Time perception* was also curtailed; as far as possible, the subjects were prevented from finding out the time.

At all times the experimenter on duty could observe the subjects through the observation windows, and the subjects and experimenter could converse when absolutely necessary over microphone-speaker systems. The subjects were fed in the chamber and were allowed to go to the toilet in an adjacent room. On the average, the subjects had only 2 to 3 hours a day of these interruptions in the sensory monotony. (Figure 9-2 also shows wires leading from the subject's scalp. These recorded the electrical activity of the brain.)

Few subjects could endure this situation for more than 2 or 3 days. Sooner or later they became bored and *craved stimulation.* And they very frequently had *intense emotional experiences,* including anxiety. Since

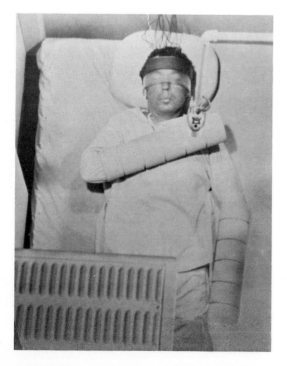

Figure 9-2 The kind of experimental situation used in Heron's (1961) studies of sensory deprivation, as it would appear from above with the ceiling removed. The air-conditioning unit is above the foot of the bed.

arousal of anxiety is our chief interest in these experiments, we shall discuss only those aspects of sensory deprivation experiments that are relevant to it.

ANXIETY-PROVOKING EXPERIENCES

The decrease in reality contact is not inherently noxious; some people even enjoy it. Yet many subjects in many subsequent experiments have also become extremely frightened. Some have been unable to tolerate the situation for more than a few hours. Interviews reveal why: The interference with reality contact produces a variety of other experiences that, according to many subjects, arouse anxiety. The following are examples of the most extreme reactions; effects vary greatly from one experiment to another.

Loss of Control
of the Thinking Process

Many subjects report an inability to concentrate. Instead they experience a "jumble of thoughts with no rhyme or reason [Smith & Lewty, 1959]." Some are unable to "think about anything to think about [Heron, 1961]." Many are frightened by such changes in their self-control because they feel they are becoming insane (Smith & Lewty, 1959; Cohen, Silverman, Bressler, & Shmavonian, 1961).

Images and Hallucinations

One subject saw objects moving toward his face and was observed jerking his head back in response (Heron, 1961). Others reported seeing "a face covered with horrible red spots and lumps," "a large wheat field waving in the wind," and a "burning tree [Zubek, Aftanas, Kovach, Wilgosh, & Winocur, 1963]." Most of the hallucinations are visual, but other senses may be involved. One subject, for example, "heard" someone breathing and walking about the isolation room and panicked when she *smelled* something burning (Zuckerman, Albright, Marks, & Miller, 1962). Another subject heard her sisters' voices speaking, often to each other (Azima, Vispo, & Azima, 1961).

Changes
in Body Image

This kind of perceptual distortion is very frequent. One subject said "My arms aren't here sometimes. . . . They feel to be in the back of my body . . . my head seems to be floating . . . parts of my body keep missing and coming back . . . [Azima, Vispo, & Azima, 1961]." Another subject felt herself getting "smaller and smaller [Zuckerman et al., 1962]"; another feared that his body parts would disappear and disintegrate (Cohen et al., 1961); others felt that their bodies were floating or revolving in space, that their arms or legs were rising, or that one limb was much shorter than another (Zubek et al., 1963). Another felt that his arm was "like a ton-weight and feels fatter than my body [Smith & Lewty, 1959]." Some subjects feel they cannot control their muscles. Thus, one young man was afraid he could not speak when he wanted to and later feared he was unable to move (Cohen et al., 1961).

These alterations in self-perception may even reach the point of depersonalization, where a person perceives his body, or part of it, as an external object. One subject saw his head before him protruding from a purple cloud (Zubek et al., 1963).

Fantasies   Fantasies—pleasant and unpleasant—frequently dominate the subject's stream of experience, and they may become so vivid as to be nearly delusional. Sometimes the person's most cherished wishes are represented as fulfilled. One subject who longed to be a missionary in Africa became deeply engrossed in a vivid fantasy that she was drifting in a rocking boat along a jungle river (Zuckerman et al., 1962).

Unpleasant fantasies also occur. One 20-year-old woman started to imagine that she was locked in the experimental room. While she knew this was not true, she could not get rid of the idea. She became so unnerved that she had to stop participating in the study (Smith & Lewty, 1959). In another study (Cohen et al., 1961) two female subjects imagined that the oxygen in the room would be used up and they would suffocate. A male subject in the same study fantasied that he was continually being watched, although the room was dark and the observation window was covered with black board, and he imagined that he was somehow in danger. When he then heard a slight variation in the noise of the ventilating fan, he fantasied that someone was scooting about the chamber seated in a captain's chair and was rapidly turning some dials that "had something to do with the chamber."

The fantasies may reflect the person's characteristic concerns. In one experimental setup (Mendelson, Kubzansky, Leiderman, Wexler, & Solomon, 1961) the subjects fed themselves whenever they wanted food by sucking nourishing eggnog from a glass tube. One subject took a sip shortly after entering the isolation chamber. It tasted cool to him, yet he fantasied that bacteria were growing in the eggnog that was trapped in the feeding tube, that these bacteria were poisoning him, and that his body then started to produce a counterpoison. This very vivid fantasy was one reason he quit the experiment after about 3½ hours. The fantasy was a continuation of trends present in his everyday experience. Thus, when he smoked cigarettes he became preoccupied with thoughts of getting lung cancer, and when he entered a building housing tuberculosis patients he feared that he would develop tuberculosis. Apparently he could normally control such thoughts; but with the decrement of external stimulation they became very prominent.

**Emergence
of Conflicted Wishes**   Some subjects acknowledged that very disturbing wishes dominated their thoughts during sensory deprivation. After 2 hours of sensory deprivation, one sub-

ject told an interviewer that he was panicky. But he could not admit the cause of this intense anxiety until the following day, when another interviewer was very supportive and reassured him that the condition itself often produced bizarre effects in many people over which they had no control. The man then told how he had been overwhelmed by homosexual fantasies when he was in the chamber by himself. Furthermore, these fantasies had persisted into the first interview and involved his feeling for the first interviewer (Cohen et al., 1961).

The experiences that have been described here are not limited to experimental situations or to real-life situations in which sensory deprivation is *imposed from without*. They may also occur when contact with reality is reduced by a withdrawal of attention and interest from it. The hermit's seclusion, the hospitalized patient's psychosis, the drug addict's "trip," and the neurotic person's daily sessions with a psychoanalyst at times exemplify the condition. A more common instance of a decrease in reality contact is the transition between sleep and wakefulness.

THE TRANSITION BETWEEN SLEEP AND WAKEFULNESS

Most of us can recall lying half-awake in the middle of the night, preoccupied with a vivid fantasy in which we have imagined satisfying all kinds of sexual and aggressive wishes that we did not care to admit to ourselves the next day. And in that twilight state we have all been caught up in fantasies in which the day's frustrations have been overcome or some harrowing experience has been relived so vividly that our hearts pounded and we were fully awakened.

Many people experience at night the kinds of changes in the body image that subjects experience during the sensory deprivation experiment. One young woman occasionally felt that her body was many times larger than its actual size and that her flesh was puffy and spongy. As there, the alterations in body image may extend to the point of depersonalization. This young woman recalled vividly an experience she used to have when she was 8 years old: While falling asleep she used to "see" her body, in the form of an amorphous, gelatinous shape, in the corner of the room. Federn (1952) reported that one of his psychoanalytic patients had an unusually pleasant, vivid sexual dream and felt, on suddenly awakening, as if his body was lying beside him and did not belong to him.

Many other alterations in body image seem to be just as intimately related to the subject's sexual life.

One young man reported frequently lying in bed with a sensation that his right leg ended at his knee. The "disappearance" of the lower part of his leg appeared to be related to a repressed memory of an early childhood experience. Once he had slept with his father after a long separation. He awoke in the night to find that he was touching his father's erect penis with his foot, which had slipped inside his father's pajamas. He fell back to sleep in that position, feeling that it was wonderful to be with his father again. The body-image distortion occurred at a point in his psychoanalysis when his love for his father was especially intense but repressed. It was as if, at these times, he longed to relive that remembered experience of touching his father's penis with his foot, an episode of intimacy and of directly experiencing his father's strength. But it was as if he also had to withdraw his attention completely from his foot and leg in order to keep the memory repressed.

The change the young woman felt in the size of her body was also related to her sexual life. It would occur when she became exceptionally aroused and then suddenly repressed her voluptuous sensations.

Vivid imagery, approaching hallucinatory intensity, is not unusual during the sleep-wakefulness transition. One instance of this was the young girl's terrifying perception that a "bad man" was coming into her bedroom to get her (page 111).

Difficulty in concentrating, in controlling one's train of thought, may also occur. When we try to think through something logically as we drop off to sleep, our thoughts eventually ramble. Sometimes we suddenly realize that our thoughts have been jumping wildly about for some time and that we cannot retrace their sequence.

Many people do not enjoy these experiences. Some are so frightened by them that they avoid the transitional stage and thereby develop insomnia. Some resort to sleeping pills or alcohol, not only in order to sleep but to avoid the transitional stage of the decrease in reality contact. Others compulsively read themselves to sleep, clinging to a tenuous contact with reality as they pass through the transitional stage.

WHY LOSS OF REALITY IS DISTURBING

What is so disturbing about the interference with reality contact? The observations that have been presented here suggest two sources of discomfort.

Weakening of Defenses

The first is a weakening of defenses. Inherently frightening memories and fantasies may emerge from repression, as do sexual and aggressive sensations, memories, and wishful fantasies. When they do, the anxiety and guilt prompted by them, which normally motivate mitigating defenses, are intensely experienced. So far we are in familiar territory: This source of discomfort stems from the subject's unconscious conflicts because of an interference with his defenses. But we have also encountered something new: the realization that *normal contact with reality (a normal kind and amount of sensory input) is an important condition for the maintenance of defenses.*

The second source of discomfort is the loss of the *mode,* or *form,* of thinking and perceiving that is characteristic of normal waking life. The inability to concentrate, the perception of the world largely from an egocentric point of view, the loss of an integrated body image, and the intrusions of hallucinations or images that allow forbidden wishes to emerge into consciousness—all these represent a shift from a more or less logically organized, modulated style to a primitive form of behavior, thought, and experience. In psychoanalytic terminology, there is a shift from a more *secondary process* to a more *primary process* mode of functioning (Freud, 1900, Chapter 7). "Secondary process modes of functioning" refers to the way we usually think and act when we are awake: with words, with a logical organization, and with our emotions kept within reasonable bounds. "Primary process modes of functioning" refers to more primitive forms of behavior, such as that found in dreams: thinking in the form of sensory images like pictures, in an illogical manner, and with emotional controls largely removed. Freud called the latter "primary" because he considered them to be characteristic of the conscious behavior of infancy and also of the unconscious processes of adults. He called the former "secondary" because he regarded them as developing during the course of life and also as characteristic of the conscious thinking and behavior of adults. In other words, he believed that adult unconscious functioning retained the characteristics of conscious childhood functioning.

Rapaport (1958) made the general formulation that *continued contact with reality is a prerequisite for maintaining the more mature secondary process mode of functioning and, indeed, for keeping all our behavior relatively free from domination by our basic drives.* Developments in neurophysiology complement this formulation nicely. Magoun and others (whose work is reviewed in Lindsley, 1961) have identified a system in the brain known as the *reticular activating system,* which "alerts" or "arouses" the cortex of the brain in the presence of sensory input to the sense organs. The brain-wave pattern this system arouses is characteristic of the waking, alert state only; sleeping or drowsy animals show a different pattern. Stimulation of the reticular system will make a sleeping animal alert and also improves the actual capacity of the brain to make fine stimulus discriminations. It thus appears that behavior during normal wakefulness and during sensory deprivation have different neurophysiological counterparts.

The shift in the *form* of functioning and experiencing—from the more secondary process to the more primary process modes—itself distresses some people greatly when they experience it. Present knowledge indicates that this shift is distressing when the person cannot, or feels that he cannot, control it. At such times people may be terrified that they are losing self-control, going insane, or experiencing disintegration of their personalities. This type of anxiety is called *fear of the loss of one's ego organization* (Waelder, 1930; A. Freud, 1936). It appears to be just as disturbing and just as potent a motive for defense as any of the other anxieties and unpleasant affects we have discussed.

Formulations such as these, especially Rapaport's, suggested an interesting study to Goldberger and Holt (1961). They reasoned that a measure of the extent to which a shift toward the primary process disturbed an individual in one situation—in this case the Rorschach Test, the "ink-blot" test—should be related to the degree of emotional disturbance experienced by the same individual in the sensory deprivation experiment. They began by administering the Rorschach Test to a group of college students. They measured the amount of primary process functioning during the test performance and the extent to which each student was disturbed by such functioning. These measures were obtained by a special Rorschach scoring system Holt had devised previously (Holt, 1956). Next they ranked the subjects according to the *ease* with which they could tolerate shifts to the primary process mode. Top ranks were given to those students who could readily engage in primary process functioning without becoming anxious or defensive; low ranks were assigned to those subjects who frequently shifted to primary process functioning and became very disturbed because of it; middle ranks were assigned to students who rarely engaged in the primary process. Presumably these last students were also afraid to do so, but they were unable to avoid it in the testing situation.

The experimenters then observed the students in the sensory deprivation situation. They found that the more disturbed a student was by primitive perceptions, thoughts, and drive expressions in the Rorschach Test, the more likely he was to react to sensory deprivation with unpleasant affect and with thoughts about quitting the experiment. He was especially more likely to avoid going to sleep. Perhaps the partial loss of reality achieved by the experimental procedure was frightening enough, and the subjects did not want it intensified by the further sensory isolation of sleep.

In any event, this study demonstrated that the *formal* shift to primitive modes of functioning is very disturbing for some people, less so for others, and pleasant for still others. It strongly suggests that when this shift is induced by decreased reality contact, it frightens the same people who are also frightened by it under other conditions. Perhaps the tolerance for the shift to primary process functioning is a general personality attribute that determines how disturbed a person will become in many different types of situations that involve sensory deprivation. If so, measures of this tolerance may prove to have practical value in the selection of pilots, astronauts, or other skilled technicians for jobs that involve prolonged exposure to monotonous conditions.

"Well! my dear Pangloss," said Candide, "when you were hanged, dissected, stunned with blows and made to row in the galleys, did you always think that everything was for the best in this world?"

"I am still of my first opinion," replied Pangloss.

VOLTAIRE. Candide

CHAPTER 10
DEFENSE AGAINST UNPLEASANT EXTERNAL SITUATIONS

W e have discussed a variety of stimulus situations that produce unpleasant emotional reactions in most people in our Western culture. We began, in Chapter 6, by describing the six categories of "realistic," or objective, external dangers. To recapitulate, the categories were as follows:

1. Frustration of basic drives
2. Separation from a protector
3. Loss of love (rejection by a loved person)
4. Loss of a love object (separation from a loved and loving person through death, long-term separation, or renunciation)
5. Loss of self-esteem
6. Threats to physical integrity

Then we added "unrealistic" external dangers to the list:

7. Innocuous stimuli that have been associated with or resemble "realistic" external dangers (Chapter 6)
8. Innocuous or potentially pleasant stimulus situations that produce an inner conflict by

      a. arousing conflictful unconscious fantasies or wishes (Chapters 6–8) or

      b. interfering with the functioning of defenses (Chapter 9)

  9. Interference with reality contact (Chapter 9)

Man's behavior in these situations ranges from adaptive mastery to domination by unpleasant emotions and utter helplessness, with the process of defense falling between the two poles.

As we saw in Chapter 3, some defenses prevent unpleasant emotional experiences by interfering with the impact or perception of the external stimuli that give rise to them. We have mentioned most of these defenses already, but in this chapter we shall discuss them systematically and in detail.

Escape and Simple Avoidance

Reflexive withdrawal of one's hand from a hot stove is the simplest way to stop the pain and the tissue damage. The withdrawal reflex is simultaneously an innate adaptive mechanism and also the simplest known defense. This reaction, like all withdrawal reactions, *halts an unpleasant experience*. All defenses share precisely this experiential effect; they differ only in the means of achieving it. In this example an elementary motor act removes the sense organs from the external stimulus source, thereby disrupting at its origin the chain of events leading to the experience of pain.

But withdrawal reflexes are inadequate and even irrelevant under most circumstances: those circumstances in which man's inner needs and special capacities are very important in determining the danger. Frustration, separation from a nurturant figure, and permanent loss of a loved one can produce a state of *continual* and intense *inner* drive stimulation. These internal states give rise not only to distressful physical sensations (for example, feelings of thirst, hunger, and cold) but also to a sense of unrelieved tension and even a sense of helplessness. Furthermore, man's capacities to learn and anticipate, to remember and imagine, to engage in inner conflict, and to develop highly organized patterns of behavior create an order of external dangers rarely involving physical pain—for example, separations devoid of actual distressful needs and helplessness, loss of love, and innocuous stimuli that trigger inner conflict. To cope with all these experiences, man must and does develop other mechanisms of defense.

The withdrawal reflex is the prototype for the simplest of these additional mechanisms: *escape and physical avoidance* achieved by motor behavior that is more complex than mere reflexes. Since this defense is so elementary, it is especially characteristic of children. When the small child becomes frightened at being separated from his mother in the middle of the night, he runs into her bed. He literally *escapes* an unpleasant stimulus situation and creates a new, pleasant one, and his anxiety subsides. He can also learn to *avoid* separation perceptions and thus to avoid separation anxiety. For example, he soon learns to cling tenaciously to his mother as she is about to leave him, if she rewards this behavior by not leaving him alone.

Older children may develop "school phobias" to avoid separation from their mothers. There are even many adults who refuse more promising jobs with new, young, aggressively liberal employers to avoid the anxiety of separating from benignly paternalistic, autocratic ones. Erich Fromm (1941) presented a substantial discussion of this "escape from freedom."

Escape and avoidance may be used to defend against any unpleasant situation, not just that of separation. Ed avoided sexual intimacy with his wife to prevent the castration anxiety produced by the incestuous significance of making love with his wife. Many subjects escaped from the sensory deprivation experiments when that interference with reality contact frightened them. People often break off a close but unsatisfying relationship to escape from frustration. A student may avoid having conferences with an especially critical teacher who threatens his self-esteem. Other examples of flight from "realistic" and "unrealistic" danger situations are familiar to everyone.

THE PROBLEM OF INTIMACY AND ISOLATION

Erikson (1959) has underscored the importance of the capacity for physical and psychological intimacy—for *personal intimacy*, let us say. *Isolation* and *self-absorption*, Erikson points out, are the fate of the person who cannot enter into intimate relationships with other people. He believes that this capacity is a prerequisite for the *ability both to love and to work well* (abilities that Freud once proposed as the basic, empirical criteria of normality). But intimacy is a danger for many people. The list of danger situations presented at the beginning of this chapter and the examples that have been cited show why: Nearly all of them are strictly interpersonal, and, generally speaking, their intensity varies directly with the degree of intimacy involved. A person will never experience any stronger separation anxiety, any deeper hurt or fear of loss of love, any sadder grief, or any humiliation so painful as that which might arise out of intimacy. Furthermore, intimacy brings with it the *potential* for *all* the unpleasant experiences we have discussed.

Many young people flee from intimacy because they experience in it one or more of those dangers. As a result, they enter adulthood without the capacity for intimacy. A few gradually discover that human closeness is not so dangerous, and they belatedly develop the capacity. Social isolation is the fate of the others. "Loners" may appear to be strong, contented, and self-sufficient, even to themselves. But this is a deceptive image. This defensive escape from intimacy brings with it all the misery that a loss of love entails.

Marriage and family life and some other patterns of interpersonal relationships may camouflage an escape from intimacy. Flighty, superficial, and ritualized social interaction—epitomized by the "cocktail hour" of executive suburbia (and some academic and professional circles)—is a sham intimacy, a pretentious togetherness concealing a defensive aloneness. A married couple may one day realize that they are actually strangers. They discover that they spend very little time together (one or both of them always have "homework" that simply must be done). They may not even sleep in the same room, let alone the same bed ("I can't sleep with all that snoring and tossing and turning," or "I'll sleep in the other room again, dear, because I'll be late coming to bed again tonight"). Of course, the sheer quantity of time spent together is no gauge or guarantee of intimacy; even a small amount of the right quality can suffice.

Denial

Escape and avoidance achieve their defensive effects by removing the sense organs from the effective action of external stimuli. In this way they interrupt the chain of events leading to unpleasant perceptions and distressful emotional experience. But perception is an active process, controlled in part by internal processes.

The *distribution of attention* determines whether or not we perceive physical stimuli impinging on our sense organs. If we concentrate on carefully reading a difficult book, we do not hear a song being played on the radio. By withdrawing our attention from noises, we can stop hearing them and go to sleep. The stimuli may be *registered* in our nervous system, but we do not *perceive* them. The same withdrawal and shifts in attention can and usually do occur unconsciously. All day long we unconsciously *selectively* perceive the world about us. Man can prevent unpleasant perceptions by varying his attention and by wishful perceiving or thinking. Unconscious distortion of perception of external stimuli that arouse unpleasant emotions is called *denial*. Denial is a *nonverbal* reaction that alters the *perception* of external stimuli. (Another defensive process, called *negation*, is verbal and cognitive. A person is using this defense when he says or thinks to himself, "No, I don't hate you" or "I don't love you" when his unconscious feelings are just the opposite.)

The simplest form of denial is blotting out the perception by withdrawing our attention from it. In this way we may fail to see a snake in the middle of a trail or an angry facial expression or fail to hear a criticism or our mother's loving tone when she mentions our brother's name. We may fail to perceive sexually attractive qualities in a person who is the object of an unconscious approach-avoidance sexual conflict. If we have an unconscious conflict over responding aggressively, we may fail to perceive another person's provocations to anger. Withdrawal of attention, then, may produce *"perceptual blanks."*

People frequently *"fill in the blanks"* with wish-fulfilling perceptions. Duane did this in his transitory perceptions of his father, as we discussed in Chapter 2. The most extreme outcome of this process is the wish-fulfilling hallucinatory world of psychosis. In his first published discussion of denial (1894) Freud wrote of a woman who had fallen in love with a man who frequently visited her home.

> She thought he came to see her out of love for *her*. But he had really been using her to gain access to another woman in the household. When that other relationship failed, he stopped coming. We can imagine that the woman suffered greatly—frustration, a sense of rejection, humiliation, grief, and intense conflicted anger at the man. Eventually she hallucinated that he was continually there with her. She was denying on a grand scale the perception of a tormenting reality.

Filling in the blanks with wish-fulfilling perceptions increases the defensive effectiveness of denial. It dissolves the tension of ungratified wishes and evokes pleasant affects. It also provides an obstacle to the reappearance of the unpleasant blanked-out perceptions. Life's unpleasant facts keep knocking at the door of consciousness, but our attention does not go to open the door and help them across the threshold. It is preoccupied, preempted by the pleasant perceptions that have already forcibly entered the mind's room. The price of this defensive gain can be high: an inability to live in the real world. But denial usually stops short of the hallucinatory extreme of psychosis: In the adult, wishful thinking and even the tendency to it are usually restricted by being tested against reality. Not so with the child, however, whose behavior conforms more to the pleasure principle than to the reality principle. Children, then, give us our clearest examples of *denial in fantasy and action*.

DENIAL IN CHILDREN

Children often resort to denial in fantasy and action, according to Anna Freud (1936), when they are confronted by any unpleasant situation. Little Hans (Freud, 1909a), whom we discussed earlier (pages 65, 79), provides an example of how children may deny in fantasy stimuli that arouse a feeling of being unloved.

> Little Hans was 3 years old when his sister Hanna was born. Previously his only rival for his mother's love had been his father. Now he had to share it with Hanna, too. He witnessed many unpleasant scenes that made him long for the "good old days." Often he watched Hanna being bathed, toileted, and caressed by his mother. Eventually he denied such distasteful sights by fantasying that he had many children of his own, whom he cared for lovingly. In the fantasy he participated in the kind of pleasant experiences enjoyed by Hanna and his mother.
> Because of his Oedipal love for his mother, Little Hans also found it very

disagreeable to see reminders of his father's relationship to his mother. Hans denied this situation with a fantasy in which he was married to his mother, she was the mother of *his* children, and Hans's father was married to *his own* mother.

Hans also used fantasy to ease his fear that his father would castrate him. He imagined that his father, who was disguised as a plumber in the fantasy, robbed him of his little penis *but* replaced it with a big one. This fantasy denial so relieved Little Hans of his castration anxiety that it appeared to have brought his fear of horses—which was partly a disguised fear of being castrated by his father—to an end. Here we have a vivid demonstration of the defensive effectiveness of denial in fantasy.

We have discussed how inferior, worthless, and envious little girls feel when they recognize that they do not have a penis. Many girls relieve themselves of this painful loss of self-esteem by denying the perceptions of their female physical characteristics. One lovely 3-year-old girl, having seen little boys urinating while they ran wildly around the yard, pretended to do the same thing at home. She would take off her clothes, press back her labia with her fingers so as to expose her clitoris, and run excitedly around the room, screaming in frantic elation, "Look at my tinkler. Look at me tinkling." Later, in a touching conversation with her mother, she sadly admitted that she wanted a "tinkler like Timmie's." Following several discussions in which her loving and sympathetic mother expressed pride in the little girl's femininity and made it clear that they both had bodily things little boys didn't have, the episode of frenzied elation and perceptual denial subsided.

Some girls continue into adolescence and adulthood feeling humiliated and worthless and envying maleness upon perceiving their own femaleness. Two such women were described in Chapter 6. Another, in adolescence, dressed in boy's clothes and bore a short stick inside one trouser leg in order to appear to have a penis. She no longer did this as a young adult, but she still walked with a marked mannish gait and carried her head and body in the characteristic fashion of her father.

We shall now consider some other uses of denial.

EXPERIMENTAL STUDIES OF DENIAL

One of the most devastating results of social discrimination is that members of minority groups may internalize the derogatory values and attitudes of the majority and regard themselves as inferior or worthless. When they do, the perception in themselves of characteristics singled out by the majority for derogation is the basis for a marked loss of self-esteem. One way out is to deny the perceptions of these characteristics in oneself. An experiment by K. B. and M. P. Clark (1958), prominent Negro psychologists in New York City, showed clearly how Negro children denied their own skin color. This was one of the psychological studies cited in the

1954 decision by the U.S. Supreme Court that racial segregation in public schools is unconstitutional (United States Reports, 347).

The Clarks administered a Dolls Test to 253 Negro children ranging from 3 to 7 years of age. In this test the Clarks presented the children with both brown dolls and white ones and asked the children to answer a series of questions by selecting the appropriate doll. The questions fell into three categories. The first category determined if the children perceived accurately the racial, skin-color characteristic—for example, "Give me the doll that looks like a white child, . . . a colored child, . . . a Negro child." The second category determined the affective attitude toward the dolls—which one was a "nice doll," which was a "nice color," which "looks bad," and which they would like to play with or liked best. Finally, the children were asked, "Give me the doll that looks like you."

The results were all too clear-cut. Most of the children accurately perceived the racial characteristic of skin color; they could select correctly the doll that looked like a white child or a Negro child. Table 10-1 sum-

Table 10-1   Affective Responses and Self-Perceptions
of Negro 3-Year-Olds and 7-Year-Olds in the Dolls Test

Instruction and Choices	Responses	
	3-Year-Olds	7-Year-Olds
"Give me the doll that looks bad."		
Colored doll	68%	43%
White doll	19	17
No choice	13	40
"Give me the doll that looks like you."		
Colored doll	36	87
White doll	61	13
No choice	3	0

Based on data from K. B. & M. P. Clark, 1958.

marizes the results that primarily concern us. The prominence of an internalized, negative self-image is clearly shown: 68 percent of the 3-year-olds saw the *brown* doll as looking "bad"! The bottom group of numbers reveals the frequency of denial at this age level: 61 percent saw the *white* doll as resembling *themselves*. These data strongly suggest that the majority of the younger Negro children denied their *own* skin color in order to avoid the painfully low self-esteem associated with its accurate perception. The following observations by the experimenters support this inference.

Some of the children who were free and relaxed in the beginning of the experiment broke down and cried or became somewhat negativistic during the latter part when they were required to make self-identifications. Indeed, two children ran out of the testing room, unconsolable, convulsed in tears. . . . A northern five-year-old dark child felt compelled to explain his identification with the brown doll by making the following unsolicited statement: "I burned my face and made it spoil." A seven-year-old northern light child went to great pains to explain that he is actually white but: "I look brown because I got a suntan in the summer" [K. B. & M. P. Clark, 1958, p. 611].

The data for the 7-year-olds show the decrease in denial with increasing age: 43 percent of these children still judged brown skin to be "bad," but only 13 percent denied their own skin color. Even this, of course, is a high percentage.

The fact that 3-year-old Negro children had internalized values should not surprise us, for the general phenomenon of internalization in small children has already been discussed. The white man's world touches such young children in many ways that could transmit the negative attitude of the majority of white people toward the Negro. But it seems quite likely that the parents of the Negro children had themselves internalized the white man's attitude that dark skin is "bad" and had passed it on to their children. In his recent autobiography, *Manchild in the Promised Land*, Claude Brown, a Negro, portrays his father's negative view of dark skin and how he explicitly transmitted that view. We can be sure that there is also a great deal of implicit communication of the same value from the time the child is born.

> Papa used to make me mad with, "Who was that old boy you was with today, that old tar-black boy?" . . .
> I knew that Pimp [Brown's younger brother] was at an age when he'd be bringing his friends around, and Papa would be talking that same stuff about, "Who's that black so-and-so?" If you brought somebody to the house who was real light-skinned, Papa would say, "They're nice," or "They're nice lookin'." . . .
> I remember one time when Papa was telling his favorite story about how he could have passed for white when he first came to New York and moved down on the Lower East Side. He became a janitor of a building there. He said everybody thought he was white until they saw Uncle McKay. . . . Papa said if it wasn't for McKay, he could have passed for white. This story used to get on my nerves, and I thought it was probably bothering Pimp now too. Sometimes I wanted to tell him, "Shit, man, why don't you just go on some place where you can pass for white, if that's the way you feel about it? And stop sitting here with all us real colored niggers and talkin' about it." . . .
> I wondered if it was good for him to be around all that old crazy talk, because I imagined that all my uncles who were dark-skinned—Uncle McKay, Uncle Ted, Uncle Brother—felt that Papa didn't care too much for them because they were dark-skinned, and I supposed that Pimp might have gotten that feeling too [Brown, 1965, pp. 276–77].

Anyone who reads this remarkable book will realize that Claude Brown's awareness of the devastating effects of the transmission of the negative self-image by Negro parents, and of course by white people, and his protest against it were intimately involved in his victory over such effects.

Why do some Negro parents add to the misery their children must bear in a generally white society? Claude Brown's father had to maintain his own self-esteem in a world bent on devastating it. This is what he was doing when he unconsciously internalized the white man's negative attitude toward black skin. (We shall discuss this process in more detail in a moment.)

The Mark of Oppression by Kardiner and Ovesey (1951), psychoanalysts especially interested in the relationship between man and society, shows by the case study method the extent to which the self-esteem of their Negro subjects was damaged by the social climate in America. That climate, of course, is now changing so rapidly that the presently available studies will soon be outdated. American Negroes are developing an intense pride in their black color and culture. If they continue to do so, and if the attitudes of more and more white people change, future Negro parents and children should be quite different from those reflected in Claude Brown's book and in the studies by the Clarks and by Kardiner and Ovesey.

A study by Tagiuri, Bruner, and Blake (1958) suggests that denial of perceptions of being disliked by the people around us *may* be a more widespread process than we realize. These investigators asked sailors, summer campers, and students to express their likes and dislikes for their associates and also to state how they thought their associates felt about them. The subjects' accuracy in perceiving negative attitudes about themselves was poor. This outcome could be due to defensive denial.

Identification

IDENTIFICATION WITH THE AGGRESSOR

We discussed in Chapter 5 how the Oedipal boy defends against his anxiety that his father will castrate him: He adopts his father's moral values and punitive attitudes, applies them to himself, and consequently represses his Oedipal complex. In the process, the boy takes a giant step along the path of superego development. We have just seen how Claude Brown's father had internalized the loathing many white people have for black skin, and we saw indirect evidence that a large number of Negro children had done the same thing by the time they were 3 years old. These are instances of identification with the aggressor.

Anna Freud (1936) relates the following story.

One day a male teacher consulted August Aichorn, a former colleague of Miss Freud and author of a well-known book, *Wayward Youth* (1935). The boy the teacher had brought along with him made odd faces whenever the teacher scolded him in class. The other pupils laughed uproariously at this, and the teacher was at his wits' end: Was the boy intentionally ridiculing him, or was it just a nervous habit? Aichorn noticed that the boy grimaced involuntarily during the interview whenever the teacher became angry. Furthermore, the grimaces were a caricature of the teacher's angry look. Frightened by the facial expression, the boy had unconsciously imitated it.

Anna Freud gives another example of the same process.

A little girl was afraid to cross a hall in the dark for fear she might meet a ghost. She resolved this fear by gesturing peculiarly as she ran across the hall. "There's no need to be afraid in the hall," she explained to her little brother, "you just have to pretend that you're the ghost who might meet you [1936, p. 119]." Copying the aggressor's *physical characteristics* made the fear go away.

In the following example the identification took a slightly different form.

One day a 6-year-old boy in therapy with Anna Freud was noticeably cross and unfriendly with her, and he played very aggressively, cutting into pieces with his knife everything he could lay his hands on. Why? He had just been to the dentist and this "aggressor" had hurt him. The identification here was with the *aggression* of the aggressor, not with his physical characteristics. The boy did not play at being a dentist; he played only at being aggressive, but he did that with a vengeance.

This same child demonstrated still another form of identification with the aggressor—the unconscious adoption of symbols representing *idealized attributes* of the aggressor to bolster his self-esteem as well as to increase his courage. We quote Anna Freud's succinct account of this episode:

On another occasion this little boy came to me just after he had a slight accident. He had been joining in an outdoor game at school and had run full tilt against the fist of the games-master . . . . My little patient's lip was bleeding and his face tear-stained, and he tried to conceal both facts by putting up his hand as a screen. I endeavoured to comfort and reassure him. He was in a woe-begone condition when he left me, but the next day he appeared holding himself very erect and dressed in full armour. On his head he wore a military cap and he had a toy sword at his side and a pistol in his hand. When he saw my surprise at this transformation, he simply said, "I just wanted to have these things on when I was playing with you." He did not, however, play; instead, he sat down and wrote a letter to his mother: "Dear Mummy, please, please, please, please send me the pocket-knife you promised me and don't wait till Easter!" Here again we cannot say that, in order to master the anxiety-experience of the previous day, he was impersonating the teacher with whom he had collided. Nor, in this instance, was he imitating the latter's aggression. The weapons and armour, being manly attributes, evidently symbolized the teacher's strength and . . , helped the child to identify himself with the masculinity of the adult and so to defend himself against narcissistic mortification or actual mishaps [A. Freud, 1936, pp. 120–21].

These episodes of identification with the aggressor share an underlying pattern:

1. Somebody threatens or distresses a person.
2. The "victim" identifies with some aspect of the "aggressor's" behavior that was involved in the aggression: values and consequent criticism, physical features, aggression, a symbol of the strength of the aggressor.
3. Concomitant with or following such identifications the victim's emotional distress disappears.

How does identification with the aggressor provide this relief? Probably by a combination of factors.

When Freud thought about episodes in children's play resembling those we have described, he noticed that they involve the *active* reenactment of a *passive* unpleasant experience (1920a, 1926). The boy with the knife, for example, "hurt" other things by cutting them up after he had been hurt by the dentist. The change from helpless passivity to doing something, anything, always makes one feel better. This relief produced by activity does not necessarily have a realistic basis. The grimacing boy, for example, infuriated his teacher. Realistically based or not, the relief seems to come about from internal changes. Activity releases or dissipates the physiological and psychological tension produced by traumatic stimulation. But probably more important is the *change in self-perception* brought about by actively identifying with the aggressor. Bodily sensations of helplessness and passivity cease. One perceives in one's own behavior qualities of the aggressor—a facial expression, articles of clothing, aggressiveness. Most important, one perceives oneself as the aggressor, not as the victim. This is only possible because one is *fantasying* that he is the aggressor. The little girl deliberately and overtly imagined she was the feared ghost; others do the same thing unconsciously.

A blatant example of this phenomenon in adults is the "you can't fire me, I quit" stereotype. Fearing he will be fired, the employee turns the tables. The student who suffers at the hands of a strict and critical teacher frequently acts the same way in class discussions or when he writes his term paper. Now *he* tears to shreds the work of leading thinkers.

IDENTIFICATION WITH THE AGGRESSOR IN EXTREME SITUATIONS

The same defensive mechanism we have been discussing produces one of the most insidious consequences of organized hostility and sadism in prisons and other authoritarian situations: It induces detrimental personality changes in the victim. Such identifications, however, may enable the victims to cope with their immediate, extreme situations.

In 1938 the Nazis imprisoned Bruno Bettelheim, a Jewish Viennese psychoanalyst who is now one of the leading analysts and child therapists in America. Bettelheim endured a year at Dachau and Buchenwald, two particularly notorious concentration camps. Partly to help ward off the disintegration of his personality, he carefully observed how the victims reacted to the extremely cruel, inhuman conditions of these camps (Bettelheim, 1943). One outcome of his observations is a vivid picture of how "old" prisoners—those confined at least 3 years—eventually came to identify with their cruel Gestapo jailers. This was an insidious, unconscious process—a last desperate measure to cope with their extreme condition. The identifications involved the physical attributes of the Gestapo, their aggression, and their values.

When speaking angrily to other inmates, the old prisoners came to use the vocabulary of the Gestapo. They wore old pieces of Gestapo uniforms or tried to alter their own prison clothes so they would resemble Gestapo uniforms. The old prisoners often treated other inmates just as cruelly as the guards treated them. The Gestapo got rid of "unfit" prisoners—the complainers, those who could not adjust, and those who disobeyed orders or could not work in the labor gangs. Sometimes the old prisoners collaborated with the Gestapo in this weeding out of the unfit. Some prisoners turned traitor, and the others decided it was necessary to kill them if the others were to survive. Identification with their own Gestapo torturers caused the old prisoners to kill these traitors slowly, torturing them for days.

Clearly, the old prisoners had internalized Gestapo values, and some came to share the Gestapo's anti-Semitism. (Bettelheim closes his account with the reminder that identification with the Gestapo was but one part of the picture. At times the very same prisoners also acted with extraordinary courage in defying the Gestapo.)

The growing literature about the Negro contains many references to a very similar phenomenon. Kenneth Clark gives many examples of it in *Dark Ghetto* (1965), ranging from hair straightening and skin bleaching to an abandonment of Negro values and culture for the white man's. Friedman (1966) describes a young Negro woman who had completely identified with the white man's values and racial attitudes, even to the point of unknowingly referring to Negroes as "they," unconsciously accepting the concept of "black gorilla," which her parents had called her as a child, and avoiding most pleasures in life because they seemed "niggerlike." The journalist Jack Newfield (1966) tells of a Negro kitchen worker at the store in Greensboro, North Carolina, where the first sit-in occurred. She spoke like some white Southerners when she called the original sit-inners "a disgrace to their race" and "ignorant." According to Newfield, many parents of Negro leaders in the nonviolent civil rights movement expressed the same attitudes about them. Several presidents of southern Negro colleges suspended students who participated in the growing movement. Those who take this stand, of course, are regarded as "Uncle Toms" and as "white man's niggers" by many Negro parents and educators who take pride in the civil rights activities of young Negro adults. Much of the meaning of their epithets lies in their allusion to the tendency of the more conservative Negroes to identify with the white aggressors. (Sarnoff [1951] indicates that the same process may be involved in the psychodynamics of the anti-Semitic Jew.)

IDENTIFICATION WITH THE AGGRESSOR
AND SUPEREGO FORMATION

We are now in a better position than we were in Chapter 5 to discuss the hypothesis that identification with the aggressor plays an important part in superego development.

Defensive identification with the aggressor consists essentially of unconsciously imitating attributes of a feared person—his values, his aggression, and the form of his aggressive expression, for example—and the consequent relief from distressing affect. The internal regulation of behavior by one's superego involves not only the internalization of values (notably those of parents) but also the "awakening" of those values by one's wishes and feelings, the subjugation of these to one's values, and self-criticism for transgressions. Thus, it is a big jump from the relatively simple phenomenon of defensive identification with the aggressor to self-controlled, conscience-regulated behavior. If this hypothesis—that identification with the aggressor plays an important role in superego development—is valid, identification with the aggressor in childhood should reflect the transition. We shall cite here some illustrative observations indicating that the transitional forms do occur, and we shall suggest their nature.

Anna Freud (1936) describes a curious pattern of behavior shown by a boy who lived in a children's home.

> He used to ring the entrance bell very loudly and then, while waiting for the housemaid to let him in, would become frightened that she would scold him for making so much noise. When she finally came to the door, *he would angrily scold her,* ostensibly for taking so long to answer the bell. Actually, he was identifying with the aggression he anticipated from her. He was scolding her as he feared she would scold him for his misbehavior.

The following observation, also from Anna Freud, shows that the same anticipation and externally directed aggression can be set in motion even by sexual *thoughts and wishes.*

> A 5-year-old boy who was in child analysis with Jenny Waelder in Vienna was usually docile and passive, but episodically he would become "fiercely aggres-

sive." Pretending he was a lion, he would roar and attack Mrs. Waelder. Or he would carry a stick with him and hit everything in sight, pretending he was *a devil who punished naughty children*. He would try to hit his mother and grandmother in the face, and eventually he threatened them with kitchen knives. Mrs. Waelder noticed that each of these outbursts occurred whenever the theme of masturbation was about to come out in his therapy. The outbursts ceased when these tabooed thoughts and feelings did come out and were openly discussed by Mrs. Waelder and himself. In his aggressive episodes he was treating others as his parents had treated him when they had caught him masturbating—they had shouted at him, slapped his face, and beat him with a rod. And he fantasied that they might even cut off his penis with a knife. But his identification was anticipatory, in two senses: Thoughts and wishes that were *about* to become conscious and overt evoked identification *before* any actual punishment occurred.

Both of these observations reveal transitional stages in the step from defensive identification with the aggressor to adult superego functioning. In neither instance is the child simply defending against a past or present external aggression, as in the first observations that were presented on page 161. He is, instead, identifying with an *anticipated punishment,* and this anticipated punishment is *linked with his own behavior*—actual misbehavior or only "bad" thoughts and wishes, even unconscious ones. The child has become a "self-starter" with respect to *his* punitive behavior. But his punitive behavior is not yet directed against himself or even against another guilty person. It is directed only against an external "aggressor."

One can observe children in other additional transitional stages as well. Often they scold other people for projected misdeeds or wishes, for the very things they are beginning to feel anxious and guilty about themselves.

We have discussed here the role of identification with the aggressor in superego formation and functioning. But it is not *only* fear that is involved in these matters. *Love for our parents, especially when we renounce them as sexual love objects, also contributes to identifications that produce many of our ideals.*

IDENTIFICATION WITH THE LOST LOVE OBJECT

We have already seen that people defend against the pain of object loss by identifying with the loved person. In Chapters 5 and 6 we discussed identification when there is active renunciation of a love relationship. The object loss need not be permanent, as it is in death and Oedipal renunciation, for identification to occur. It need only be painful. People often temporarily identify with the loved one when *unwanted* transient separations are forced upon them.

We shall now consider some important questions about the process of identification that we have not yet discussed.

THE BASIC MECHANISM
OF IDENTIFICATION: AN HYPOTHESIS

"Identification" is a descriptive concept denoting the tendency of one person to acquire personality attributes of another person. Its relationship to object loss and to encounters with aggressors is grounded in empirical, clinical observation. The nature of the mechanism or process that produces identifications is a different matter. Frequently the terms *internalization, incorporation,* and *introjection* are used as though they indicated the nature of the process, but they are little more than metaphors. Some people do have conscious and unconscious fantasies of eating their loved ones, and others have subjective experiences of fusing with other persons, even of complete bodily identity. But, obviously, no one actually takes another person inside himself. The nature of the *mechanism* of achieving an identification is still an open question. Basic ingredients in this process may be our memories of the other person and the matching of our behavior to those memories by carefully observing and correcting ourselves. Such a process would be analogous to that by which children *unknowingly* adopt the precise speech patterns of their parents. There, too, memory traces of someone else's behavior and self-monitoring and self-regulation based on sensory feedback from one's own behavior (the preconscious hearing of one's own speech, for example) are crucial. According to this hypothesis, the identification mechanism is patterned after what Wiener (1948, 1950) calls a *negative-feedback process*. In such a process feedback signals result in the minimizing of any deviations from a preset pattern. The development of speech is a good example.

One real-life example will illustrate the hypothetical process.

A middle-aged man grew a beard for the first time a few months after his father died in a distant part of the country. The son had been told that his father had gone unshaved for several days just before he died, and one relative had emphasized to him the shock she had felt when she had beheld the father's helpless, whiskered face instead of his usual robust, cleanly shaved cheeks and chin. Hearing this, the son pictured clearly how his father must have looked. Then the image vanished. A few weeks after this experience he decided to let his beard grow—"just for kicks." But for days, each time he washed and saw his whiskery image in the mirror, a vision of his dying father's unshaved face flashed before his eyes and he experienced a welling-up of grief. After more than 2 years he shaved the beard off, ostensibly because he had "had his kicks." Actually, it was because his most intense period of mourning had ended. One feature of his behavior illustrates the self-observation and correction—the negative feedback process—mentioned above. He felt comfortable only when he had his beard very short—to match his memory image of his dying father's unshaved face.

Such a process pertains only to the mechanism of identification that might be set in motion by the distress of object loss and threatening aggressors. It does not account for the *relief* of emotional distress provided by identification. We have already discussed on page 162 how identification with the aggressor might provide this relief.

Why does identification with a lost love object ease the grief of object loss? Probably because we unconsciously fantasy that we *are* the lost person and carry on a largely unconscious emotional relationship with the inner replica of the lost object. Miss Eaton unconsciously hated herself in precisely the same way and on the same grounds as she hated her sister. People can love themselves (as identified with the lost object) in much the same way they love any memento or facsimile of the lost object—his picture, clothing, or favorite chair, for example. The man with the beard bestowed all the tender care and affection on his whiskers that he wished he had been able to give his dying father. In fact, his conscious emotional attitude toward his whiskers varied with his unconscious fantasy relationship to his dead father. He loved or hated them (and his father) one day, pitied them another, admired them frequently, and finally gave them up. Like this man, Dora, who developed her father's coughs, and women who adopt their husbands' professions after their deaths all find relief from their grief because unconsciously they have not suffered the loss. In their unconscious fantasies things are still the same.

Ego Restriction

When a person perceives that his accomplishments are inferior to someone else's, his self-esteem is lowered. Many people who cannot tolerate such a situation bring it to an end and prevent it from arising again in the future by simply abandoning the activity involved. Anna Freud first delineated this defense and named it *ego restriction*. The following episode, which occurred during her psychoanalytic treatment of a small boy, illustrates the phenomenon. In her own words,

> One day, when he was at my house, he found a little Magic Drawing-Block, which appealed to him greatly. He began enthusiastically to rub the pages, one by one, with a coloured pencil and was pleased when I did the same. Suddenly, however, he glanced at what I was doing, came to a stop and was evidently upset. The next moment he put down his pencil, pushed the whole apparatus (hitherto jealously guarded) across to me, stood up and said, "You go on doing it; I would much rather watch." Obviously, when he looked at my drawing, it struck him as more beautiful, more skillful or somehow more perfect than his own and the comparison gave him a shock. He instantly decided that he would not compete anymore, since the results were disagreeable, and thereupon he abandoned the activity which, a moment ago, had given him pleasure. *He adopted the role of the spectator, who does nothing and so cannot have his performance compared with that of someone else. By imposing this restriction on himself the child avoided a repetition of the disagreeable impression* [Anna Freud, 1936, p. 101; italics added].

Escape and avoidance of an unpleasant stimulus situation, then, is the essential feature of this defense. But whereas other forms of escape and avoidance usually physically remove the person from an unpleasant situation, ego restriction entails the subject's stopping an *activity* he himself is performing. The abandonment of the activity then becomes permanent and constitutes a restriction in one or more areas of life.

Ego restriction may occur in connection with any activity. The intelligent student who does not study because he is mortified if he does not get an A is engaging in ego restriction. The wife who never entertains at home because she feels her cooking and table-setting are inferior to those of the people she would invite is doing the same thing. Many potential talents lie fallow simply because people cannot tolerate the inevitable imperfections in their first efforts.

Ego restrictions differ from what is commonly meant by *inhibitions*, such as the "stupidity" or ineffectiveness of the intelligent student who *does* study or the chronic stammering and loss of voice of the person who *does* keep trying to speak in public. Unconscious conflicts over sexuality or aggression cause such disturbances, just as they caused the avoidances discussed in Chapters 6–9. Some students, for example, become sexually aroused when they study—either because of the subject matter or because of intellectual activity per se. When this happens, they become anxious or feel guilty, and the stage is set for various kinds of disturbances of studying and learning. Sexual thoughts and feelings can be distracting. Anxiety and guilty feelings can disrupt learning. Or they can motivate defenses, such as a general inhibition of intellectual functioning. Stammering is frequently caused by the inhibition of the urge to speak aggressively. One patient in psychotherapy stammered severely in those interviews when she was afraid to vent her anger at the therapist and the world. But the stammering itself turned out to be an indirect expression of her anger: She admitted to taking a malicious pleasure in the fact that her stammering prevented the therapist from understanding her.

Anna Freud suggested a useful criterion for distinguishing ego restrictions from inhibitions resulting from unconscious conflicts. In ego restrictions the person is perfectly satisfied to give up the activity and turns readily to other activities in which he does not experience insults to his self-esteem. In inhibitions, however, the person does not give up the activity in spite of all the suffering it causes him. In fact, he cannot give it up for the same reason he cannot complete it effectively: because of its sexual or aggressive meaning to him. We might say that he is trapped by his approach-avoidance conflict. In ego restriction, however, there is no *hidden* sexual or aggressive gratification in the abandoned activity. Here the approach gradient is so weak that it never rises above the avoidance gradient. As a result, the individual turns with relief to another activity.

Major Aspects of Defense
Against External Dangers

Summarized here are the major aspects of processes of defense oriented toward external dangers—the danger situations listed at the beginning of this chapter.

1. The interaction of external stimuli and internal motives gives rise to perceptions of the unpleasant external stimuli and to disturbing perceptions of oneself.

2. These perceptions evoke corresponding unpleasant emotional experiences, either for realistic reasons or because they activate unconscious memories, fantasies, or conflicts in the manner illustrated in Chapters 6–9. Motivated by these unpleasant emotions, one can reduce their intensity by adaptive coping or by various defenses. We are concerned here only with defenses.

3. Physically *escaping or avoiding* the relevant external stimuli can terminate any of the various unpleasant emotions previously discussed in this section of the book, ranging from the intense pain of frustration, through separation anxiety, to fear of ego disorganization.

4. *Denial* prevents the realistic perception of unpleasant external stimuli by simply blotting out or distorting the perception. Alterations in the distribution of attention and the substitution of fantasies or hallucinations for the realistic perceptions achieve these results. Denial, too, can terminate any of the unpleasant emotions.

5. *Identification with the dreaded stimulus,* which is nearly always another person, can terminate all the unpleasant emotions. *Identification with an aggressor* who is threatening one's physical welfare is the paradigm of this defense mechanism. In this defense the subject perceives himself to be like the threatening person and thereby perceives that person as less threatening. The subject's conscious and unconscious fantasies, as well as related changes in his overt behavior, form the bases for these changes in perception of self and of external stimuli.

6. *Identification with a lost or renounced love object* eases the pain of loss. Unconscious fantasies that he is the lost person, and related changes in overt behavior, alter the subject's self-perception. In his unconscious fantasies he is now both himself and the lost object and perpetuates within himself the emotional relationship that existed between himself and the object.

7. *Ego restriction* protects one from the loss of self-esteem. By abandoning his attempts at achievement, which he or others may evaluate negatively,

the subject brings the mortifying stimulus situation to an end and prevents its recurrence.

8. Escape and avoidance, denial, ego restriction, and identification with the "aggressor" and with the lost love object all achieve their defensive effect by interrupting and modifying the chain of events leading from external stimuli to the unpleasant emotional reactions. These defenses are oriented toward the external danger situations.

9. A person can also avoid experiencing the unpleasant emotions by orienting defenses toward these very reactions. He can, for example, repress or project fear or guilt. Such processes were not discussed in this chapter because examples of them have already been shown and because these additional defense mechanisms will be dealt with in the last two chapters.

Every man has reminiscences which he would not tell to every-one, but only to his friends. He has other matters in his mind which he would not reveal even to his friends, but only to him-self, and that in secret. But there are other things which a man is afraid to tell even to himself, and every decent man has a number of such things stored away in his mind.

FYODOR DOSTOEVSKY. Notes from Underground

CHAPTER 11
DEFENSE AGAINST DRIVES AND AFFECTS

L ife would be reasonably easy if the only sources of emotional turmoil were external stimuli. But many people are frightened or feel guilty because of their own natural sexual and aggressive drives, and when this happens they often try to avoid having sexual or aggressive feelings or thoughts or engaging in overt sexual or aggressive behavior. We have discussed many examples of such conflicts, ranging from those of Ed, Duane, and Edie, described in Chapter 2, through Miss Eaton's guilt-ridden conflict over her hatred for her sister, which we examined in Chapter 8. Our primary concern in these two final chapters is to discuss systematically the nature of such conflicts. Most of this chapter is devoted to the nature of the defenses against sexuality and aggression. Of the ten such defenses we shall discuss, the first six—repression, projection, reaction formation, negation, isolation, and undoing—all result in a *damming up* of a sexual or aggressive drive or emotional state and consequent relief from the anxiety and guilt evoked when those drives are aroused. The last four—turning around upon the self, reversal, regression, and sublimation—all change the *nature* of the drive itself and serve both to relieve the anxiety and guilt and to provide some gratification of the now transformed drive. Our discussion will consolidate and summarize the main points illustrated by our cases, and it will also include new material. The last chapter will consider some additional points about conflict and defense.

The Motives
for Defense Against Drives

In Chapter 3 we noted that when people defend against their sexual and aggressive drives, they act as if they are anticipating dangerous consequences if they express those drives. The dangers are the ones we discussed in Chapters 6–9.

FEAR OF EXTERNAL DANGERS

Some people anticipate that if they engage in sexual and aggressive behavior, the people they depend upon for security will leave them or the people they care about will reject them. Others think they will be shamed or ridiculed; still others think they will be physically harmed. Some even unconsciously believe their own anger or sexual excitement may kill the people they love.

When people anticipate such dangers as being abandoned, rejected, or castrated, they are not engaging in cool, cognitive expectations like predicting tomorrow's weather. They are experiencing *anticipatory fear reactions*. In these reactions the bodily changes and distressing sensations of fear blend with specific memories and thoughts that define the nature of the particular danger situation anticipated. *Our anxieties consist of just such specific anticipatory fear reactions.* For example, Ed's castration anxiety, as expressed in his dreams, was not simply the bodily reaction and feeling of fear. It included ideational content: that his penis would be cut off by a "witch" or a doctor if he engaged in sexual behavior. The woman suffering from separation anxiety, discussed in Chapter 6, experienced fear too, but her memories and thoughts about separation specifically defined that fear as separation anxiety.

FEAR OF INTENSE DRIVES

Many people anticipate that if they become sexually excited or angry, they will be *helpless in the face of intense urges* for which there is no relief *or* that they will lose control of themselves, that *their usual personality organization will disintegrate*. For example, some subjects fled from the sensory deprivation experimental situation as their sexual feelings and thoughts became intense and they began to fear that they were losing self-control.

FEAR OF CONSCIENCE

When the child internalizes his parents' moral standards and their observing, evaluating, and punitive functions, he begins to scold and punish himself for violating standards that are now his own. Such self-directed aggression produces *feelings of guilt* and of *lowered self-esteem*; the extreme intensity such feelings can reach was shown in the case of Miss Eaton, among others. Most people will do anything to avoid guilt and lowered self-esteem, including defending against the sexual or aggressive thoughts, feelings, or overt expression that instigate them.

Before we develop a superego, we feel safe from external censure as long as we do not actually *do* bad things and as long as no one, especially our parents, *knows* that we are wishing to do them or are thinking about them. Adults whose morality depends on what they can "get away with" are still functioning this way. After we develop a superego, however, *we* observe, judge, convict, punish ourselves, and feel guilty or worthless for mere *intentions*, even *unconscious* ones, that conflict with our personal moral code.

The motives for defense against sexual and aggressive drives, then, are the various anxieties we have discussed, plus lowered self-esteem and guilt. In *inner* conflict, these unpleasant affects are stimulated internally by drive arousal and as anticipatory reactions, not by external events. The slightest trace of such an unpleasant affect, an emotional "signal," instigates defenses (Freud, 1926). It is quite probable that such a pattern of internal regulation—the drives producing emotional signals, which then instigate defenses—is a product of learning (Dollard & Miller, 1950). In a moment we shall examine the defenses that are used against sexuality and aggression.

Direct Defense
Against Unpleasant Affects

In addition to defending against the external stimuli or the internal drives that arouse anxieties and guilt, people also defend directly against these distressing emotions. Clinical observations have shown that the defense mechanisms used for this purpose are the same as those used against sexuality and aggression. Ed, for example, not only repressed his incestuous wishes; he also repressed his castration thoughts and sometimes

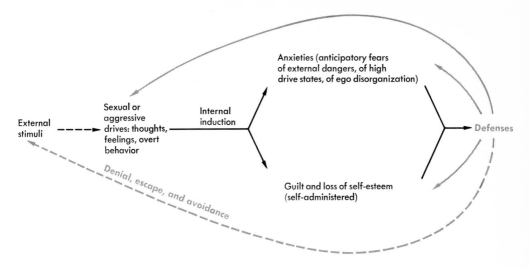

*Figure 11-1   Internal conflict: the relation between external stim-
uli, drives, motives for defense, and defenses.*

*Since external stimuli are not essential for internal conflicts, their
role and the defenses against them are represented by dashed
arrows. In internal conflict the person's drives induce anxiety,
guilt, or loss of self-esteem, which in turn instigate defenses. The
defenses may be directed against the drives or the unpleasant
emotional reactions or both.*

the anxiety associated with them. In the discussion of the defenses used
against the sexual and aggressive drives we shall occasionally illustrate their
use against the distressing emotions themselves.

Figure 11-1 schematizes the relation between the sexual and aggressive
drives, the motives for defense, and the defenses in internal conflicts. The
diagram also represents the influence of external stimuli in internal conflicts. Generally speaking, external stimuli are not essential for internal
conflicts, although they may trigger such conflicts, as we saw in Chapters
6–9. One way they trigger inner conflicts is by "releasing" drive thoughts,
feelings, and tendencies to action when the individual is in a high drive state,
as most adults know from encounters with members of the opposite sex,
especially after a period of abstinence. In such situations, some people reduce their drive-aroused anxiety or guilt by using the "stimulus-oriented"
defenses of denial or escape and avoidance. Ed avoided sexual intimacy with
his wife, and Ray avoided close male companionship to relieve the conflict over his unconscious homosexual wishes (see Chapters 6 and 7). Since
these defenses have already been discussed in detail, they will not be considered here.

Flight and Barricades

Man does gain control over his sexuality and aggression, his anxieties and guilt, but he cannot obliterate them from his life. Yet this is what he attempts to do in the process of defense against drives and affects. Figuratively speaking, he tries to run away from his own sexual and aggressive, anxious and guilty thoughts, feelings, and action tendencies. But his own internal workings and the inevitable provocations of the external world see to it that his drives and distressing emotions keep chasing him in hot and close pursuit. Continuing in his futile attempt to escape them, man tries to build barricades between himself and his drives and affects. As Edie's eating difficulty showed, a single barricade does not work. So he builds another, and another.

The process of defense nearly always utilizes two tendencies analogous to flight and the erection of barricades. We have already seen these two tendencies at work in the defenses against unpleasant external stimuli. In denial, for example, they took the form of withdrawal of attention from unpleasant perceptions and the substitution of wishful fantasies or perceptions for them. In a similar fashion, many of the defenses against drives function as barricades against "the return of the repressed," as Freud noted (1915c, 1937). But even repression utilizes these two tendencies.

It is important to remember that *all defenses operate automatically and outside of awareness.* Defenses are motivated, but they are not executed voluntarily. The average person does not know what defenses he is using, nor can he voluntarily stop using a defense if its presence is pointed out to him.

The following discussion consolidates and summarizes the main points about each defense mechanism, some of which could not be made explicit earlier when examples of their use were presented.

Repression

The basic empirical evidence of repression is an *inappropriate under-reaction* to a relevant situation and *indirect evidence that the repressed tendencies are actually present.* A nasty insult usually evokes some response—a flushed face, a clenched fist, an angry thought or retort, or all of these. A sexy picture or story, or the intimacy of the wedding night, usually arouses sexual reactions—widespread autonomic changes, localized ones in the genitals giving rise to sexual feelings, wishes to make love or fantasies of doing so, actual lovemaking. Repression prevents these reactions. *Repression* is the exclusion of drive thoughts and feelings from consciousness and the inhibition of related overt activity and autonomic bodily changes.

These effects are achieved by the twofold process noted earlier. The "flight" can be observed very clearly when it occurs during free association. The patient's "blank mind" indicates that he has *withdrawn his attention* from his thoughts and from the sensations arising within his body. One can even sometimes observe the body go limp, especially when people are repressing anger.

If this were all that happened when a strong drive is repressed, the repressed thoughts, feelings, and action tendencies would soon reappear. But the drive is still there, producing thoughts and feelings that attract attention again and threaten to burst forth in behavior. So the "barricade" process also occurs. Perhaps its simplest form is a shift to an active immobility—a not-thinking, not-feeling, not doing anything. At these times, patients in psychoanalysis frequently report such sensations as, "My jaws feel like they are wired shut," or "I am beginning to feel like I *won't* think, not just that I can't think of anything." A common form of repressive barricade is to shift attention to some *external* stimulus, the more "insignificant" the better. But perhaps the most common type of repressive barricade is *focusing attention and interest on displacement substitutes* for the repressed. Even the "insignificant" external stimuli that a person might "just happen to notice" usually prove to be displacement substitutes. One young man, for example, suddenly became preoccupied with a spot of peeling paint on the ceiling; he was repressing the wish to shake hands with and contaminate his analyst. The peeling paint "reminded" him of a spot of ringworm he had noticed on his hand that morning. The Wolf Man's sexual reactions to kneeling and squatting women (Chapter 5), Ed's marriage to a "tabooed" woman (Chapter 6), and a husband's angry reaction to his wife after a frustrating day at the office are all examples of displacement substitutes.

It is the presence of repressed, unfulfilled wishes and urges that produces displacement substitutes. But once produced, they serve as repressive barricades, provided they do not resemble the repressed too much. In time the substitutes take on more and more of the qualities of the repressed, and further repression involving the substitute occurs. Ed's sexual relationship with his wife illustrates a common sequence. (1) When he first met his future wife, Ed had repressed his incestuous memories and wishes. Furthermore, Ed felt that he had found a girl who was markedly dissimilar from his sister, especially because of her tabooed ethnic origin. His sister always came off the loser in his frequent and emotionally involved comparisons of the two. Not realizing his wife-to-be was a partial substitute for his sister, Ed became very involved with her and was able to enjoy all aspects of their relationship to a certain extent. (2) By means of his involvement in this relationship and the satisfaction of his sexual urges, he was able to keep his "sister complex" repressed. But as time went by, his unconscious thinking endowed her more and more with the qualities of his sister until his sister replaced his wife in his dreams, as was illustrated in Chapter 6. He finally found himself thinking that living with his wife was like living with his sister. (3) During this development, his sexual life with his wife became the target of defense too.

Ed's experiences illustrate two other important features of repression. The first is a distinction Freud made between *after-repression* and *primal repression*. If something "reminds" a person of his repressed memories or wishes, it too will often be repressed. A common example would be forgetting the name of someone because it is the same as the already "forgotten" name of someone else about whom we have many repressed feelings and memories. The "new forgetting" is an instance of after-repression; the "old forgetting" was the primal repression. Ed's eventual repression of his wishes, feelings, and behavior toward his wife was after-repression; his childhood repression of his incestuous sexual desires and fantasies was primal repression. The second feature of repression emphasized by Freud and illustrated by Ed is that childhood repression is a prerequisite for later repression and predisposes the individual for this fate. Thus, the primal repressions are the childhood repressions.

We have been talking about repression of drives and the feelings and memories that accompany them. But the anxious or guilty thoughts and feelings generated by those drives and feelings may also be repressed. Sometimes only the anxious or guilty thoughts are repressed; sometimes the anxious or guilty feelings are repressed; sometimes both. In Chapters 2 and 6 we described Ed's repression of his castration *thoughts*, which were manifested in his dreams. While he had repressed those thoughts, he did not repress his feelings of anxiety. Therefore he experienced an objectless anxiety when his sexual impulses were aroused. Other males might have repressed *both* their castration thoughts and feelings of fear. Little Hans and the Wolf Man did this. They were afraid of being castrated by their fathers, but they were able to tolerate and even enjoy the company of their fathers. This was possible because they had repressed both their *thoughts* and their *fears* that their fathers would castrate them. These repressed complexes were then expressed indirectly in their over-reactions of fear of large animals.

Guilt feelings and thoughts may also be repressed. An example is the adolescent who masturbates, seemingly without guilt, but then experiences such extreme guilt about his "dirty" hands that he must wash them every half-hour.

Projection

Another way to barricade against the reemergence of repressed thoughts, feelings, and action tendencies is to attribute them to another person. This is defensive *projection*. We have observed it as a defense against both drives and guilt (see Chapters 7 and 8) and as a prominent element in homosexual conflicts (Chapter 7). The present discussion will therefore be limited to two general considerations.

The projective attribution of unconscious qualities to another person is not a barren intellectual act. It creates a "perceptually real" world for the subject. Ray did not merely *think* his potential hiking companion was homosexual; he *saw* a leering and crudely seductive homosexual before him, and he responded with shock and alarm. The paranoid psychotic may spend years and thousands of dollars in a legal battle with an enemy who is perceptually real, even though only projectively created to maintain the repression of the subject's own hatred.

How does projection come about? Freud (1922) observed that the projector does not create tormentors "out of the blue." He seizes upon tiny clues in the other person's behavior, *minor* indications of the same unconscious wishes the projector is defending against. Then the projector magnifies their significance unrealistically by focusing all of his attention upon them and discounting all the *major* personality characteristics of the other person. It is analogous to the way a spot of dirt on the door changes the appearance of a new car. Suppose Ray's companion did have unconscious homosexual wishes, which caused him to act as he did. Most people would not rivet their attention on those transitory actions and elevate them into major traits. Only someone driven by unconscious homosexual wishes himself and the need to reinforce their repression would do that. Since every human being shares the same classes of unconscious wishes, which are inevitably betrayed in very slight indications, the vigilant projector has ample opportunity to find suitable victims.

Reaction Formation

In her adolescence Miss Eaton (discussed in Chapter 8) repressed her jealous hatred of her younger sister. To maintain this repression she also *reversed* (see "Reversal," below) her dominant feelings toward her sister: She exaggerated her love for her. Then, over the next few years, she developed a *general attitude of kindness* toward everyone, including her sister. This attitude became a general *personality trait*, which persisted for at least 20 years. Its major function was to maintain the repression of all her aggression. Such general personality traits with a defensive function are called *reaction formations*. They are the epitome of behaviors that oppose "the return of the repressed," for they consist of deeply ingrained attitudes that are the direct opposites of the repressed ones.

Reaction formations take various forms, depending on the nature of the drives that must be kept repressed. The general trait of orderliness and cleanliness as a defense against repressed desires to be messy and dirty is a classic example discovered by Freud (1908). Generosity is often a defense against unconscious stinginess. The asceticism developed by many adolescents often becomes an extreme reaction formation, a defense against all drive gratifications—all pleasures of the flesh, even eating, sleeping in a comfortable bed, or being warm (A. Freud, 1936).

Some people use reaction formations to *ward off repressed distressing affects*. The chronic daredevil, in every arena of life, for example, is often behaving that way to keep deep-seated anxieties repressed. His condition is called "counterphobic." Many generally unscrupulous people are actually warding off an unconscious sense of guilt. Unrelieved cheerfulness is often a reaction formation against underlying depression.

Since most reaction formations consist of socially desirable behavior, the temptation is strong to attribute them to social approval rather than to relief from anxiety and guilt over sexuality and aggression. The psychoanalytic view is that both "gains" are important but that the internal relief from anxiety and guilt is the "primary gain" and external social approval is a "secondary gain." Psychoanalysis takes this view for several reasons. One is that not all reaction formations—defensive unscrupulousness, for example—are sociably desirable. Also, many of the "socially desirable" reaction formations are carried to such an extreme, for defensive purposes, that they become socially undesirable and socially or economically disadvantageous to the individual. Yet such traits persist. The compulsively clean housekeeper makes herself work hard all day long and makes visitors so uncomfortable that they avoid her; and the compulsively orderly office worker often falls so far behind in getting his work done that he loses his job.

Such exaggeration of what is normally simply a socially desirable way of behaving is, in fact, a reliable clue that a reaction formation exists. But even reaction formations do not succeed completely in blocking the repressed impulses. Miss Eaton's kindliness, for example, was not a completely successful defense against her repressed hostility toward her sister. Throughout her twenties and thirties she still suffered from her secret ritual of repeating minor acts several times. Thus her repressed hostility still found indirect symbolic expression in very insignificant actions, and she had to magically undo the effects she superstitiously attributed to them. This coexistence of reaction formations and hidden islands of expression of the repressed impulses is a common phenomenon. The overly generous person is always a miser in some respect. And the compulsively fastidious person is very likely to have dirty toenails or underwear. Furthermore, reaction formations are likely to break down at times (when a person is drunk, for example), whereupon the repressed tendencies suddenly erupt, as in Somerset Maugham's well-known story, "Rain," about the prudish clergyman who suddenly began violently making love to the prostitute whom he thought he was trying to save from a life of evil.

Freud thought the distinction between primary and secondary gain applies to all defenses and symptoms, a possibility worth keeping in mind, especially in these days when so much emphasis is placed on the external causes of mental distress.

Negation

The comical stereotype of an angry man shouting "Who's angry? I'm *not* angry!" illustrates this defense. In *negation* a repressed thought is expressed in its negative form (Freud, 1925a). The repressed content is conscious, but with a "negative sign" attached to it.

As in repression, the individual using negation is not aware of the nature of his repressed thoughts and thus feels relieved of anxiety or guilt. But when negation is the defense, the informed onlooker can immediately tell the nature of the thoughts being defended against. He simply deletes the negative words in such statements as "I'm *not* angry"; "I *don't* think I like you"; "I *don't* remember *ever* loving my sister."

Psychoanalysts' refusal to accept negations at face value is the source of a common complaint about them: that they automatically translate a patient's "no" into a "yes," and vice versa. Actually, to determine if negation is really being employed, the psychoanalyst draws upon a variety of information. In the first example, he would notice that the person *angrily shouts* "I'm not angry!" And the patient would no doubt forcefully repeat the assertion several times. This is especially impressive when no one has asked him if he was angry. The total context and style of negation causes the analyst to think to himself: "Who says you are angry—who except another part of yourself? Why do you need to convince me and your conscious self that you aren't angry, unless you really are? Aren't you protesting too much?" After such a negation is called to the patient's attention, he often confirms its validity by acknowledging his anger.

It is easy to confuse the concepts of denial and negation. They are quite distinct both in regard to what is defended against and in behavioral content. *Denial* substitutes pleasant for unpleasant perceptions of external stimuli. *Negation* consists of negated thoughts and negated perceptions of internal states.

"I'm *not* afraid"; I'm *not* sad"; "No sir, I *don't* feel guilty or ashamed that I did it"; "I *don't* miss you"; "My feelings are *not* hurt" are all familiar examples of *negations of unpleasant affect*.

Isolation

When conflict is not intense, drive thoughts, feelings, and impulses to action blend to produce a unitary conscious experience. The defense of *isolation* shatters this experience: The individual components remain conscious or overt, or potentially so, but split apart, isolated from one another. The person who isolates has, at one moment, relatively undisguised sexual and aggressive thoughts but without feelings. Another time he will be seized with sexual or aggressive feelings without any clear thoughts, such as about the person toward whom they are directed. At another moment a relatively "cold" impulse to action will overtake him. As we shall show, selective, transitory repression of components is basic to the phenomenon of isolation.

Imagine talking with someone and suddenly having the thought of breaking his arm flash into your mind, or having an angry feeling surge up, or an urge to grab his arm and start twisting it. Many people have just such upsetting experiences, in which the drive components occur individually—robbed of their total context. These different forms of expression of the underlying anger are examples of *obsessional thoughts, obsessional feelings,* and *compulsions.* It was no accident that Freud first clearly delineated the defense of isolation in his report about the Rat Man's obsessive-compulsive neurosis (1909b), for isolation creates many of the symptoms of that neurosis.

One of the Rat Man's most troublesome thoughts arose when he was a Reserve Army officer on summer maneuvers. A fellow officer described an Oriental punishment in which a container of rats was fastened upside down on the buttocks of the criminal. The rats bored into the victim's anus. The *thought* of this happening to the woman he loved flashed through the Rat Man's mind. This thought embodied a disguised wish, and most people would have repressed it. But it became fully conscious to the Rat Man for a moment, because he isolated his pleasurable sadistic feelings from it by momentarily repressing them. His conscious experience was of an *idea* stripped of its affect. Freud saw the emotion, however, in the expression of horrified pleasure on the Rat Man's face as he described that experience.

DISPLACEMENT

Isolated feelings may occur in relatively pure form, as in sudden surges of anger with little thought content or in surges of genital sensations. Usually, however, they are *displaced* or transferred (generalized, in the language of conditioned response psychology), often onto very insignificant events. Several examples of such displacement were given in Chapter 8.

ISOLATION OF TENDER FEELING FROM SENSUAL LOVE

Isolation takes many forms, two of which will be cited here. One concerns love. Many people cannot simultaneously experience tender, loving feelings and sensual feelings without becoming anxious or guilty, but they can tolerate those feelings in isolation. As a result, they often lead double love lives. A man, for example, may carry on an intimate, tender, loving relationship with the kind of woman he idolizes and wants to marry. He cannot tolerate any sensual feelings for her, nor successfully engage in any overt sensual behavior with her. Yet he is able to enjoy sexual relations with another woman whom he looks down upon. Why does blending the sensual with his idealized love life make him anxious or guilty? Because the idealized love relationship resembles the "cleansed" relationship of the boy to his mother (Freud, 1910b). To introduce sensuality into it makes it all the more Oedipal and thus all the more anxiety-provoking and guilt-ridden.

INTELLECTUALIZATION

An exaggerated emphasis on thought, called *intellectualization*, is another frequent form of isolation. We all try to minimize our emotions when we are trying to think logically about a practical or intellectual problem. The isolator carries this process to an extreme for defensive purposes. He will talk about the most blatant sexual and aggressive matters in a highly abstract, logical manner, devoid of the feelings most people would experience if they talked about the same themes. Many adolescents use intellectualization in their struggle with their sexual and aggressive turmoil (A. Freud, 1936). A common result is the "bull session," in which questions involving sexuality and aggression are talked about in the abstract and sexual excitement or angry feelings are experienced only slightly, if at all. In this case the defense may have adaptive value; such "bull sessions" obviously help most adolescents resolve their conflicts and develop their philosophies of life.

Many people can talk about the impact of separations, bodily threats, and other unpleasant events without experiencing any feelings. Then, some time later, they will suddenly experience "free-floating," objectless anxiety. They have *isolated their distressing feelings* from the relevant memories and other thoughts.

Undoing

A person who hurts someone's feelings and then tries to make up for it, or someone who has gone too far in flirting with someone and then becomes quite indifferent or even slightly "cool" to that person, is showing normal behavior that is the prototype of undoing. The second action "undoes" the first one and thus minimizes the person's anxiety and guilt over having committed the first one. The defense of *undoing* is simply an unconscious exaggeration of this normal process. Undoing, as illustrated by the Rat Man and Miss Eaton in Chapter 8, often attempts to "undo what isolation has already done." The Rat Man's kicking the stone loose in the road, for example, gave direct expression to his angry wish that his girlfriend's carriage would hit it and turn over. The act of kicking the stone loose from the road's surface was not accompanied by angry thoughts and feelings about her. They and the act had been isolated from each other. When he then removed the stone from the road, he was undoing the "isolated" act. The pairing of isolation and undoing is especially noticeable in obsessive-compulsive disorders.

Inhibition is the ultimate effect of the defenses we have just discussed—of repression, projection, reaction formation, negation, isolation, and undoing. They exclude from consciousness and overt behavior either wishes, bodily changes and feelings, or impulses to action that would bring drive gratification or emotional discharge. When directed against painful affect, these defenses also have the ultimate effect of inhibition. A "dammed-up" drive or emotional state is the net result.

The defenses we shall now discuss change the *nature* of the drives, rather than simply *blocking* them. This drive transformation has two consequences. First, the person gains *relief* from the anxiety or guilt prompted by the original form of the drive. Second, *gratification* of the transformed drive does occur, within limits.

Turning Around upon the Self

One way of defensively transforming a wish or impulse is to change the person toward whom it is directed. We have already seen several examples of such displacements from one person to another. In a more radical displacement the person himself becomes the object; the drive gets turned around upon the self (Freud, 1915b).

TURNING AGGRESSION AROUND UPON THE SELF

Turning aggression around upon the self is a very common instance of this defense. Its simplest form is the "unintentional," but open and direct hurting of oneself instead of the other person. Many self-injurious "accidents" are caused this way. One patient in psychotherapy frequently cut himself shaving, nearly always when he was obviously repressing anger toward his wife. Many people scratch themselves with their fingernails when they are inhibiting anger. One young female analysand did this so frequently and vigorously that both forearms became badly infected from her wrists to her elbows (Mahl, 1968).

Frequently, the self-directed aggression stops at the level of thoughts and compulsive urges of self-destruction. The Rat Man had many symptoms like these. Once he was seized with the impulse to rush to his razor and cut his throat; he was very angry that his girlfriend had gone away to nurse her sick grandmother, and he had just repressed the wish to kill the old woman. On another occasion, during the visit he and his girlfriend made to the mountain resort (Chapter 8), an inner command ordered him to jump off a cliff upon which he was standing; the turning around of a repressed desire to kill another man who was paying a lot of attention to his girlfriend prompted this suicidal impulse.

Miss Eaton's self-accusations that she was guilty of serious offenses and her self-deprecatory thoughts and feelings of being worthless illustrate more disguised forms of turning aggression around upon the self. As her treatment with Helene Deutsch revealed, these behaviors consisted of repressed hostile thoughts about her sister, which she was now directing against herself.

Turning aggression around upon the self accomplishes two important things. First, it provides relief from the sense of guilt prompted by the original, outwardly directed anger. Second, it provides some gratification of the repressed anger, albeit in a different form. Children feel better when they have been punished by their parents for misbehavior. Having paid penance and been forgiven, they are relieved of their guilt. Adults seem to operate by the same principles in relation to their own conscience, to their internal representation of their parents. The role of conscience and guilt in this defense accounts for its prominence in obsessive-compulsive and severely depressed people, such as the Rat Man and Miss Eaton, for such people suffer from an especially severe conscience.

TURNING LOVE AROUND UPON THE SELF

Turning love around upon the self also occurs, although it is usually referred to as a "return to narcissism" or a "regression to narcissism." This is misleading, for not all instances of turning love around upon the self are regressive. The self-concern of the sick person, for example, is not always accompanied by regressive, childish helplessness. Nor is the loving of oneself that is mediated by the identifications of normal mourning. At least one instance of turning love inward is "progressive": the self-love produced by internalizing our parents' ideals (Loewald, 1962, 1964). Originally, we admire our parents and all they stand for. When we internalize their values and make them our own, we cherish these aspects of ourselves just as we did our parents.

Reversal

When a person uses *reversal*, he shifts from the wishes, feelings, and impulses that make him anxious or guilty to directly opposite kinds. There are two types of such reversals (Freud, 1915b): changing from loving to hating (or vice versa) and changing from active to passive modes of obtaining sensual pleasure (or vice versa), as in shifting between sadism and masochism. Reversals bring relief from anxiety or guilt over one kind of aggressive or sexual impulse and simultaneously provide for some type of alternative gratification.

Let us consider first the activity-passivity reversals, using sadism and masochism for illustrative purposes. Overt sadism blends sexual and aggressive satisfaction: The fully developed sadist must humiliate and inflict pain on his partner in order to become sexually excited and have an orgasm. Sadism starts in childhood. In one expression of it the child masturbates while consciously fantasying that another child is being beaten by that child's parent or a parent substitute. Such wishes and experiences arouse so much guilt in some young sadists that they defend themselves by turning into overt masochists, but they remain unconscious sadists. They achieve this reversal by turning their sexualized aggression around upon themselves and then taking one more step. They seek out some other person to inflict the sexualized pain upon themselves.

The child masochist will usually provoke his parents into beating him, mainly for erotic satisfaction. The Wolf Man (Freud, 1918) did exactly this when he was about 4 years old. He would deliberately misbehave in front of his father in order to be spanked. That he wanted to be spanked is shown by the fact that at times he would even get as physically close to his father as possible when he misbehaved. Most boys, of course, stay as far away from their fathers as possible under such circumstances. As an adult the Wolf Man got great pleasure out of beating fantasies, especially ones in which he pictured boys being beaten on their penises. The adult masochist, of course, insists that his or her lover inflict the pain and humiliation on him. Consciously, he enjoys being hurt; unconsciously, he also enjoys the fantasy that he is the sadist.

Having become a masochist, the conflicted person may then revert to sadism because he can no longer tolerate the passive situation. It may arouse his castration anxiety, for example, or lower his self-esteem. But when he does behave sadistically, he now gets a great deal of secret masochistic gratification, too, for he projectively identifies with the partner he is now hurting and humiliating. This seems to involve the same type of empathy that enables us to "feel" the pain when we see someone being hurt. That is a normal prototype of what the reconverted sadist does on a grand scale.

The sadist and the masochist enjoy the same blend of sexuality and aggression. Only the overt—passive or active—form is different. If one form is enjoyed consciously and overtly, the other form is enjoyed inwardly through projective identification with the partner and unconscious fantasy.

Other defensive reversals involve love and hate, as was noted above. Miss Eaton's adolescent reaction to her sister was an example of the use of love to defend against guilt-ridden hate. The same kind of reaction is one of the many causes of homosexuality. Thus, Freud (1922) found that some homosexual men had started out hating their brothers and fixed on homosexual love because their hatred made them feel so guilty.

Hate may be used to defend against love. A person who is afraid of unconscious heterosexual wishes may hate members of the opposite sex; a person who fears homosexual wishes may hate members of the same sex. Paranoid delusions of persecution arise from the projection of such defensive hatred, which keeps homosexual wishes repressed, as we saw in Chapter 7.

Reversals of the unpleasant emotions resulting from conflict—anxiety and guilt—are analogous to reversals of love and hate. Many people, for example, repress their anxiety and "whistle in the dark"; acting brave helps them to avoid fear. And the nonchalant flouting of one's ideals can help a person to defend against a sense of guilt.

How do reversals differ from reaction formations? The main distinction is the *degree of generality* of the opposing feelings and behavior. In reversal, the defensive behavior is fairly specific. For example, the type of homosexual who turned to homosexual love because hatred of a brother brought on great guilt can hate in many areas of his life. When Miss Eaton first reversed her hatred for her sister, she undoubtedly could express anger toward many other people. It is only when a reversal becomes generalized to all people and to all areas of one's life—only when a characterological change occurs—that we call it a reaction formation.

Regression

Let us recall what happened to Edie the day she and her husband, feeling sexually aroused, rushed home from the museum. She became anxious and felt guilty and momentarily repressed her sexual desires. Then she experienced intense hunger and delayed her lovemaking long enough to eat something. And we saw many indications that eating was an intensely erotic experience for her. We also saw that early in her childhood she had enjoyed eating but had then become a chronic "eating problem-child." Here in a nutshell is an example of the defensive regression of drives. To avoid the anxiety and guilty feelings about her *heterosexual* wishes, Edie repressed them and regressed to the developmentally earlier stage of *oral eroticism*. Put another way, she regressed to an early *fixation* point in her psychosexual development.

The minor episode the day of that museum outing encapsulated what had happened on a major scale late in her adolescence. The night of the senior prom in high school she had become sexually excited but had repressed her sexual wishes. She became ravenously hungry and was all set to eat a juicy cheeseburger. But something happened that did not occur that day of the museum trip. As she was about to eat with her boyfriend, she became afraid she would choke to death. In her unconscious thinking, eating was a sexual act. She anticipated the same danger upon eating that she anticipated from her mother in retribution for her Oedipal love for her father. (In Chapter 5 we discussed a woman whose fear that her mother would choke her was expressed in her first dream in analysis. Edie had identical unconscious fears.) Her new anxiety necessarily motivated still a further defense: the inhibition of eating with a man, the repression of her oral eroticism. This further defense against even the regressed wishes is a common outcome. It is, as noted earlier (pages 52–53), the *immediate* cause of most hysterical symptoms.

To round out this account of Edie, it should be noted that her transition from adolescence into young adulthood repeated the same defensive trend of oral inhibition that she showed earlier in her childhood, when she changed from a fleshy little girl of 5 to a "stark" beanpole by the age of 7.

It is possible and useful to distinguish between regressions of erotogenic zones, of wishes, and of objects. Edie's regression involved only a retreat from the genital to the oral erotogenic zone. From her fantasies and free associations it appeared that her wishes and their object were unchanged: Unconsciously, she wanted to have oral intercourse with a man's penis. This specific wish was the target of her inhibition of eating with a man. Another woman might have regressed in all three aspects, ending up wanting to be fed like a baby by her mother. The Wolf Man regressed on all three counts, as the final chapter will show.

Some regressions involve reversions from adult loves to childhood ones, as in the frightened bride who longs to be back home with her Oedipal father and the guilt-ridden bridegroom whose thoughts turn to his Oedipal mother. Other regressions involve retreats from sensuous relations with other people to autoeroticism. Still others are to pregenital psychosexual stages, as in the Wolf Man.

In the most marked regressions of schizophrenia the person retreats to the pregenital pleasures of being cared for like a baby by maternal figures, to narcissism like that of Judge Schreber (discussed in Chapter 4), or to a level of experience in which they feel fused with parental surrogates, usually horribly distorted by psychotic thought.

Sublimation

Sublimation, often called a "normal" defense (A. Freud, 1936), also provides for the expression of repressed drives and affects. But the forms sublimation takes are highly displaced and resemble only slightly the raw, unconscious emotional urges and feelings from which they derive most of their impetus.

Helene Deutsch (1965) reports the following "absolutely true anecdote":

> One early summer morning many years ago, the inhabitants of a small . . . university town . . . made the horrifying discovery that all the dogs which had been running loose during the night in a certain point of the city had

lost their tails. They learned that the medical students had attended a drinking bout that night and that when they left the party one young man had had the highly humorous inspiration to cut off the tails of the dogs. Later he became one of the most famous surgeons in the world [p. 304].

This anecdote illustrates not only how alcohol "dissolves the superego" and releases repressed sadistic urges but also how such repressed sadistic urges may be expressed in very constructive, socially valuable activities such as surgery—in other words, they may be sublimated.

One nurse recalled that her favorite game in childhood had been to pretend that her dolls, who were "sister" and "mother," were dead and that she was bringing them to life again. From the case material it appeared that her childhood conflict between her unconscious jealous hatred of her mother and sister and her defensive undoing in the rescue fantasy was sublimated in her adult occupational role.

Freud (1910a) noted a remarkable parallel between Leonardo da Vinci's "Madonna and Child with St. Anne" (Figure 11-2) and Leonardo's own childhood. "He had had two mothers: first, his true mother Caterina, from whom he was torn away when he was between three and five, and then a young and tender step-mother, his father's wife, Donna Albiera [p. 113]."

Figure 11-2 Leonardo's "Madonna and Child with St. Anne."

Freud noted several unusual things about the painting. Few Italian painters portrayed St. Anne, Mary, and Jesus together as a trio; and the few other European artists who had painted the trio never had a mature Mary sitting on her mother's lap while she reached out to the child on the ground. Furthermore, St. Anne here has a youngish, beautiful, radiant face—very similar to Mary's—not the face of an old woman. Finally, the blissful smile —so famous from "Mona Lisa"—appears on the faces of both women. Freud concluded that this picture (and many other Leonardos of the same period that featured the same smile) must be a derivative expression, or sublimation, of Leonardo's repressed Oedipal memories and feelings, for the existence of which Freud adduced a great deal of indirect evidence. The painting could be viewed as a condensed recapitulation of Leonardo's childhood: As a baby he had been cared for by a loving young "mother" and before that by a second, perhaps slightly older, loving mother.

Freud also thought that Leonardo's painting of so many women like Mona Lisa and the women in "Madonna and Child with St. Anne" was as much a sublimation of his unconscious painful longings for his lost mothers as it was of his simpler Oedipal desires. One can appreciate how this might happen by putting oneself for a moment in Leonardo's position and imagining what inward emotions one might feel spending hour after hour completely absorbed in creating stroke by stroke all those mysteriously marvelous mother-faces. Freud's inferences can be questioned, of course, by both Leonardo scholars and psychoanalysts on the ground that unconscious meanings cannot adequately be determined from biographies of dead people who cannot give the analyst their own free associations. Granted; but the general mechanism of sublimation is commonly observed in artistic creativity (Kris, 1952).

The intellectual curiosity of the adult, Freud proposed (1905b), was in large part a sublimation of the child's "sexual researches." And the inhibitions of creativity that he observed in adults seemed to derive from the strong repression of childhood sexual curiosity.

In Chapter 5 we discussed the way in which the child begins to establish his ideals by renouncing his Oedipal sensuality and by identifying with his Oedipal love objects. This, too, is regarded as a sublimation.

The differences between adult phenomena of sublimation, such as those mentioned above, and the presumably related childhood sexual-aggressive drives and experiences reflect the critical mechanisms of sublimation. All the adult sublimations show a marked displacement away from the childhood sexual or aggressive aims and targets. In addition, the adult behavior serves a socially constructive function. Where a young man might obtain sadistic pleasure and master his own castration anxiety by cutting off the tails of dogs and symbolically castrating his father, the surgeon cuts up sick people in order to save lives. The child Leonardo may have reveled in his sensuous intimacy with his two mothers; Leonardo, the middle-aged artist, might have become absorbed in painting the biblical scene partly to symbolically relive this intimacy and partly for the enjoyment it would provide his fellow men and posterity. The child starts to form his ideals out of adoration of his parents, the need to cope with giving up his Oedipal relationships, and the need to relieve his castration anxiety; the adult man of principles is relatively free of parental ties and fits into the value system of society.

The "goodness of fit" between the childhood and adult phenomena is one reason for taking the concept of sublimation seriously. But there is an even more compelling reason. Sublimations sometimes lose their adjustive value by becoming invaded by the sexual or aggressive drives from which they stem. When this happens, the sublimations become the target of severe inhibitions. Intellectual activity, for example, sexually excites some men who devote themselves to scholarly pursuits; they eventually lose their keenness. One male psychotherapy patient avoided libraries and eventually all serious reading because studying in the library stacks regularly aroused him to the point of masturbating on the spot. Painters, doctors, and nurses occasionally become unable to carry on their vocations for similar reasons.

This completes the discussion of defenses against sexual and aggressive drives. The brief final chapter touches on a few important aspects of conflicts and defenses that have not yet been considered.

A Word About Freud's Terminology

Readers who plan to study Freud's original papers may profit from a few preliminary words about the changes in some of his concepts and terminology. The bit of history presented in Chapter 1 demonstrated that defense and repression were among his original psychoanalytic discoveries. Each subsequent paper in his long life, regardless of its principal topic, dealt with some aspect of these processes. In addition, he wrote general or theoretical discussions of defense and repression during three different periods of his work—1893–96, 1914–17, and 1923–37. But he meant different things at these different times by "defense" and "repression."

In the early phase of his work "defense" was a general concept subsuming a wide variety of specific defenses. "Repression" was regarded as one of many defenses, along with most of those mentioned in this chapter (Breuer & Freud, 1893–95; Freud, 1894, 1896b). Freud's next general discussions of defense and repression appeared in some of his "metapsychological papers" of 1915 (1915b, 1915c, 1915d), which presented his then-current psychological theory in a highly condensed form. Here he referred to nearly all the various defense mechanisms as simply "repression." What he had earlier thought of as different mechanisms of defense—repression, projection, reaction formation, and so forth—he now viewed as mechanisms of "repression." He also spoke of other mechanisms—such as turning aggression around upon the self—as "defenses," and he referred to defenses as "vicissitudes" of instincts.

In these same papers Freud insisted that "repression" (synonymous

Figure 11-3   Sigmund Freud.

Top left: Freud in 1891, at age 35. Freud was just beginning to discover the far-reaching effect of unconscious memories and emotions on conscious behavior and thought. Top middle: Freud in 1906, at age 50, one year after the publication of one of his most important monographs, Three Essays on the Theory of Sexuality. *Top right: Freud in 1922, at age 66. A year later Freud will have published his new model of the personality in* The Ego and the Id. *Much of this monograph was devoted to his discoveries and new theoretical ideas about the superego. Bottom: Freud in 1938, at age 82, after having emigrated from Vienna to London. Here Freud is reading his manuscript for Moses and Monotheism, which would soon be published in English. Freud died in 1939.*

with "defense") applied only to *ideas;* at other times he spoke of repression of an instinctual *impulse.* And the "vicissitudes" altered drive *behavior,* as in the change from sadism to masochism.

Furthermore, in the years from 1893 to 1923, Freud held two different views on the relation between anxiety and defense. On the one hand, he claimed that anxiety motivated defenses, which, in turn, minimized anxiety. On the other hand, his "official" theory of anxiety held that it was transformed, repressed sexual affect; that is, defense ultimately produced anxiety. Moreover, in some passages he asserts that anxiety motivates defenses, while in other passages he asserts that the "self-preservative instincts" do so. Freud does not make the relation between the two very clear.

There were probably two main reasons for all these terminological inconsistencies and conceptual difficulties. First, from 1900 to 1923 Freud's main goal had been to clarify the role of drives, especially sexual wishes, in normal and neurotic behavior. He believed that the biological drives were the basic source of all behavior. In keeping with this goal, he was very specific about drives but became less specific about defenses. Thus, he differentiated all the forms and stages of sexuality we mentioned in Chapters 4 and 5 at the same time he was indiscriminately referring to all the defenses as "repression." Also in keeping with this goal of explaining *all* aspects of behavior in terms of biological drives, he adopted as a working hypothesis the assumption that the "self-preservative *instincts*" supplied the motivating force for repression. Second, he was in the process of developing a general psychological theory concerning as yet unstudied aspects of human behavior. He realized this and explicitly acknowledged several major difficulties with his theory (1915d).

At the same time, Freud gradually increased his empirical and theoretical study of "ego" psychology. With the writing of *The Ego and the Id* (1923) and, especially, *Inhibitions, Symptoms, and Anxiety* (1926) he arrived at essentially the theory of conflict and defense that has been presented here. Anna Freud restated it especially clearly and amplified it considerably in *The Ego and the Mechanisms of Defense* (1936). In this third phase (1923–37) Freud returned to the general concept of defense. Abandoning the view that repression produces neurotic anxiety, he concluded that anxiety is anticipatory fear and that the various anxieties we have mentioned (as well as guilt) motivate the defenses. Defenses, he now made clear, can interfere with ideas and with feelings and their underlying bodily changes, as well as with overt behavior. And he returned to his early distinction between various defense mechanisms. In his last major paper, *Analysis Terminable and Interminable* (1937), however, he gives repression a special place and regards the other defense mechanisms as supplementary to it.

So, to the uninitiated reader about to plunge into the middle of Freud's collected papers: Beware! But go ahead and jump. The swimming is fine, but you have to work to keep your head above water.

There was a child went forth every day,
And the first object he looked upon, that object he became,
And that object became part of him for the day or a certain part of
the day,
Or for many years or stretching cycles of years.

The early lilacs became part of this child,
And grass and white and red morning-glories, and white and red
clover, and the song of the phoebe-bird. . . .

.   .   .

His own parents, he that had fathered him and she that had con-
ceived him in her womb and birthed him,
They gave this child more of themselves than that,
They gave him afterward every day, they became part of him.

The mother at home quietly placing the dishes on the supper-table,
The mother with mild words, clean her cap and gown, a wholesome
odor falling off her person and clothes as she walks by,
The father, strong, self-sufficient, manly, mean, angered, unjust,
The blow, the quick loud word, the tight bargain, the crafty lure,
The family usages, the language, the company, the furniture, the
yearning and swelling heart,
Affection that will not be gainsayed, the sense of what is real, the
thought if after all it should prove unreal. . . .

.   .   .

These became part of that child who went forth every day, and who
now goes, and will always go forth every day.

WALT WHITMAN. There Was a Child Went Forth

CHAPTER 12

ORGANIZATION
OF DEFENSES
AND INDIVIDUAL
DIFFERENCES

I n this final chapter we shall discuss briefly two additional aspects of conflict and defense: the patterning and organization of multiple defenses and individual differences in conflict and defense. Why have these topics been left until the end, and why are they discussed so briefly? Partly because they take us beyond the goal of dealing with basic concepts, and partly because little is known about them. This chapter, especially the discussion of individual differences, raises questions whose answers lie in the future.

Patterning of Multiple Defenses

For the sake of clarity, the discussion in the last two chapters focused on one defense at a time. Actually, defense mechanisms do not operate singly. From three different perspectives we can speak of a *patterning of multiple defenses*.

1. *Multiple defenses against each single target.* Defense against any single "target" in the conflict paradigm—a perception of an external stim-

ulus, an approach component (such as a drive), or an avoidance component (such as an unpleasant affect)—nearly always involves repression and at least one other defense that reinforces the repression.

2. *Multiple defenses against multiple targets.* There is always defense against more than one target in the paradigm, and these multiple defenses are not always the same. In his experience at the restaurant door Ray was repressing both his homosexual wishes and his self-criticism for having such wishes, but in addition he projected the unconscious self-criticism. A similar patterning of multiple defenses was demonstrated for most of the over-reactions discussed in Chapters 6–8.

3. *Correlated defenses.* Clinical experience suggests that there is some correlation in the use of certain defenses. Thus, obsessional people seem to use isolation, undoing, regression, and reaction formation. Repression and denial seem to be characteristic of hysterical individuals. Identification seems to be correlated with projection and denial in schizophrenia. (These statements do *not* mean, of course, that all people using these defenses suffer from a neurosis or a psychosis.) However, these clinical impressions have not been verified by careful, systematic research.

Hierarchical Organization of Defenses

Most conflicts have discernible "natural histories"; they are seldom, if ever, resolved by a single defensive effort. The discussion of Edie in the last chapter (pages 187–88) illustrated the "succession of movements" over time that constitutes the dynamic history of conflicts. Just as influences from previous historical periods continue into the present so, it seems, many of the earlier stages in the process of defense continue to exist and operate unconsciously in the present. Thus, a concept of a *hierarchical organization of defenses,* of a "layering of defenses," seems necessary to account for the behavior of an individual at the last stage in the historical process. Indeed, this theoretical necessity was one of several weaknesses Freud saw in his early model of the personality, which consisted of an Unconscious and an opposing Preconscious or Conscious. It was one of the reasons he replaced the earlier model with the Ego-Id-Superego model in 1923.

We shall draw upon the clinical observations Freud made during his psychoanalysis of the Wolf Man to illustrate this concept of the hierarchical organization of defenses. Figure 12-1 summarizes and illustrates the main points of the discussion. The bottom entries in this figure summarize some of the facts about the Wolf Man's childhood that were mentioned in Chapter 5:

He was sexually excited about his nursemaids, first Grusha and then Nanya, but he repressed these sexual desires when he developed castration anxiety. These repressed desires, however, continued to affect his sexual behavior as an adult,

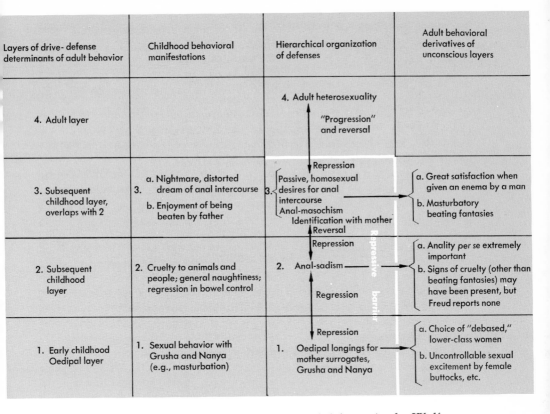

Layers of drive- defense determinants of adult behavior	Childhood behavioral manifestations	Hierarchical organization of defenses	Adult behavioral derivatives of unconscious layers
4. Adult layer		4. Adult heterosexuality ↑ "Progression" and reversal	
3. Subsequent childhood layer, overlaps with 2	3. a. Nightmare, distorted dream of anal intercourse b. Enjoyment of being beaten by father	↓ Repression 3. Passive, homosexual desires for anal intercourse Anal-masochism Identification with mother ↑ Reversal	a. Great satisfaction when given an enema by a man b. Masturbatory beating fantasies
2. Subsequent childhood layer	2. Cruelty to animals and people; general naughtiness; regression in bowel control	↑ Repression 2. Anal-sadism ↑ Regression	a. Anality per se extremely important b. Signs of cruelty (other than beating fantasies) may have been present, but Freud reports none
1. Early childhood Oedipal layer	1. Sexual behavior with Grusha and Nanya (e.g., masturbation)	↑ Repression 1. Oedipal longings for mother surrogates, Grusha and Nanya	a. Choice of "debased," lower-class women b. Uncontrollable sexual excitement by female buttocks, etc.

Figure 12-1   Hierarchical organization of defenses in the Wolf Man.

as is indicated by his preference for women who were socially inferior to him and by his sexual over-reactions to women's buttocks and to kneeling women.

But repression was not the Wolf Man's only childhood defense. He also regressed to the anal stage of relating to people. Soon after his Nanya threatened him with castration if he "misbehaved" sexually, he became generally naughty and cruel. He took great delight in killing and torturing insects and small animals, in fantasying that he was beating large animals, and in teasing and disobeying Nanya. He also reverted to incontinence of his bowels.

Soon other changes appeared in the boy's behavior. He misbehaved so as to elicit beatings from his father, as we saw in the previous chapter, and he started to fantasy that boys were being beaten, especially on their penises. He also made a peculiar complaint about his loss of bowel control, saying that he "couldn't go on living like that." Since there was convincing evidence that he had heard his mother make just this remark about *her* intestinal troubles, it appeared quite likely to Freud that the little boy had unconsciously identified with his mother. About this time, the Wolf Man had his nightmare of the wolves staring in at him through his bedroom window, and he also developed his phobia of pictures of wolves standing and walking on their hind legs. His free associations to this nightmare (which he reexperienced in his transference relationship with Freud), the evidence that he had identified with his mother and that he liked to be spanked by his father, and many other facts led Freud to conclude that this dream scene was a disguised picture of a scene the boy had witnessed earlier—either his father and mother having intercourse from behind or animals having intercourse. In either case, the male was up on his hind legs. Collectively, these items strongly suggest that the boy had defended against his anal sadism (which was itself a defense by regression) and his repressed erotic feelings about Nanya by developing passive, masochistic erotic desires for his father. It was *as if* the boy now unconsciously wished that his father would have intercourse with him.

But it was also *as if* this wish was extremely frightening to him; otherwise his dream would not have been a nightmare. Since the theme of castration emerged in all the many free associations about wolves, the most plausible reason for the boy's terror of the nightmare and the pictures was that he thought he would have to be castrated if his erotic feminine wishes for his father were to come true. He knew women did not have penises. This *rearoused castration anxiety* appears to have caused repression of his anal masochism. Later, under the pressure of puberty, his heterosexual desires again became predominant. The term "progression" can be used for this change, which contrasts with the childhood regression. His repressed, passive anal eroticism, however, still operated. One bit of evidence was that he indulged in beating fantasies when he masturbated. The most striking evidence, however, was that he developed a severe obsessional neurosis after he contracted a venereal disease. It was as if this disease had reactivated his castration anxiety, which in turn had intensified his repressed anal masochism, especially his unconscious feminine desires for his father. That this was the case is most clearly indicated by one of his adult symptoms: *One of his greatest pleasures was to be given an enema by a man.* But, in fact, his entire obsessional neurosis was caused by conflicts over his intensified, unconscious anal eroticism.

(Any reader interested in the detailed clinical data that emerged in the Wolf Man's analysis and gave rise to the formulations presented here should study Freud's original case report [1918], which is also, as we said earlier, the best sample of Freud as a clinical investigator.)

Figure 12-1 depicts the hierarchical organization of defenses just described. The third column summarizes his defensive movements starting, at the bottom, with the repression of his Oedipal longings for his mother surrogates, Grusha and Nanya. The second column cites the major behavioral manifestations of the earlier, childhood movements. The singular features of the Wolf Man's adult behavior are noted in the fourth column. Such observable symptoms provide the major *empirical* basis for assuming that there is a hierarchical organization of defenses. Note that two defensive "layers"—the regression to anal sadism and the reversal to anal masochism or passive homosexuality—are unconscious. Here we see concrete examples of the fact that defenses are unconscious.

Another important empirical reason for assuming such hierarchical organizations is a general timetable that characterizes most psychoanalyses. At first the analysand talks primarily about aspects of his life concerned with the "top layer." But his associations include slight, disguised indications of even the lowest layers, showing that those "deep layers" are active at that moment but are being defended against. As the analysis progresses, the analysand talks increasingly and more directly about the "lower layers" and their influence on his present life.

Individual Differences in Conflict and Defense

We are now going to open Pandora's box, without being able to sort out all that pours forth from it and without closing the lid.

The clinical experience of psychoanalysts and psychotherapists strongly suggests that people differ from one another in the three major variables in the conflict paradigm: the kinds of drives that disturb them, the kinds of unpleasant affects that plague them, and their preferred defenses (Freud, 1926, 1937; A. Freud, 1936). All we shall do here is indicate the nature of these apparent individual differences and discuss briefly how they *might* originate.

We shall start with *drives*. Few people develop inner conflicts over the basic, life-sustaining biological drive behavior, such as eating, drinking, excretion, and breathing. But some people do, when those behaviors become the means for sexual or aggressive gratification. Individual differences become more prominent within the realm of sexuality and aggression. Aggression is the *primary* source of conflict for some people, for example those suffering from severe depression and obsessional behavior. With others, the paramount source of conflict is some kind of sexual wish. Every adult with a sexual conflict seems never to have resolved his childhood incestuous attachments. But, beyond this core conflict (which in itself varies in intensity from person to person), different aspects of sexuality stand out in the conflicts of different people. Some people's misery stems primarily from heterosexual conflicts, that of others from homosexuality or from their oral or anal eroticism or even from self-love. Other powerful motives, such as autonomy or dependency strivings, may also be subject to conflict in any given person.

People also appear to differ in regard to the *motives for defense*. Where one man's predominant anxiety is fear of disorganization of his personality, another's is separation anxiety, another's is fear of loss of love, and still another's is castration anxiety. Still others find their nemesis in shame or in other forms of lowered self-esteem or in hypertrophied consciences and the resulting sense of guilt.

All the *defense mechanisms* discussed here and others that will undoubtedly be discovered in the future are probably used by everyone at one time or another. But some people seem to be predominantly "repressors and deniers," others "projectors and identifiers," and so on. Furthermore, each individual appears to use his "preferred defenses" against all the instigators of those defenses. If a person is a "projector," for example, he is likely to project his sexual and aggressive thoughts, his corresponding feelings, and his anxiety or guilt.

The whole enterprise of diagnostic testing within the framework of psychoanalytic theory stands largely on the premise that the kinds of individual differences mentioned here can be observed and assessed by psychological tests.

Determinants
of Individual Differences

Freud (1905b, 1926, for example) consistently took the position that innate determinants and environmental influences interacted to produce each of the individual differences we have discussed. He distinguished two kinds of innateness. First, he believed that an innate ground plan, or biological schedule, present in all people, determined both psychosexual development (described in Chapters 4 and 5) and the progressive emergence of the anxieties and guilt we have described. He believed that the latter appeared in this order: the original fear and sense of helplessness of the newborn child (evoked by the high levels of inner and outer stimulation to which he is subjected), separation anxiety, fear of loss of love, castration anxiety and low self-esteem (all of which intimately involve the parents and parental surrogates), and, finally, the impersonal conscience of the adult. Biological schedules of maturation, he believed, also influence the sequence in which defenses appear. Projection and identification, for example, might be used by the very young infant and contribute to the formation of his self-concept. Repression might not develop until later in childhood, when controls over attention and drive behavior have developed. Such controls are required in repression—to block conscious perceptions of inner or outer excitations and to inhibit autonomic and skeletal activity. This first kind of innateness is general, common to all people. It would make people alike.

The second kind of innateness Freud referred to was specific to individual people. Freud held that there were such unique, organically based dispositions as innate differences in drive intensity, in the readiness to develop anxiety, and in precursors of the specific defense mechanisms.

Freud believed that experience, environmental influences, and learning had definite effects on the potentialities provided by the unfolding biological ground plan. He emphasized two kinds of experiences: traumatic ones and those producing the identifications with our parents, especially the identifications resulting in superego formation. The latter, in his view, provided the primary means of cultural transmission.

Although he clearly believed that "nature and nurture" interacted to determine individual differences, Freud did not always seem to appreciate the full impact of the environment. Anybody who reads the Little Hans paper (1909a) today, for example, will be struck by the erotic stimulation of Little Hans by his mother and her inconsistent castration threats. But Freud minimizes the significance of her behavior. In assessing Freud's attitude three things must be remembered. Freud, like the other thinkers of his age, was profoundly influenced by Darwin's theory of evolution, including Darwin's acceptance of Lamarck's idea that acquired characteristics are inherited (Ritvo, 1965). Such a heavy emphasis on heredity meant a corresponding lack of emphasis on environment. Also, the behavioral psychology of Freud's day was largely an "instinct psychology"; learning theory was practically nonexistent. Finally, cultural sociology and anthropology had not yet developed into the powerful disciplines they are today.

Among Freudian psychoanalysts, Karen Horney was one of the first to take strong exception to Freud's relatively heavy *theoretical* emphasis on innate biological determinants of behavior. One of her major books, *The Neurotic Personality of Our Time* (1937), opened and closed with chapters focusing on the cultural definition and determination of neuroses. Horney believed that "nurture" was far more important than "nature" in determining the conflicts people have. For example, she thought that the Oedipal complex was a product of the child's family environment. In fact, she believed that the Oedipal complex was not found in children raised in a family atmosphere of healthy warmth and security. Instead, she thought it was a neurosis itself, a response of the child to such parental behavior as sexual overstimulation of the child, emotional withdrawal from him, or severe hostility toward him.

Many factors have since combined to bring into better balance the present-day psychologist's views concerning the roles of innate and environmental influences. The view that today appears most valid and productive holds that individual differences in conflict and defense result from equally important variations in innate and environmental influences, especially those of family life. In its broadest form, this view holds that the behavior of any individual is the resultant of cultural forces and systems interacting with his biologically provided potentialities, a resultant that guarantees the "adaptive fit" between himself and society (Hartmann, 1939; Erikson, 1950; T. Parsons, 1964). Adaptation between the individual and his immediate family, as a representative microcosm of society, is a crucial link in this process.

This broad view faces in two directions, toward individual differences within a culture and toward cultural differences in "national character." According to this view, individual differences in conflict and defense within a culture would result from the interaction of the individual's unique innate endowments, the uniqueness of his family with respect to the drives and defenses it promotes or stunts, and the kind of emotional distress the family fosters in doing so. Cultural differences in the world at large would result from the interaction of genetic differences in racial stock, if they exist, and the uniqueness of the cultures with regard to the drives and defenses they promote.

CROSS-CULTURAL VARIATIONS
IN THE OEDIPAL COMPLEX

The Oedipal complex can serve to illustrate some of these general propositions, especially the assumptions that (1) an individual's conflicts are influenced by social institutions as these are mediated through the family, and (2) the outcome is an "adaptive fit" between the individual and his society.

The child's erotic and mental capacities and the social conditions of child rearing guarantee his forming erotic attachments to maternal figures and ambivalent relationships with people he sees as frustrating those attachments. In our patriarchal Western culture the child develops these relationships with his mother and father—that is, he develops a positive Oedipal complex. But in different social systems this complex may take different forms. In a matrilineal society such as that of the Trobriand Islanders (Malinowski, 1927; A. Parsons, 1964) the "psychic father" is the boy's maternal uncle. In this culture conception is attributed to action by spirits; the father is simply the mother's husband and is not considered to be related to the boy. The boy becomes a member of his mother's kin group, in which the maternal uncle holds authority over him and his mother. The mother, in turn, shows a great deal of respect to her brother. Furthermore, the myths of the Trobrianders are highlighted by brother-sister incest themes, suggesting that strong unconscious incestuous attractions draw the mother and her brother to each other. In fact, the strongest incest taboos in the society concern the brother-sister relationship. It is not surprising that the young boy appears to develop a "nuclear complex" somewhat different from the Oedipal complex we are familiar with. The best-known variation is that the "Oedipal" hostility and ambivalence are directed at his psychic father, his maternal uncle. What we have said so far pertains to the conditions for the development of the Trobriander's variation on the Oedipal complex.

There is another important point about all this. By being disciplined and frustrated by his maternal uncle, the young boy presumably identifies with him the way boys in our culture identify with their fathers, and in the process he internalizes the intense taboos against brother-sister incest. This identification is crucial. It guarantees not only that the boy will grow up avoiding incest with his sister but also that he will later be able to fulfill the maternal uncle role for his sisters' children. Thus, the net effect of his Oedipal conflict and its resolution is that he will fit into and perpetuate the kinship system, the basic social organization, of his culture. (This discussion of the Trobriand Islanders is based on Anne Parsons' reevaluation [1964] of Malinowski's anthropological field data [1927]. Parsons' paper also discusses another version of the Oedipal complex in the "madonna culture" of southern Italy.)

VARIATIONS WITHIN A CULTURE

What holds for cross-cultural variations probably also holds for *"cross-family" variations* within our own culture. Families with distinctive needs and organizations of their own foster particular conflicts, anxieties, and defenses in the children. One of Freud's own early discoveries in this area (1920b, 1922) concerned those heterosexual conflicts that are resolved by a defensive homosexuality. He found that this particular conflict-resolution combination is produced by an unusually intense, intimate relationship between a mother and son in a family where the father is "psychologically absent or weak." More recent research—such as that by Lidz, Fleck, and Cornelison (1965) on family dynamics in schizophrenia, Keniston (1965) on adolescent alienation, and Myers and Roberts (1959) on family structure, social class, and mental illness—has begun to extend our knowledge about cross-family variations. Lidz and his co-workers, for example, studied the families of schizophrenic patients. They intensively interviewed family members and made first-hand observations of how the family interacted both at home and in group meetings. Their observations led them to hypothesize that personality deficiencies in the parents and related disturbed marital interaction had profoundly influenced the children. The parents appeared to deprive their children of adequate nurture, to provide them with faulty models for forming a healthy sexual identity, to stimulate conscious incestuous fantasies that bound the children to them in guilt- and anxiety-ridden relationships, and to transmit irrational modes of behavior—irrational ways of thinking and disordered ways of handling interpersonal relationships. Setting aside the question of the cause of schizophrenia, this research suggests that family dynamics and organization influence significantly the kinds of conflicts and defenses found in the offspring.

Family structure reflects social-class values as well as the idiosyncratic dynamics of the individual family members. So the question naturally arises: Do individual differences in conflict and defense vary with social-class membership and participation? A pioneering study by Hollingshead and Redlich (1958) and another by Srole, Langer, Mitchell, Opler, and Rennie (1962) suggest that this *might* be the case. Both studies demonstrated that the general forms of mental illness (psychosis versus neurosis, for example) differ markedly in the various social classes. Psychosis, for example, is more prominent in the lower classes; neurosis, in the upper classes. *If* different emotional distresses and different defense processes determine the form of mental illness, these studies obviously suggest that the *life differences* of the various social classes in America promote different conflicts and defenses. More direct studies of social class and of specific conflicts and defenses characteristic of members of different social classes are clearly needed. Psychologists, sociologists, and psychiatrists are beginning such investigations (for example, Miller & Swanson, 1958). Indeed, there are many indications that the energetic efforts now being made in community mental health programs and centers will stimulate many people to do the clinical and systematic research that will greatly increase our understanding of the ways social conditions influence the dominant conflicts and defenses of people in different sectors of present-day society.

REFERENCES

Citations in the text are made by author and date of publication.

AFTANAS, M., *see* Zubek *et al.* (1963).

AICHORN, A. *Wayward youth.* New York: Viking Press, 1935.

ALBRIGHT, R., *see* Zuckerman, Albright, Marks, & Miller (1962).

ALPER, T. G. Task orientation and ego orientation as factors in reminiscence. *Journal of Experimental Psychology,* 1948, 38, 224–38.

ALLPORT, G. W. *Personality: A psychological interpretation.* New York: Holt, Rinehart and Winston, 1937.

ALLPORT, G. W. *Pattern and growth in personality.* New York: Holt, Rinehart and Winston, 1961.

APPLEY, M. H., *see* Cofer & Appley (1964).

ATKINSON, J. W., *see* McClelland & Atkinson (1948).

AZIMA, F. J., *see* Azima, Vispo, & Azima (1961).

AZIMA, H., VISPO, R., & AZIMA, F. J. Observations on anaclitic therapy during sensory deprivation. In P. Solomon, P. E. Kubzansky, P. E. Leiderman, J. H.

Mendelson, R. Trumbull, & D. Wexler (Eds.), *Sensory deprivation.* Cambridge, Mass.: Harvard University Press, 1961. Pp. 143–60.

BERKUN, M. M., *see* Murray & Berkun (1955).

BERLIN, J. C. Adolescent friendship patterns in relation to anxiety and dominance. *Dissertation Abstracts,* 1966, 27 (1-B), 298.

BETTELHEIM, B. Individual and mass behavior in extreme situations. *Journal of Abnormal and Social Psychology,* 1943, 38, 417–52.

BEXTON, W. H., HERON, W., & SCOTT, T. H. Effects of decreased variation in the sensory environment. *Canadian Journal of Psychology,* 1954, 8, 70–76.

BLAKE, R. R., *see* Tagiuri, Bruner, & Blake (1958).

BLUM, G. S. A study of the psychoanalytic theory of psychosexual development. *Genetic Psychology Monographs,* 1949, 39, 3–99.

BOWER, G. H., *see* Hilgard & Bower (1966).

BRESSLER, B., *see* Cohen, Silverman, Bressler, & Shmavonian (1961).

BREUER, J., & FREUD, S. (1893–95) Studies on hysteria. *Standard edition*, Vol. 2. London: Hogarth Press, 1955.

BROWN, C. *Manchild in the Promised Land.* New York: Macmillan, 1965.

BROWN, J. S. Gradients of approach and avoidance responses and their relation to level of motivation. *Journal of Comparative and Physiological Psychology*, 1948, *41*, 450–65.

BRUNER, J. S., *see* Tagiuri, Bruner, & Blake (1958).

BURLINGHAM, D., *see* Freud & Burlingham (1943).

CANTRIL, H., *see* Hastorf & Cantril (1954).

CHEIN, I., *see* Levine, Chein, & Murphy (1942).

CLARK, K. B. *Dark ghetto.* New York: Harper & Row, 1965.

CLARK, K. B., & CLARK, M. P. Racial identification and preference in Negro children. In E. E. Maccoby, T. M. Newcomb, & E. L. Hartley (Eds.), *Readings in social psychology.* (3rd ed.) New York: Holt, Rinehart and Winston, 1958. Pp. 602–11.

CLARK, M. P., *see* Clark & Clark (1958).

COFER, C. N., & APPLEY, M. H. *Motivation: Theory and research.* New York: Wiley, 1964.

COHEN, S. I., SILVERMAN, A. J., BRESSLER, B., & SHMAVONIAN, B. M. Problems in isolation studies. In P. Solomon, P. E. Kubzansky, P. H. Leiderman, J. H. Mendelson, R. Trumbull, & D. Wexler (Eds.), *Sensory deprivation.* Cambridge, Mass.: Harvard University Press, 1961. Pp. 114–29.

COLBY, K. M. *The skeptical psychoanalyst.* New York: Ronald Press, 1958.

CONDOMINAS, G. Nous avons mangé la forêt de la pierre-genie Gôo (Hii saa Brii Mau-Yaang Gôo). In *Chronique de Sar Luk, Village Mnong Gar.* Paris: Mercure de France, 1957. Chapters 1 and 3 were partly translated in *Natural History*, 1966, June–July, 8–19.

CORNELISON, A., *see* Lidz, Fleck, & Cornelison (1965).

CORWIN, S. M., *see* Sarnoff & Corwin (1959).

DEUTSCH, H. *Neuroses and character types.* New York: International Universities Press, 1965.

DIVEN, K. Certain determinants in the conditioning of anxiety reactions. *Journal of Psychology*, 1937, *3*, 291–308.

DOLLARD, J., & MILLER, N. E. *Personality and psychotherapy.* New York: McGraw-Hill, 1950.

EPSTEIN, S., & FENZ, W. D. Steepness of approach and avoidance gradients in humans as a function of experience: Theory and experiment. *Journal of Experimental Psychology*, 1965, *70*, 1–12.

ERIKSON, E. H. *Childhood and society.* New York: Norton, 1950.

ERIKSON, E. H. Identity and the life cycle. *Psychological Issues*, 1959, *1*, No. 1.

FEDERN, P. *Ego psychology.* New York: Basic Books, 1952.

FENZ, W. D., *see* Epstein & Fenz (1965).

FISHER, C. Psychoanalytic implications of recent research on sleep and dreaming, Part 1: Empirical findings. *Journal of the American Psychoanalytic Association*, 1965a, *13*, 197–270.

FISHER, C. Psychoanalytic implications of recent research on sleep and dreaming, Part 2: Implications for psychoanalytic theory. *Journal of the American Psychoanalytic Association*, 1965b, *13*, 271–303.

FISHER, C., GROSS, J., & ZUCH, J. A cycle of penile erection synchronous with dreaming (REM) sleep: Preliminary report. *American Medical Association Archives of General Psychiatry*, 1965, *12*, 29–45.

FLECK, S., *see* Lidz, Fleck, & Cornelison (1965).

FREUD, A. (1936) *The ego and the mechanisms of defense.* New York: International Universities Press, 1946.

FREUD, A., & BURLINGHAM, D. *War and children.* New York: International Universities Press, 1943.

FREUD, S. (1892–99) Extracts from the Fliess papers. *Standard edition*, Vol. 1. London: Hogarth Press, 1966. Pp. 175–280.

FREUD, S. (1894) The neuropsychoses of defence. *Standard edition*, Vol. 3. London: Hogarth Press, 1962. Pp. 43–61.

FREUD, S. (1896a) Heredity and the etiology of the neuroses. *Standard edition*, Vol. 3. London: Hogarth Press, 1962. Pp. 141–56.

FREUD, S. (1896b) Further remarks on the neuropsychoses of defence. *Standard edi-*

tion, Vol. 3. London: Hogarth Press, 1962. Pp. 159–85.

FREUD, S. (1896c) The etiology of hysteria. *Standard edition*, Vol. 3. London: Hogarth Press, 1962. Pp. 189–221.

FREUD, S. (1900) The interpretation of dreams. *Standard edition*, Vols. 4 and 5. London: Hogarth Press, 1953.

FREUD, S. (1905a) Fragment of an analysis of a case of hysteria. *Standard edition*, Vol. 7. London: Hogarth Press, 1953. Pp. 3–122.

FREUD, S. (1905b) Three essays on the theory of sexuality. *Standard edition*, Vol. 7. London: Hogarth Press, 1953. Pp. 125–243.

FREUD, S. (1908) Character and anal erotism. *Standard edition*, Vol. 9. London: Hogarth Press, 1959. Pp. 167–75.

FREUD, S. (1909a) Analysis of a phobia in a five-year-old boy. *Standard edition*, Vol. 10. London: Hogarth Press, 1955. Pp. 3–149.

FREUD, S. (1909b) Notes upon a case of obsessional neurosis. *Standard edition*, Vol. 10. London: Hogarth Press, 1955. Pp. 153–249.

FREUD, S. (1910a) Leonardo da Vinci and a memory of his childhood. *Standard edition*, Vol. 11. London: Hogarth Press, 1957. Pp. 59–137.

FREUD, S. (1910b) A special type of object choice made by men. *Standard edition*, Vol. 11. London: Hogarth Press, 1957. Pp. 163–75.

FREUD, S. (1911) Psycho-analytic notes on an autobiographical account of a case of paranoia. *Standard edition*, Vol. 12. London: Hogarth Press, 1958. Pp. 3–82.

FREUD, S. (1912) The dynamics of transference. *Standard edition*, Vol. 12. London: Hogarth Press, 1958. Pp. 97–108.

FREUD, S. (1913) Totem and taboo. *Standard edition*, Vol. 13. London: Hogarth Press, 1955. Pp. 1–161.

FREUD, S. (1914a) On narcissism: An introduction. *Standard edition*, Vol. 14. London: Hogarth Press, 1957. Pp. 67–102.

FREUD, S. (1914b) Remembering, repeating, and working-through. Further recommendations on the technique of psychoanalysis, 2. *Standard edition*, Vol. 12. London: Hogarth Press, 1958. Pp. 145–56.

FREUD, S. (1915a) Observations on transference love. *Standard edition*, Vol. 12. London: Hogarth Press, 1958. Pp. 157–71.

FREUD, S. (1915b) Instincts and their vicissitudes. *Standard edition*, Vol. 14. London: Hogarth Press, 1957. Pp. 109–40.

FREUD, S. (1915c) Repression. *Standard edition*, Vol. 14. London: Hogarth Press, 1957. Pp. 141–58.

FREUD, S. (1915d) The unconscious. *Standard edition*, Vol. 14. London: Hogarth Press, 1957. Pp. 159–204.

FREUD, S. (1915–17) Introductory lectures on psychoanalysis. *Standard edition*, Vols. 15 and 16. London: Hogarth Press, 1963.

FREUD, S. (1917) Mourning and melancholia. *Standard edition*, Vol. 14. London: Hogarth Press, 1957. Pp. 237–58.

FREUD, S. (1918) From the history of an infantile neurosis. *Standard edition*, Vol. 17. London: Hogarth Press, 1955. Pp. 3–122.

FREUD, S. (1920a) Beyond the pleasure principle. *Standard edition*, Vol. 18. London: Hogarth Press, 1955. Pp. 7–64.

FREUD, S. (1920b) Group psychology and the analysis of the ego. *Standard edition*, Vol. 18. London: Hogarth Press, 1955. Pp. 67–143.

FREUD, S. (1922) Some neurotic mechanisms in jealousy, paranoia, and homosexuality. *Standard edition*, Vol. 18. London: Hogarth Press, 1955. Pp. 221–32.

FREUD, S. (1923) The ego and the id. *Standard edition*, Vol. 19. London: Hogarth Press, 1961. Pp. 3–59.

FREUD, S. (1924) The dissolution of the Oedipus complex. *Standard edition*, Vol. 19. London: Hogarth Press, 1961. Pp. 173–79.

FREUD, S. (1925a) Negation. *Standard edition*, Vol. 19. London: Hogarth Press, 1961. Pp. 235–39.

FREUD, S. (1925b) Some psychical consequences of the anatomical distinction between the sexes. *Standard edition*, Vol. 19. London: Hogarth Press, 1961. Pp. 243–58.

FREUD, S. (1926) Inhibitions, symptoms, and anxiety. *Standard edition*, Vol. 20. London: Hogarth Press, 1959. Pp. 77–172.

FREUD, S. (1933) The dissection of the psychical personality. In New introductory lectures on psycho-analysis. *Standard edi-*

tion, Vol. 22. London: Hogarth Press, 1964. Pp. 57–80.

FREUD, S. (1937) Analysis terminable and interminable. *Standard edition*, Vol. 23. London: Hogarth Press, 1964. Pp. 209–53.

FREUD, S., *see also* Breuer & Freud (1893–95).

FRIEDMAN, N. James Baldwin and psychotherapy. *Psychotherapy*, 1966, 3, 177–83.

FROMM, E. *Escape from freedom*. New York: Holt, Rinehart and Winston, 1941.

GLIXMAN, A. F. Recall of completed and incompleted activities under varying degrees of stress. *Journal of Experimental Psychology*, 1949, 39, 281–95.

GOLDBERGER, L., & HOLT, R. R. Experimental interference with reality contact: Individual differences. In P. Solomon, P. E. Kubzansky, P. H. Leiderman, J. H. Mendelson, R. Trumbull, & D. Wexler (Eds.), *Sensory deprivation*. Cambridge, Mass.: Harvard University Press, 1961. Pp. 130–42.

GOUGH, H. Identifying psychological femininity. *Educational and Psychological Measurement*, 1952, 12, 427–39.

GRINKER, R. R., & SPIEGEL, J. P. *Men under stress*. Philadelphia: Blakiston, 1945.

GROSS, J., *see* Fisher, Gross, & Zuch (1965).

HALL, C. S., & LINDZEY, G. *Theories of personality*. New York: Wiley, 1957.

HARTMANN, H. (1939) *Ego psychology and the problem of adaptation*. New York: International Universities Press, 1958.

HARTMANN, H. Comments on the psychoanalytic theory of the ego. *Psychoanalytic Study of the Child*, 1950, 5, 74–96.

HARTMANN, H. The mutual influences in the development of the ego and id. *Psychoanalytic Study of the Child*, 1952, 7, 9–30.

HARTMANN, H. Notes on the theory of sublimation. *Psychoanalytic Study of the Child*, 1955, 10, 9–29.

HASTORF, A. H., & CANTRIL, H. They saw a game: A case study. *Journal of Abnormal and Social Psychology*, 1954, 49, 129–34.

HERON, W. Cognitive and physiological effects of perceptual isolation. In P. Solomon, P. E. Kubzansky, P. H. Leiderman, J. H. Mendelson, R. Trumbull, & D. Wexler (Eds.), *Sensory deprivation*. Cambridge, Mass.: Harvard University Press, 1961. Pp. 6–33.

HERON, W., *see also* Bexton, Heron, & Scott (1954).

HILGARD, E. R., & BOWER, G. H. *Theories of learning*. (3rd ed.) New York: Meredith, 1966.

HOLLINGSHEAD, A. B., & REDLICH, F. C. *Social class and mental illness*. New York: Wiley, 1958.

HOLT, R. R. The accuracy of self-evaluations: Its measurement and some of its personological correlates. *Journal of Consulting Psychology*, 1951, 15, 95–101.

HOLT, R. R. Gauging primary and secondary processes in Rorschach responses. *Journal of Projective Techniques*, 1956, 20, 14–25.

HOLT, R. R., *see also* Goldberger & Holt (1961).

HORNEY, K. *The neurotic personality of our time*. New York: Norton, 1937.

JANIS, I. L. *Stress and frustration*. New York: Harcourt Brace Jovanovich, 1971.

JONES, E. *The life and work of Sigmund Freud*. New York: Basic Books, 1953 (Vol. 1), 1955 (Vol. 2), 1957 (Vol. 3).

JOYCE, J. *Ulysses*. New York: Modern Library, 1961.

KARDINER, A., & OVESEY, L. *The mark of oppression: Explorations in the personality of the American Negro*. Cleveland: World, 1951.

KENISTON, K. *The uncommitted*. New York: Harcourt Brace Jovanovich, 1965.

KOVACH, K., *see* Zubek *et al.* (1963).

KRIS, E. *Psychoanalytic explorations in art*. New York: International Universities Press, 1952.

KUBZANSKY, P. E., *see* Mendelson *et al.* (1961).

LANGER, T. S., *see* Srole *et al.* (1962).

LEIDERMAN, P. H., *see* Mendelson *et al.* (1961).

LEV, J., *see* Pintner & Lev (1940).

LEVINE, R., CHEIN, I., & MURPHY, G. The relation of the intensity of a need to the amount of perceptual distortion. *Journal of Psychology*, 1942, 13, 283–93.

LEWIN, K. Environmental forces in child behavior and development. In C. Murchison (Ed.), *A handbook of child psychology*. Worcester, Mass.: Clark University Press, 1931. Pp. 92–127.

LEWTY, W., *see* Smith & Lewty (1959).

LIDZ, T., FLECK, S., & CORNELISON, A. *Schizophrenia and the family*. New York: International Universities Press, 1965.

LINDSLEY, D. B. Common factors in sensory deprivation, sensory distortion, and sensory overload. In P. Solomon, P. E. Kubzansky, P. H. Leiderman, J. H. Mendelson, R. Trumbull, & D. Wexler (Eds.), *Sensory deprivation*. Cambridge, Mass.: Harvard University Press, 1961. Pp. 174–94.

LINDZEY, G. Some remarks concerning incest, the incest taboo, and psychoanalytic theory. *American Psychologist*, 1967, 22, 1051–59.

LINDZEY, G., *see also* Hall & Lindzey (1957).

LOEWALD, H. Internalization, separation, mourning, and the superego. *Psychoanalytic Quarterly*, 1962, 31, 483–504.

LOEWALD, H. On internalization. Paper presented before the Western New England Psychoanalytic Society, New Haven, Conn., 1964.

LUNGER, R., & PAGE, J. O. Worries of college freshmen. *Journal of Genetic Psychology*, 1939, 54, 457–60.

MAHL, G. F. Gestures and body movements in interviews. In J. M. Shlien (Ed.), *Research in psychotherapy*, 3. Washington, D.C.: American Psychological Association, 1968. Pp. 295–346.

MALINOWSKI, B. (1927) *Sex and repression in savage society*. London: Routledge & Kegan Paul, 1953.

MARKS, C., *see* Zuckerman, Albright, Marks, & Miller (1962).

MC CLELLAND, D. C., & ATKINSON, J. W. The projective expression of needs, 1: The effects of different intensities of the hunger drive on perception. *Journal of Psychology*, 1948, 25, 205–22.

MENDELSON, J. H., KUBZANSKY, P. E., LEIDERMAN, P. H., WEXLER, D., & SOLOMON, P. Physiological and psychological aspects of sensory deprivation: A case analysis. In P. Solomon, P. E. Kubzansky, P. H. Leiderman, J. H. Mendelson, R. Trumbull, & D. Wexler (Eds.), *Sensory deprivation*. Cambridge, Mass.: Harvard University Press, 1961. Pp. 91–113.

MILLER, D. R., & SWANSON, G. E. *Inner conflict and defense*. New York: Holt, Rinehart and Winston, 1958.

MILLER, G., *see* Zuckerman, Albright, Marks, & Miller (1962).

MILLER, N. E., *see* Dollard & Miller (1950).

MILLER, N. E. Experimental studies of conflict. In J. McV. Hunt (Ed.), *Personality and the behavior disorders*. New York: Ronald Press, 1944. Pp. 431–65.

MILLER, N. E., & MURRAY, E. J. Conflict and displacement: Learnable drive as a basis for the steeper gradient of avoidance than of approach. *Journal of Experimental Psychology*, 1952, 43, 227–31.

MITCHELL, S. T., *see* Srole et al. (1962).

MOSS, H. A. Standards of conduct for students, teacher, and parents. *Journal of Counseling Psychology*, 1955, 2, 39–42.

MUNROE, R. *Schools of psychoanalytic thought*. New York: Dryden Press, 1955.

MURDOCK, G. P. *Social structure*. New York: Macmillan, 1949.

MURPHY, G., *see* Levine, Chein, & Murphy (1942).

MURRAY, E. J., *see* Miller & Murray (1952).

MURRAY, E. J., & BERKUN, M. M. Displacement as a function of conflict. *Journal of Abnormal and Social Psychology*, 1955, 51, 47–56.

MURRAY, H. A. The effect of fear upon estimates of the maliciousness of other personalities. *Journal of Social Psychology*, 1933, 4, 310–29.

MYERS, J. K., & ROBERTS, B. *Family and class dynamics in mental illness*. New York: Wiley, 1959.

NEWFIELD, J. *A prophetic minority*. New York: New American Library, 1966.

OPLER, M. K., *see* Srole et al. (1962).

OVESEY, L., *see* Kardiner & Ovesey (1951).

PAGE, J. O., *see* Lunger & Page (1939).

PARSONS, A. Is the Oedipus complex universal? The Jones-Malinowski debate revisited and a South Italian "nuclear complex." In W. Muensterberger & S. Axelrod (Eds.), *The psychoanalytic study of society*, Vol. 3. New York: International Universities Press, 1964. Pp. 278–328.

PARSONS, T. *Social structure and personality*. New York: Free Press, 1964.

PINTNER, R., & LEV, J. Worries of school children. *Journal of Genetic Psychology*, 1940, 56, 67–76.

PRITCHARD, R., & ROSENZWEIG, S. The effect of war stress upon childhood and youth. *Journal of Abnormal and Social Psychology*, 1942, 37, 329–44.

RACHMAN, S., *see* Wolpe & Rachman (1960).

RAPAPORT, D. The theory of ego autonomy: A generalization. *Bulletin of the Menninger Clinic*, 1958, 22, 13–35.

REDLICH, F. C., *see* Hollingshead & Redlich (1958).

RENNIE, T. A. C., *see* Srole *et al.* (1962).

RIESMAN, D. *The lonely crowd.* New Haven, Conn.: Yale University Press, 1950.

RITVO, L. Darwin as the source of Freud's neo-Lamarkianism. *Journal of the American Psychoanalytic Association*, 1965, 13, 499–517.

ROBERTS, B., *see* Myers & Roberts (1959).

ROSENZWEIG, S. An experimental study of "repression" with special reference to need-perspective and ego-defensive reactions to frustration. *Journal of Experimental Psychology*, 1943, 32, 64–74.

ROSENZWEIG, S., *see also* Pritchard & Rosenzweig (1942).

SANFORD, R. N. The effects of abstinence from food upon imaginal processes: A preliminary experiment. *Journal of Psychology*, 1936, 2, 129–36.

SANFORD, R. N. The effects of abstinence from food upon imaginal processes: A further study. *Journal of Psychology*, 1937, 3, 145–59.

SARNOFF, I. Identification with the aggressor: Some personality correlates of anti-Semitism among Jews. *Journal of Personality*, 1951, 20, 199–218.

SARNOFF, I., & CORWIN, S. M. Castration anxiety and the fear of death. *Journal of Personality*, 1959, 27, 374–85.

SCOTT, T. H., *see* Bexton, Heron, & Scott (1954).

SEARS, P. S. Doll play aggression in normal young children. *Psychological Monographs*, 1951, 65, No. 323.

SEARS, R. R. Experimental studies of projection, 1: Attribution of traits. *Journal of Social Psychology*, 1936, 7, 151–63.

SEARS, R. R. Survey of objective studies of psychoanalytic concepts. *Social Science Research Council Bulletin*, 1943, No. 51.

SHMAVONIAN, B. M., *see* Cohen, Silverman, Bressler, & Shmavonian (1961).

SILVERMAN, A. J., *see* Cohen, Silverman, Bressler, & Shmavonian (1961).

SMITH, S., & LEWTY, W. Perceptual isolation using a silent room. *Lancet*, 1959, 2, 342–45.

SOLOMON, P., *see* Mendelson *et al.* (1961).

SPIEGEL, J. P., *see* Grinker & Spiegel (1945).

SROLE, L., LANGER, T. S., MITCHELL, S. T., OPLER, M. K., & RENNIE, T. A. C. *Mental health in the metropolis: The midtown Manhattan study.* New York: McGraw-Hill, 1962.

STERNLAFF, R. Differential perception in paranoid schizophrenics and depressives. Unpublished doctoral dissertation, University of Oklahoma, 1964.

SULLIVAN, H. S. *Conceptions of modern psychiatry.* Washington, D.C.: William Alanson White Psychiatric Foundation, 1947.

SWANSON, G. E., *see* Miller & Swanson (1958).

TAGIURI, R., BRUNER, J. S., & BLAKE, R. R. On the relation between feelings and perception of feelings among members of small groups. In E. E. Maccoby, T. M. Newcomb, & E. L. Hartley (Eds.), *Readings in social psychology.* (3rd ed.) New York: Holt, Rinehart and Winston, 1958. Pp. 110–16.

UNITED STATES REPORTS. *Brown et al. v. Board of Education of Topeka et al.,* 347, 483–96.

VISPO, R., *see* Azima, Vispo, & Azima (1961).

WAELDER, R. (1930) The principle of multiple function. *Psychoanalytic Quarterly*, 1936, 5, 45–62.

WAELDER, R. The problem of the genesis of psychical conflict in earliest infancy. *International Journal of Psychoanalysis*, 1937, 18, 406–73.

WEXLER, D., *see* Mendelson *et al.* (1961).

WIENER, N. *Cybernetics.* Cambridge, Mass.: MIT Press, 1948.

WIENER, N. *The human use of human beings.* Boston: Houghton Mifflin, 1950.

WILGOSH, L., *see* Zubek *et al.* (1963).

WINOCUR, G., *see* Zubek *et al.* (1963).

WOLOWITZ, H. Attraction and aversion to power: A psychoanalytic conflict theory of homosexuality in male paranoids. *Journal of Abnormal Psychology*, 1965, 70, 360–70.

WOLPE, J., & RACHMAN, S. Psychoanalytic "evidence": A critique based on Freud's case of Little Hans. *Journal of Nervous and Mental Diseases*, 1960, 130, 135–48.

ZAMANSKY, H. An investigation of the psychoanalytic theory of paranoid delusions. *Journal of Personality*, 1958, 26, 410–25.

ZUBEK, J. P., AFTANAS, M., KOVACH, K., WILGOSH, L., & WINOCUR, G. Effect of severe immobilization of the body on intellectual and perceptual processes. *Canadian Journal of Psychology*, 1963, 17, 118–33.

ZUCH, J., *see* Fisher, Gross, & Zuch (1965).

ZUCKERMAN, M., ALBRIGHT, R., MARKS, C., & MILLER, G. Stress and hallucinatory effects of perceptual isolation and confinement. *Psychological Monographs*, 1962, 76, No. 30.

INDEX

Page numbers in *italics* refer to illustrations.

Approach-approach conflict, 21, 22, 39
Approach-avoidance conflict, 6, 21, 23–24, 27, 27, 29, 30, 34, 38, 39, 40, 141, 168
Approach gradient, 22, 23, 23, 24, 24, 39, 141, 142, 142, 143, 168
Approach tendency, 39
Asceticism, 180
Assessment, personality, Rorschach Test in, 150
Attention, distribution of, 155
Aversive emotional state, 39, 40, 139
Avoidance, as defense, 153, 154, 155, 168, 169
Avoidance-avoidance conflict, 21, 25, 39, 132
Avoidance gradient, 22, 23, 23, 24, 141, 142, 142

B

Bashfulness, projection of, 123, 123
Behavior therapy, 140
Behavioral disturbances, examples of, 5 (table)
Bereavement, 95
    See also Depression; Grief; Separation anxiety
Bernheim, Hippolyte, and hypnosis, 10–11
Bettelheim's observation of identification with aggressor, 163
"Blacky Test," 82
Body image, changes in, 145–46, 147–48
Bowel training, 58
Brain, reticular activating system in, 149
Breuer's treatment of Anna O., 8–10
Brown, Claude, quoted, 159

C

Case studies:
    altruistic surrender (Miss Eaton), 133–34
    Anna O., see Anna O.
    body image during transition between sleep and wakefulness, 147–48
    castration anxiety, 79–80, 112
    denial, 156–57
    depression, severe, 134
    Dora, 95, 167
    Duane, see Duane
    eating conflict (Edie), 30, 31, 32, 33
    Eaton, Miss, see Eaton, Miss
    Ed, see Ed
    Edie, see Edie
    ego restriction, 167
    female castration complex, 59–61
    Freud's first, in psychoanalysis (Lucy R.), 11

Case studies (*Cont.*)
    generalized stimulus and response of humiliation in women, 101
    homosexual wishes, unconscious, and projection (Ray), 117, 120
    identification with aggressor, 160, 161–62, 164–65, 166
    identification with parent (Dora), 95, 167
    incestuous fantasies (Ed), 112–13
    interference with defenses, 139–40
    isolation (Rat Man), 182
    Little Hans, see Little Hans
    love as defense against hate, 131–32
    Lucy R., see Lucy R.
    memories activated by imminent separations, 105–06
    obsessional symptoms (Miss Eaton), 131–32
    Oedipal complex, 65, 67, 68, 70–71, 72, 77–78
    over-reaction to minor loss (Miss Eaton), 134
    paranoiac projections (Schreber), 122
    perceptual conflict (Duane), 25–26
    projection of unconscious homosexual wishes (Ray), 117, 120
    psychoanalysis, discovery of (Anna O.), 8–10
    Rat Man, see Rat Man
    Ray, see Ray
    Schreber, Daniel Paul, see Schreber, Daniel Paul
    separations, memories activated by, 105–06
    sexual conflict (Ed), 28
    Wolf Man, see Wolf Man
    women, preference of, for boy babies, 61–62
Castration anxiety, 28, 29, 41, 78–82, 80, 83, 85, 139, 154, 157, 173, 178, 186, 190, 191, 196, 198, 200
    case studies of, 79, 80, 112
    origin of, 78–81
Charcot, Jean-Martin, and hypnosis, 8
Child:
    identification of, with aggressor, 165–66
    identification of, with parent, 86–87, 160
    toilet training of, 58
Childhood:
    aggression in, see Childhood aggression
    amnesia for, 85
    denial in, 156–57
    hostility in, 65, 67, 76, 83
    latency period of, 85–86, 88
    sexuality in, see Childhood sexuality
    See also Father; Mother; Parents
Childhood aggression, 49, 51, 65, 66, 74, 164–65

Childhood sexuality, 48, 49, 90
  and adult sexuality, 52–53
  aggressive aspects of, 51
  anal stage of, 51, 52, 54
  and development of object relations, 55–62
  and erotic-genital stimulation by parents, 58–59
  Freud's investigation of, 48, 49–51
  interchangeability of excitations in, 54–55
  oral stage of, 51, 52, 54
  phallic stage of, 51, 52
Clark, Kenneth B., on identification with aggressor, 163
Community mental health, 204
Concentration, and sensory deprivation, 145
Conceptions of Modern Psychiatry (Sullivan), 98
Conditioned emotional response, paradigm of, 101–02, 103
Conditioned stress stimuli, 100, 109
  generalized, 100, 109
Conflict(s), 6, 7, 22, 143, 193
  adaptive, 45
  over aggression, 128–29, 136, 172, 199
  approach-approach, 21, 22, 39
  approach-avoidance, 6, 21, 23–24, 27, 27, 29, 30, 34, 38, 39, 39, 141, 168
  appropriateness of, 42
  avoidance-avoidance, 21, 25, 39, 132
  case studies of, 25–26, 28, 30, 31, 32, 33
  cause of, unbearable affect as (Freud), 12–13
  conscious and unconscious, 41–43
  consequences of, 42–43
  double approach-avoidance, 21, 24, 24–25, 39
  eating, case study of (Edie), 30, 31, 32, 33
  examples of, 25–35, 27, 29, 34
  homosexual, see Homosexuality, projection of unconscious
  individual differences in, 199, 201
  over-reactions to unconscious, 136
  paradigm of approach-avoidance, 38–40, 39, 199
  and past, role of, 43–44
  perceptual, case study of (Duane), 25–26
  resolution of, process of, 42
  sexual, see Sexual conflict
  types of, 20–25, 39
  unbearable affect as cause of (Freud), 12–13
  unconscious and conscious, 41–43
  See also Anxiety; Defense(s); Fear (fear reactions); Stress

Conscience, 122, 136, 200
  fear of, 174
  See also Superego
Counterphobic behavior, 180
Cultural anthropology, 74–76, 201

D

Danger, anticipation of, 6, 40, 173
  See also Fear (fear reactions)
Dark Ghetto (Clark), 163
Darwin's theory of evolution, 201
Defense(s), 6, 40, 42–43, 44, 153, 191, 193
  adaptive, 45–46
  against affects, unpleasant, 174–75, 175
  of avoidance, 153, 154, 155, 168, 169
  change of function of (Hartmann), 46
  correlated, 196
  of denial, see Denial
  determinants of individual differences in, 200–02
  of displacement, see Displacement
  against drives, motives for, 173–74
  of ego restriction, 167–68, 169
  of escape, 153, 154, 155, 168, 169
  hierarchy of, 196–99, 197
  of identification, see Identification
  individual differences in, 199, 200–02
  of inhibition, 40
  interference with, 139–43, 148
  of isolation, see Isolation
  love as, 131, 186
  motives for, individual differences in, 199
  of negation, 181
  patterning of, 195–96
  of projection, see Projection
  of reaction formation, 134, 179–81, 187, 196
  of regression, see Regression
  of repression, see Repression
  of reversal of affect, 130, 131, 172, 179, 185–87
  of sublimation, see Sublimation
  of turning around upon the self, 172, 184–85
  of undoing, 131, 132, 183–84, 196
  weakening of, through loss of reality contact, 148
  See also Anxiety; Conflict(s); Fear (fear reactions); Stress
Denial, 40, 155–60, 169, 181, 196
  case studies of, 156, 157
  in children, 156–57
  defined, 155
  experimental studies of, 157–60
Depression, 40, 95, 135, 136, 199
  case study of (Miss Eaton), 134
  See also Grief; Separation anxiety

M

"Madonna and Child with St. Anne," 189, *189*, 190
Manchild in the Promised Land (Brown), 152
Mann, Thomas, quoted, 17
Mark of Oppression, The (Kardiner & Ovesey), 160
Masculine protest (Adler), 98
Masochism, 185, 186, 193, 198
Masturbation, 28, 29, 51, 52, 65, 118, 178
Matrilineal society, 202
Maturation, 100, 200
Memory(ies):
   activation of, by imminent separations, 104–07
   and anxiety reactions, 107, 108
   and covariations in separation stimuli, 107, 108
   as mediator in over-reactions, 108–10
Mental health, community, 204
Meyer, K. F., quoted, 36
Miller's theory of conflict, 39, 141–42
Mother:
   domination of child by, 98
   and Oedipal complex, 65, 76, 77, 78, 87, 187
   preference of, for boy baby, 61
   preoedipal attachments to, 57–58, 62
   toilet training by, 58
   See also Parent(s)
Motivation (motives):
   and aggression, *see* Aggression
   sexual, *see* Adult sexuality; Childhood sexuality
   See also Conflict(s); Frustration
Mourning, 95
   See also Depression; Grief; Separation anxiety
Murray's experiment on fantasy activity, 111

N

Narcissism, 56–57, 188
Nazism, 163
Negation, 181
Negative feedback, and identification, 166
Negative therapeutic reaction, 141–43
Negroes, 157, 158, 159, 160, 163, 164
Neurosis, 203
   Horney's view of, 201
   seduction theory of (Freud), 49, 50
   See also Case studies
Neurotic Personality of Our Time, The (Horney), 201
Newfield, Jack, on identification with aggressor, 163

O

Object relations, development of, 55–62
Obsessional symptoms, 132, 133, 182, 196
   case study of (Miss Eaton), 131–32
Obsessive-compulsive personality, characteristics of, 131
Obstinacy, projection of, 123, *123*
Oedipal complex, 50, 53, 57–58, 59, 62, 64, 84, 85, 94–95, 160, 188, 190, 191
   and adolescence, 88–90
   in adults, indirect manifestations in, 68–73
   aftermath of, 85–90
   case studies of, 65, 67, 68, 69, 70–71, 72, 77–78
   cross-cultural variations in, 202–03
   and displacement, 72
   doll-play materials used in observation of, 65–67, *66*, *67*
   in girl, repressive motives in, 77–78
   Horney's view of, 201
   and inbreeding, 75–76
   manifestations of, 64–76, *66*, *67*, *70*, *73*
   repression of, 68, 76–85, *86*
   sublimation of, 71, 72, 190
   and superego, 86–88
   universality of, 73–76
   See also Castration anxiety
Oral eroticism, 136, 187, 199
Oral stage of childhood sexuality, 51, 52, 54
Over-reactions of distress, 99, 100, 102, 103, *103*, 104, 111, 114, *114*, 128, 136, 138
   case study of (Miss Eaton), 134
   interference with defenses as mediator in, 139–43, 148
   interference with reality contact as mediator in, 143–50, 154
   memories as mediators in, 108–10, *109*
   to minor loss, 129–30, 134, 135, 138
   unconscious fantasies as mediators in, 110–14

P

Parachutists, adaptive defenses used by, 45, 46
Paranoia:
   experimental studies of, 124–26
   homosexual conflicts in, 124–26, 187
Parent(s):
   child's hostility toward, 65, 67, 76, 83
   child's identification with, 86–87, 160, 165, 166
   See also Father; Mother
Pavlovian conditioning, 102